POWER AND POWERLESSNESS

POWER AND POWERLESSNESS

Quiescence and Rebellion
in an Appalachian Valley

by
JOHN GAVENTA

UNIVERSITY OF ILLINOIS PRESS

Urbana and Chicago

First paperback edition, 1982
© 1980 by John Gaventa

This book is printed on acid-free paper.

Library of Congress Cataloging-in-Publication Data

Gaventa, John, 1949–
    Power and powerlessness.

    Includes bibliographical references and index.
        1. Appalachian region—Economic conditions—
Case studies. 2. Appalachian region—Social
conditions—Case studies. 3. Poor—Appalachian
region—Case studies. 4. Power (Social sciences)
—Case studies. I. Title.
HC107.A13G23   320.974   80-12988
ISBN 0-252-00985-1 / 978-0-252-00985-3

PREFACE

Near the Cumberland Gap, stretching between the Pine and Cumberland Mountains across parts of Tennessee and Kentucky, lies the Valley about which this book is written. Of the many experiences remembered from that summer when I first entered the Valley, one perhaps marks my introduction to the questions here pursued. With a community organizer in the area, I had climbed a narrow path to a mountain cabin to talk to a retired miner about joining with others in a law suit challenging the low taxation of the corporate coal property which surrounded his home. The miner listened attentively to the account of the local injustices which several other students and I had 'discovered'. He showed no surprise, though his response might have been anticipated. The land of his father had been taken by the coal lords. He knew of the inequities in the Valley since.

In this opportunity to move against one of the long-standing inequities, though, the miner showed no particular interest. His response did not seem one of apathy or ignorance. It seemed to grow from past experiences in the Valley, as well as from his situation in the present. The miner understood something of powerlessness, of power, and of how the two could serve to maintain inaction upon injustice, even in a 'democracy'. Of that knowledge, my rather traditional schooling at the nearby university had taught me very little.

I had read the theories of democracy, about how victims of injustice in an 'open system' are free to take action upon their concerns, about how conflicts emerge and are resolved through compromises amongst competing interests. Overlooking the Valley from the miner's porch, what I saw seemed to question the lessons I had learned. Like many throughout Central Appalachia, the Valley is rich in natural resources, especially coal, yet its people remain poor: estimates here suggested that up to 70 per cent of the families remained below the poverty line, while up to 30 per cent were unemployed. Though the Valley is endowed with land abundant for its several thousand residents, the people are landless: some 75 per cent of the land—over 60,000 acres—is owned and controlled by a single corporate owner, the American Association, Ltd., a British company, controlled (at the time) by Sir Denys Lowson, a former Lord Mayor of London and one of Britain's wealthiest men. Blessed with natural beauty, the resources of the Valley stand raped: unreclaimed strip (open cast) mining in layers along the mountains has left the landscape scarred, the hillsides eroded, the creeks and bottom lands filled with silt, acid and coal. A glance at the miner's gnarled hands and the sound of his weak lungs reminded me that deep mining, too, had taken its toll. In the United States a miner is killed every other day, one is injured every ten minutes, and those that survive stand a three in four chance of getting black lung (a chronic disease from inhaling minute particles of black coal dust). There is little compensation in the community for what is lost at work: services from the county courthouse, reached via a dangerous road, are few. All around inequalities abound.

But the inequalities in the Valley, especially those between the community and the Company, seemed not to provoke challenge. The chief executive officer of the county insisted that there were no particular problems in the coal-producing portion of the county. Neither did the once strong and militant union, the United Mine Workers of America (UMWA), seem at the time to be a source of challenge to the *status quo*. In fact, many of the miners in the Valley were non-union, or belonged to a small, company-dominated workers' association. Against corporate exploitation and government neglect, nowhere in the Valley did there appear to be organized protest. I began to wonder if I would not do better to turn my traditional political science around: to ask not why rebellion occurs in a 'democracy' but why, in the face of massive inequalities, it does not.

I began to read literature which challenged some of the more élitist democratic theories to which I had previously been exposed. Still fresh from my experience in the Valley, I attempted to develop a more adequate explanation for what I had seen. In situations of inequality, the political response of the deprived may be seen as a function of power relationships. Power works to develop and maintain the quiescence of the powerless. Rebellion, as a corollary, may emerge as power relationships are altered. Together, patterns of power and powerlessness can keep issues from arising, grievances from being voiced, and interests from being recognized.

To suggest that quiescence (or rebellion) might be related to power was to plunge immediately into an extended and lively debate in political science. What is the meaning of power? How can we tell who has it and who has not? When is it exercised, and with what effects? In Part I of this book Chapter 1 picks up the debate, examining three approaches to the study of power and arguing that each carries with it a particular understanding of political inaction in the face of inequality. In the traditional pluralists' approach, power is understood primarily in terms of who participates, who gains and who prevails in decision-making about key issues. The phenomenon of quiescence is separated from the study of power. The pluralists' approach has been challenged by a second school which argues that power may work to limit the actions of the relatively powerless through a 'mobilization of bias' that prevents certain issues and actors from gaining access to the decision-making process. The second view has been extended by a third view which suggests that power not only may limit action upon inequalities, it also may serve to shape conceptions of the powerless about the nature and extent of the inequalities themselves. In his book, (Steven Lukes, *Power: A Radical View*) the proponent of this view sketches a 'three-dimensional' approach to power, which he claims 'offers the prospect of a serious sociological and not merely personalized explanation of how political systems prevent demands from becoming political issues or even from being made'. (p. 38).

The second and third views of power seemed to contain the beginnings of a theory relating power to participation or non-participation, but it was unclear exactly how this might occur in the life of a given community. I decided to return to the Valley with a twofold task: first, to see if the theories of power could be applied usefully to better understanding the realities of political action and belief of the primarily white and rural, poor and working people of a place like Central Appalachia; and secondly, to see if the empirical examination itself could illuminate further the theoretical interrelationships of power and powerlessness, quiescence and rebellion in situations of inequality.

The task has been avoided in the past at least partially because of the methodological difficulties it was thought to present. How can we study that which does not occur? How can we see the so-called 'hidden faces' of power? What about problems of objectivity, of making assumptions about what people might want? Though difficulties are present, I shall argue that they are not insurmountable. In Part II, a historical approach helps to document the shaping in the past of roles or routines of power which continue in the present, without visible conflict. In Part III, the maintenance of quiescence in the contemporary Valley is examined by identifying specific mechanisms of power from 'below', i.e. from the perspective of the powerless. In Part IV, participant observation in the process of challenge or attempted challenge helps to confirm the extent to which patterns of power and powerlessness preclude issues from arising or actors from acting. Throughout, differing responses of the Valley's people to various opportunities for action or inaction in their 'boom and bust' history help to provide evidence for assessing the impact of power upon them.

Chapter 2 argues that the quiescence of the Central Appalachian Valley is not unique in America. Rather, the starkness of its inequalities and the exaggerated character of the power relationships may make more visible patterns of behaviour and belief which are found amongst non-élites elsewhere. As it involves an extremely poor community in the midst of abundant wealth, the case of the Appalachian Valley poses questions about the politics of poverty relevant to America's lower class generally. As it is about miners and their families, the study consideres broader questions about working-class consciousness, and union and industrial power. As much of the under-developed area is owned and dominated by a British-based corporation, an understanding of the situation involves examining the contemporary role of the multinational in the affairs of a local community, as well as the means through which protest may emerge against land-holders who are corporate and absentee.

The empirical study begins in Chapter 3 by examining the impact of industrial power at the end of the nineteenth century upon a traditional, rural people in and around the Cumberland Gap of Kentucky and Tennessee.

In Chapter 4, the historical study continues with an examination of power relationships in the coal camps of the 1920s and 1930s followed by a study of miners' movements to win their rights to organize a union, and to have their voices heard within it.

In the Valley, the inequalities and the power relationships surrounding them continue today very much as they were historically established, as is suggested in Chapter 5. Chapters 6 and 7 look at the responses to those inequalities as they occur in two potential modes of challenge: local politics and the local union. In the local political arena, a view 'from the bottom' indicates that the 'vulnerability' of the non-élite may account for the failure of issues of inequality to appear on the decision-making agenda.

In the UMWA, corruption and autocracy were challenged in the late 1960s by a rank and file organization known as the Miners for Democracy, led by Jock Yablonski, who was murdered for his protests. Using previously unavailable trial and union records, Chapter 7 examines the opposition of the miners in the Valley to the reform movement. It suggests that the case provides further illustration of the means by which power may serve to protect the powerholder, even to the extent of shaping the perceptions of the powerless about a given conflict.

In Chapter 8, the emergence of challenge against the British company which mines and minds the Valley's resources begins to indicate the elements of power and powerlessness which must be overcome for protest to occur. While the possibilities for effective action by a relatively powerless group may be limited in any situation, Chapter 9 suggests that the difficulties may be even greater for the non-élite of a rural community attempting to bypass the local élite and to influence an absentee target.

In that they focus upon differing aspects of the community

at differing points in its history, each of the empirical chapters may be seen to an extent as separate case studies. This allows a comparative approach within the single situation itself. Yet it is also likely that only in the accumulation of power amongst the various aspects and moments in community life will its full effect upon the actions and conceptions of the powerless become understood. These interrelationships as well as the consequences of the case for a more general understanding of power and powerlessness, quiescence and rebellion will be the subject of the Conclusion, Chapter 10.

In the process of relating theoretical notions of social science to various aspects of everyday community life, much is left undone. Theoretically, I have not considered the difficult question of the boundaries that separate power and structure. Methodologically, the stress on processes of power as they militate against change may have led me to underplay the significance of the challenges that have occurred. Empirically, I have not explored fully the impact of certain socialization institutions—especially education and religion—upon power relationships.

While these are clear limitations to the study, I hope that the interplay of perspectives will have facilitated other contributions. From the consideration of the specific case I hope will come a more general theory of the impact of power and powerlessness upon the political actions and conceptions of a deprived group. From the illustration of a method for examining the 'three dimensions' of power I hope will come stimulus for further exploration of the theory in other situations. And, from the application of both theory and method a better understanding has been brought to myself, and I hope to others, of the persistent politics of inequality in this often overlooked region of Central Appalachia.

Along the way, I have benefited from the assistance of many people, to whom I am grateful. Within the Appalachian region, I have learned from those whose wisdom grows from experiences in confronting power, and powerlessness, in striving for social change; as well as from the advice of social scientists who have undertaken more formal research in the area. For archives and research materials, thanks go to the

Filson Club of Louisville, Kentucky for permission to peruse and quote the papers of C. B. Roberts; to the United Mine Workers' Research Department in Washington D.C. for access to the union records and for assistance in exploring them; to the Model Valley Oral History Video Project, for permission to view, transcribe and quote their tapes; to the Highlander Research and Education Center, the Kentucky State Archives, the Tennessee State Library and Archives, as well as to persons in numerous other county courthouses, government offices, and community organizations.

In Oxford, I benefited further from the comments of those who read and discussed earlier portions or drafts of this work, especially Peter Bachrach, Juliet Merrifield, Clyde Mitchell, David Price, Jim Sharpe and Philip Williams. I am particularly grateful to my Oxford supervisor, Steven Lukes, for the combination of enthusiastic support and thoughtful criticism which he provided along the way. For finance and facilities, I thank Nuffield College, the Rhodes Scholarship Trust, and the Highlander Center. Very special thanks go to Anna Baer for patiently and unselfishly typing the manuscript.

Most of all, I am indebted in this study to the people of the Clear Fork Valley. Since that summer in 1971, they have continued to teach, in more ways than they know.

CONTENTS

List of Maps, Tables, and Figures

LIST OF MAPS, TABLES, AND FIGURES

PART I

INTRODUCTION

'We cannot assume today that men must in the last resort be governed by their own consent. Among the means of power that now prevail is the power to manage and manipulate the consent of men. That we do not know the limits of such power—and that we hope it does have limits—does not remove the fact that much power today is successfully employed without the sanction of the reason or the conscience of the obedient.'

C. Wright Mills, *The Sociological Imagination* (pp. 40-1).

1

POWER AND PARTICIPATION

This is a study about quiescence and rebellion in a situation of glaring inequality. Why, in a social relationship involving the domination of a non-élite by an élite, does challenge to that domination not occur? What is there in certain situations of social deprivation that prevents issues from arising, grievances from being voiced, or interests from being recognized? Why, in an oppressed community where one might intuitively expect upheaval, does one instead find, or appear to find, quiescence? Under what conditions and against what obstacles does rebellion begin to emerge?

The problem is significant to classical democratic and Marxist theories alike, for, in a broad sense, both share the notion that the action of the dispossessed will serve to counter social inequities. Yet, as these views move from political theory to political sociology, so, too, do they appear to move—particularly with reference to the United States—from discussing the necessities of widespread participation and challenge to considering the reasons for their non-occurrence.[1] In their wake, other more conservative theories of democracy present the appearance of quiescence in the midst of inequality as evidence of the legitimacy of an existing order, or as an argument for decision-making by the few, or at least as a phenomenon functional to social stability.[2] More recently, these 'neo-élitists' have in turn been challenged by others who, with C. Wright Mills, argue that the appearance

---

[1] See, for instance, Sidney Verba and Norman H. Nie, *Participation in America: Political Democracy and Social Equality* (Harper and Row, New York, 1972); Anthony Giddens, *The Class Structure of the Advanced Societies* (Hutchinson University Library, London, 1973).

[2] i.e. the so-called 'neo-élitists' such as Schumpeter (*Capitalism, Socialism and Democracy*, 1942), Berelson (*Voting*, 1954), Dahl (*A Preface to Democratic Theory*, 1956). The views are neatly summarized and contrasted with classical theories of participation in Carole Pateman, *Participation and Democratic Theory* (Cambridge University Press, 1970).

of quiescence need neither suggest consent nor refute the classical ideals.[3] Rather, it may reflect the use or misuse of modern-day power.

While the theories of democracy turn, at least to a degree, upon disputes as to the significance of quiescence, the sociological literature of industrial societies offers an array of explanations for its roots: embourgeoisement, hegemony, no real inequality, low rank on a socio-economic status scale, cultural deficiencies of the deprived, or simply the innate apathy of the human race—to name but a few. Rather than deal with these directly, this study will explore another explanation: in situations of inequality, the political response of the deprived group or class may be seen as a function of power relationships, such that power serves for the development and maintenance of the quiescence of the non-élite. The emergence of rebellion, as a corollary, may be understood as the process by which the relationships of power are altered.

The argument itself immediately introduces a further set of questions to be explored: what is the nature of power? How do power and powerlessness affect the political actions and conceptions of a non-élite?

In his recent book, *Power: A Radical View*, Lukes has summarized what has been an extended debate since C. Wright Mills, especially in American political science, about the concept and appropriate methods for its study.[4] Power, he suggests, may be understood as having three dimensions, the first of which is based upon the traditional pluralists' approach, the second of which is essentially that put forward by Bachrach and Baratz in their consideration of power's second face,[5] and the third of which Lukes develops. In this chapter, I shall examine the dimensions briefly, arguing that each carries with it, implicitly or explicitly, differing

---

[3] See, for example, Peter Bachrach, *The Theory of Democratic Elitism: A Critique* (University of London Press, 1969); Jack E. Walker, 'A Critique of the Elitist Theory of Democracy', *American Political Science Review*, 60 (1966), 285-95.

[4] Steven Lukes, *Power: A Radical View* (Macmillan, London, 1974).

[5] Peter Bachrach and Morton S. Baratz, 'The Two Faces of Power', *American Political Science Review*, 56 (1962), 947-52; and Bachrach and Baratz, *Power and Poverty: Theory and Practice* (Oxford University Press, New York, 1970).

assumptions about the nature and roots of participation and non-participation. I shall argue further that together the dimensions of power (and powerlessness) may be developed into a tentative model for more usefully understanding the generation of quiescence, as well as the process by which challenge may emerge. Finally, I shall sketch in general terms a methodology by which the notions may be considered empirically. Then, in Chapter 2, I shall begin to specify how the notions might apply to the study of the politics of inequality in a Central Appalachian Valley.

1.1 THE NATURE OF POWER AND ROOTS OF QUIESCENCE

The One-Dimensional Approach. The one-dimensional approach to power is essentially that of the pluralists, developed in American political science most particularly by Robert Dahl and Nelson Polsby. 'My intuitive idea of power', Dahl wrote in an early essay, 'is something like this: A has power over B to the extent that he can get B to do something that B would not otherwise do.'[6] In the politics of a community, Polsby later added, power may be studied by examining 'who participates, who gains and loses, and who prevails in decision-making'.[7]

The key to the definition is a focus on behaviour—doing, participating—about which several assumptions are made, to be questioned later in this book. First, grievances are assumed to be recognized and acted upon. Polsby writes, for instance, that 'presumably people participate in those areas they care about the most. Their values, eloquently expressed by their participation, cannot, it seems to me, be more effectively objectified.'[8] Secondly, participation is assumed to occur within decision-making arenas, which are in turn assumed to be open to virtually any organized group. Again, Polsby writes, 'in the decision-making of fragmented government—and American national, state and

---

[6] Robert A. Dahl, 'The Concept of Power', in Roderick Bell, David M. Edwards, R. Harrison Wagner, eds., *Political Power: A Reader in Theory and Research* (Free Press, New York, 1969), p. 80, reprinted from *Behavioural Science*, 2 (1957), 201–5.

[7] Nelson W. Polsby, *Community Power and Political Theory* (Yale University Press, New Haven, 1963), p. 55.

[8] Nelson W. Polsby, 'The Sociology of Community Power; A Reassessment', *Social Forces*, 37 (1959), 235.

local government are nothing if not fragmented—the claims of small intense minorities are usually attended to'.[9] In his study of New Haven Dahl takes a similar view:

In the United States the political system does not constitute a homogenous class with well-defined class interests. In New Haven, in fact, the political system is easily penetrated by anyone whose interests and concerns attract him to the distinctive political culture of the stratum . . . The independence, penetrability and heterogeneity of the various segments of the political stratum all but guarantee that any dissatisfied group will find a spokesman . . . [10]

Thirdly, because of the openness of the decision-making process, leaders may be studied, not as élites, but as representative spokesmen for a mass. Polsby writes, 'the pluralists want to find about leadership's role, presumed to be diverse and fluid'.[11] Indeed, it is the conflict amongst various leaders that ensures the essential responsiveness of the political game to all groups or classes. As Dahl puts it, 'to a remarkable degree, the existence of democratic ceremonials that give rise to the rules of combat has insured that few social elements have been neglected for long by one party or the other'.[12]

Within the one-dimensional approach, because a) people act upon recognized grievances, b) in an open system, c) for themselves or through leaders, then *non-participation* or *inaction* is not a political problem. For Polsby it may be explained away with 'the fundamental presumption that human behaviour is governed in large part by inertia'.[13] Dahl distinguishes between the activist, *homo politicus,* and the non-activist, *homo civicus,* for whom 'political action will seem considerably less efficient than working at his job, earning more money, taking out insurance, joining a club, planning a vacation, moving to another neighbourhood or city, or coping with an uncertain future in manifold other ways . . .'.[14] The pluralists argue that by assuming political action rather than inaction to be the problem to be

[9] Polsby (1963), op. cit., p. 118.
[10] Robert A. Dahl, *Who Governs? Democracy and Power in an American City* (Yale University Press, New Haven, 1961), pp. 91, 93.
[11] Polsby (1963), op. cit., p. 119.
[12] Dahl (1961), op. cit., p. 114.
[13] Polsby (1963), op. cit., p. 116.
[14] Dahl (1961) op. cit., p. 221.

explained, their methodology avoids the 'inappropriate and arbitrary assignment of upper and middle class values to all actors in the community'[15] —i.e. the value of participation. Yet, the assumption itself allows class-bound conclusions. Dahl's characterization of *homo civicus* is certainly one of a citizen for whom there are comfortable alternatives to participation and relatively low costs to inaction. And for Polsby, the assumption of inertia combines with the assumption of an open system to allow the conclusion, without further proof, that class consciousness has not developed in America because it would be 'inefficient' or 'unnecessary'.[16]

The biases of these assumptions might appear all the more readily were this approach strictly applied to the quiescence of obviously deprived groups. Political silence, or inaction, would have to be taken to reflect 'consensus', despite the extent of the deprivation. Yet, rarely is the methodology thus applied, even by the pluralists themselves. To make plausible inaction among those for whom the status quo is not comfortable, other explanations are provided for what appears 'irrational' or 'inefficient' behaviour. And, because the study of non-participation in this approach is sequestered by definition from the study of power, the explanations must generally be placed within the circumstance or culture of the non-participants themselves. The empirical relationship of low socio-economic status to low participation gets explained away as the apathy, political inefficacy, cynicism or alienation of the impoverished.[17] Or other factors—often thought of as deficiencies—are put forward in the non-political culture of the deprived group, such as in the 'amoral familism' argument

[15] Polsby (1963), op. cit., p. 116.

[16] ibid., p. 118.

[17] For examples of this approach see Gabriel Almond and Sidney Verba, *The Civic Culture* (Princeton University Press, 1963), especially chaps. 7-8; Lester W. Milbraith, *Political Participation* (Rand, McNally and Co., Chicago, 1965); Stein Rokkan, *Approaches to the Study of Political Participation* (The Christian Michelson Institute for Science and Intellectual Freedom, Bergen, 1962); Peter H. Rossi and Zahava D. Blum, 'Class, Status and Poverty', in Daniel P. Moynihan, ed., *On Understanding Poverty* (Basic Books, New York, 1968), pp. 36-63. For more general discussions of this literature see S.M. Lipset, *Political Man* (William Heinemann, London, 1959), especially pp. 170-219; or, more recently, Verba and Nie, op. cit.

of Banfield in reference to Southern Italy.[18] Rather than
examining the possibility that power may be involved, this
approach 'blames the victim' for his non-participation.[19]
And it also follows that by changing the victim—e.g. through
remedial education or cultural integration—patterns of non-
participation will also be changed. Increased participation, it
is assumed, will not meet power constraints.

Even within its own assumptions, of course, this understanding of the political behaviour of deprived groups is
inadequate. What is there inherent in low income, education
or status, or in rural or traditional cultures that itself explains
quiescence? If these are sufficient components of explanation,
how are variations in behaviour amongst such groups to be
explained? Why, for instance, do welfare action groups spring
up in some cities but not in others? Why are the peasantry of
southern Italy quiescent (if they are), while the *ujamaa*
villagers of Tanzania are not? Why do rural farmers of Saskat-
chewan form a socialist party while those in the rural areas of
the southern United States remain 'backward'?[20] If most
blacks are of a relatively low socio-economic status, why did
a highly organized civil rights movement develop, and itself
alter patterns of political participation?

In short, as operationalized within this view, the power of
A is thought to affect the action of B, but it is not considered
a factor relevant to why B does not act in a manner that B
otherwise might, were he not powerless relative to A. That
point, among others, is well made by those who put forward
the two-dimensional view of power.

The Two-Dimensional Approach. 'It is profoundly characteristic', wrote Schattschneider, that 'responsibility for
widespread nonparticipation is attributed wholly to the
ignorance, indifference and shiftlessness of the people.' But,
he continued:

There is a better explanation: absenteeism reflects the suppression of
the options and alternatives that reflect the needs of the nonparticipants.

---

[18] Edward C. Banfield, *The Moral Basis of Backward Society* (Free Press,
Glencoe, Illinois, 1958).
[19] See William Ryan, *Blaming the Victim* (Pantheon Books, New York, 1971).
[20] Contrast Lipset's earlier work, *Agrarian Socialism* (University of California
Press, Berkeley, 1950) with his later work, *Political Man*, op. cit., pp. 258-9.

It is not necessarily true that people with the greatest needs participate in politics most actively—whoever decides what the game is about also decides who gets in the game.[21]

In so writing, Schattschneider introduced a concept later to be developed by Bachrach and Baratz as power's 'second face', by which power is exercised not just upon participants within the decision-making process but also towards the exclusion of certain participants and issues altogether.[22] Political organizations, like all organizations, develop a 'mobilization of bias . . . in favour of the exploitation of certain kinds of conflict and the suppression of others . . . Some issues are organized into politics while others are organized out.'[23] And, if issues are prevented from arising, so too may actors be prevented from acting. The study of politics must focus 'both on who gets what, when and how and who gets left out and how'[24] —and how the two are interrelated.

When this view has been applied (explicitly or implicitly) to the political behaviour of deprived groups, explanations for quiescence in the face of inequalities have emerged, which are quite different from those of the one-dimensional view. For instance, Matthew Crenson, in his extended empirical application of the 'non-issues' approach, *The Un-Politics of Air Pollution,* states that 'while very few investigators have found it worthwhile to inquire about the political origins of inaction . . .', in Gary, Indiana, 'the reputation for power may have been more important than its exercise. It could have enabled U.S. Steel to prevent political action without taking action itself, and may have been responsible for the political retardation of Gary's air pollution issue.'[25] Or, Parenti, in his study of urban blacks in Newark, found that

[21] E.E. Schattschneider, *The Semi-Sovereign People: A Realist's View of Democracy in America* (Holt, Rinehart and Winston, New York, 1960), p. 105.

[22] Bachrach and Baratz (1962) and (1970), op. cit. See, too, the same authors', 'Decisions and Nondecisions: An Analytical Framework', *American Political Science Review,* 57 (1963), 641–51.

[23] ibid., p. 8, quoting Schattschneider, op. cit., p. 71.

[24] ibid., p. 105.

[25] Matthew A. Crenson, *The Un-Politics of Air Pollution: A Study of Non-Decision-Making in the Cities* (John Hopkins Press, Baltimore, 1971), pp. 130, 80.

[26] Michael Parenti, 'Power and Pluralism: A View From the Bottom', *Journal of Politics,* 32 (1970), 501–30.

in city hall the 'plurality of actors and interests . . . displayed remarkable capacity to move against some rather modest lower-class claims'. 'One of the most important aspects of power', he adds, is 'not to prevail in a struggle but to pre-determine the agenda of struggle—to determine whether certain questions ever reach the competition stage.'[26] Salamon and Van Evera, in their work on voting in Mississippi, found patterns of participation and non-participation not to be related to apathy amongst low status blacks as much as to 'fear' and 'vulnerability' of these blacks to local power élites.[27] Similarly, in his extensive study, *Peasant Wars,* Wolf found acquiescence or rebellion not to be inherent in the traditional values or isolation of the peasantry, but to vary 'in the relation of the peasantry to the field of power which surrounds it'.[28]

In this view, then, apparent inaction within the political process by deprived groups may be related to power, which in turn is revealed in participation and non-participation, upon issues and non-issues, which arise or are prevented from arising in decision-making arenas. But though the second view goes beyond the first, it still leaves much undone.

Empirically, while the major application of the approach, that by Crenson, recognizes that 'perceived industrial influence, industrial inaction, and the neglect of the dirty air issue go together', it still adds 'though it is difficult to say how'.[29]

Even conceptually, though, this second approach stops short of considering the full range of the possibilities by which power may intervene in the issue-raising process. While Bachrach and Baratz insist that the study of power must include consideration of the barriers to action upon grievances, they equally maintain that it does not go so far

[27] Lester Salamon and Stephen Van Evera, 'Fear, Apathy and Discrimination: A Test of Three Explanations of Political Participation', *American Political Science Review,* 67 (1973), 1288–1306.

[28] Eric Wolf, *Peasant Wars of the Twentieth Century* (Faber and Faber, London, 1969), pp. 276–302 generally, and especially p. 290.

[29] Crenson, op. cit., p. 124. Also, Crenson's study is more one of inaction amongst decision-makers on a single issue rather than of passivity amongst non-élites who may be outside the decision-making process altogether. See critique by Edward Greer, 'Air Pollution and Corporate Power: Municipal Reform Limits in a Black Community', *Politics and Society,* 4 (1974), 483–510.

as to include how power may affect conceptions of grievances themselves. If 'the observer can uncover no grievances', if 'in other words, there appears to be universal acquiescence in the status quo', then, they argue, it is not 'possible, in such circumstances, to determine empirically whether the consensus is genuine or instead has been enforced'.[30]

However difficult the empirical task, though, their assumption must be faulted on two counts. First, as Lukes points out, 'to assume the absence of grievance equals genuine consensus is simply to rule out the possibility of false or manipulated consensus by definitional fiat'.[31] Secondly, though, the position presents an inconsistency even within their own work. They write further:

> For the purposes of analysis, a power struggle exists, overtly or covertly, either when both sets of contestants are aware of its existence *or when only the less powerful party is aware* of it. The latter case is relevant where the domination of status quo defenders is so secure and pervasive that they are oblivious of any persons or groups desirous of challenging their preeminence.[32]

But, if the power of the 'defenders of the *status quo*' serves to affect their awareness that they are being challenged, why cannot the powerlessness of potential challengers similarly serve to affect their awareness of interests and conflict within a power situation? That is, just as the dominant may become so 'secure' with their position as to become 'oblivious', so, too, may such things as routines, internalization of roles or false consensus lead to acceptance of the *status quo* by the dominated. In short, I shall agree with Lukes that the emphasis of this approach upon observable conflict may lead it to neglect what may be the 'crucial point': 'the most effective and insidious use of power is to prevent such conflict from arising in the first place'.[33]

The Three-Dimensional Approach. In putting forward a further conception of power, Lukes argues that 'A exercises power over B when A affects B in a manner contrary to B's interests.'[34] The means by which A may do so go significantly

---

[30] Bachrach and Baratz (1970), op. cit., pp. 49-50.
[31] Lukes, op. cit., p. 24.
[32] Bachrach and Baratz (1970) op. cit., p. 50 (emphasis supplied).
[33] Lukes, op. cit., pp. 20, 23.
[34] ibid., p. 34.

beyond those allowed within the first two approaches.

First, 'A may exercise power over B by getting him to do what he does not want to do, but *he also exercises power over him by influencing, shaping or determining his very wants.*'[35] Not only might A exercise power over B by prevailing in the resolution of key issues or by preventing B from effectively raising those issues, but also through affecting B's conceptions of the issues altogether. Secondly, 'this may happen in the absence of observable conflict, which may have been successfully averted', though there must be latent conflict, which consists, Lukes argues, 'in a contradiction between the interests of those exercising power and the *real interests* of those they exclude'.[36] Thirdly, the analysis of power must avoid the individualistic, behavioural confines of the one- and to some extent the two-dimensional approaches. It must allow 'for consideration of the many ways in which *potential issues* are kept out of politics, whether through the operation of social forces and institutional practices or through individuals' decisions'.[37] In so extending the concept of power, Lukes suggests, 'the three-dimensional view . . . offers the prospect of a serious sociological and not merely personalized explanation of how political systems prevent demands from becoming political issues or even from being made'.[38]

Though the prospect has been offered, the task has yet to have been carried out. To do so, though, might bring together usefully approaches often considered separately of the relationship of political conceptions to the social order. For instance, following in a line of American political scientists (beginning perhaps with Lasswell), the emphasis upon consciousness allows consideration of the subjective effects of power, including Edelman's notion that 'political actions chiefly arouse or satisfy people not by granting or withholding their stable, substantive demands but rather by changing their demands and expectations'.[39] At the same

[35] ibid., p. 23 (emphasis supplied).
[36] ibid., pp. 24–5.
[37] ibid., p. 24.
[38] ibid., p.38.
[39] Murray Edelman, *Politics as Symbolic Action: Mass Arousal and Quiescence* (Markham Publishing Co., Chicago, 1971), p. 8.

time, by not restricting power to individuals' actions, the three-dimensional definition allows consideration of the social forces and historical patterns involved in Gramsci's concept of hegemony, or what Milliband develops as the use of ideological predominance for the 'engineering of consent' amongst the subordinate classes.[40]

Perhaps more significant, however, are the implications of this three-dimensional approach for an understanding of how power shapes participation patterns of the relatively powerless. In a sense, the separation by the pluralists of the notion of power from the phenomenon of quiescence has indicated the need for such a theory, while in the second and third approaches are its beginnings. In the two-dimensional approach is the suggestion of barriers that prevent issues from emerging into political arenas—i.e. that constrain conflict. In the three-dimensional approach is the suggestion of the use of power to pre-empt manifest conflict at all, through the shaping of patterns or conceptions of non-conflict. Yet, the two-dimensional approach may still need development and the three-dimensional prospect has yet to be put to empirical test.

This book therefore will pick up the challenge of attempting to relate the three dimensions of power to an understanding of quiescence and rebellion of a relatively powerless group in a social situation of high inequality. Through the empirical application further refinements of the notion of power may develop, but, of equal importance, more insights may be gleaned as to why non-élites in such situations act and believe as they do.

1.2 THE MECHANISMS OF POWER

What are the mechanisms of power? How might its components be wielded in the shaping or containment of conflict?

First Dimension. In the first-dimensional approach to power, with its emphasis on observable conflict in decision-making

---

[40] Antonio Gramsci, *Selections from the Prison Notebooks of* . . . ed. and trans., by Quinton Hare and Geoffrey Nowell-Smith (Lawrence and Wishart, London, 1971), see especially selections of 'State and Civil Society', in pp. 206-78. Ralph Milliband, *The State in Capitalist Society: An Analysis of the Western Systems of Power* (Weidenfeld and Nicolson, London, 1969), pp. 180-2.

arenas, power may be understood primarily by looking at who prevails in bargaining over the resolution of key issues. The mechanisms of power are important, but relatively straightforward and widely understood: they involve the political resources—votes, jobs, influence—that can be brought by political actors to the bargaining game and how well those resources can be wielded in each particular play— through personal efficacy, political experience, organizational strength, and so on.

Second Dimension. The second-dimensional approach adds to these resources those of a 'mobilization of bias',

A set of predominant values, beliefs, rituals, and institutional procedures ('rules of the game') that operate systematically and consistently to the benefit of certain persons and groups at the expense of others. Those who benefit are placed in a' preferred position to defend and promote their vested interests.[41]

Bachrach and Baratz argue in *Power and Poverty* that the mobilization of bias not only may be wielded upon decision-making in political arenas, but it in turn is sustained primarily through 'non-decisions', defined as:

A decision that results in suppression or thwarting of a latent or manifest challenge to the values or interests of the decision maker. To be more nearly explicit, nondecision-making is a means by which demands for change in the existing allocation of benefits and privileges in the community can be suffocated before they are voiced, or kept covert; or killed before they gain access to the relevant decision-making arena; or, failing all of these things, maimed or destroyed in the decision-implementing stage of the policy process.[42]

One form of non-decision-making, they suggest, may be force. A second may be the threat of sanctions, 'negative or positive', 'ranging from intimidation . . . to co-optation'. A third may be the 'invocation of an existing bias of the political system— a norm, precedent, rule or procedure—to squelch a threatening demand or incipient issue'. This may include the manipulation of symbols, such as, in certain political cultures, 'communist' or 'troublemaker'. A fourth process which they cite 'involves reshaping or strengthening the mobilization of bias' through the establishment of new barriers or new

[41] Bachrach and Baratz (1970), op. cit., p. 43.
[42] ibid., p. 44.

symbols 'against the challengers' efforts to widen the scope of conflict'.

While the above mechanisms of power involve identifiable actions which prevent issues from entering the decision-making arenas, there may be other processes of non-decision-making power which are not so explicitly observable. The first of these, 'decisionless decisions', grows from institutional inaction, or the unforeseen sum effect of incremental decisions. A second process has to do with the 'rule of anticipated reactions', 'situations where B, confronted by A who has greater power resources decides not to make a demand upon A, for fear that the latter will invoke sanctions against him'.[43] In both cases, the power process involves a non-event rather than an observable non-decision.

Third Dimension. By far the least developed and least understood mechanisms of power—at least within the field of political science—are those of the third dimension. Their identification, one suspects, involves specifying the means through which power influences, shapes or determines conceptions of the necessities, possibilities, and strategies of challenge in situations of latent conflict. This may include the study of social myths, language, and symbols, and how they are shaped or manipulated in power processes.[44] It may involve the study of communication of information— both of what is communicated and how it is done.[45] It may involve a focus upon the means by which social legitimations are developed around the dominant, and instilled as beliefs or roles in the dominated.[46] It may involve, in short, locating the power processes behind the social construction of meanings and patterns[47] that serve to get B to act and believe in a

[43] ibid., pp. 42-6.

[44] See, for instance, Edelman, op. cit.; Edelman, *The Symbolic Uses of Politics* (University of Illinois Press, Urbana, 1967); and Edelman, 'Symbols and Political Quiescence', *American Political Science Review,* 54 (1960), 695-704.

[45] For example, as developed by Claus Mueller, *The Politics of Communication: A Study in the Political Sociology of Language, Socialization and Legitimation* (Oxford University Press, New York, 1973).

[46] ibid.; see, too, Miliband, op. cit., pp. 179-264; and C. Wright Mills, *The Sociological Imagination* (Oxford University Press, New York, 1956), pp. 36-40.

[47] This is to suggest that processes may be similar to those suggested by Berger and Luckmann but that the processes are not random. They occur in a power field and to the advantage of power interests. See Peter L. Berger and Thomas Luckmann, *The Social Construction of Reality* (Doubleday and Co., New York,

manner in which B otherwise might not, to A's benefit and B's detriment.

Such processes may take direct observable forms, as Lukes suggests. 'One does not have to go to the lengths of talking about Brave New World, or the world of B. F. Skinner to see this: thought control takes many less total and more mundane forms, through the control of information, through the mass media, and through the process of socialization.'[48] His assertions are supported in various branches of contemporary social science. For instance, Deutsch and Rieselbach, in writing of new developments in the field, say that communications theory 'permits us to conceive of such elusive notions as consciousness and the political will as observable processes'.[49] Similarly, the study of socialization, enlightened by learning theory, may help to uncover the means by which dominance is maintained or legitimacy instilled, as Mann or Frey, among others, argue.[50]

In addition to these processes of information control or socialization, there may be other more indirect means by which power alters political conceptions. They involve psychological adaptations to the state of being without power. They may be viewed as third-dimensional effects of power, growing from the powerlessness experienced in the first two dimensions. Especially for highly deprived or vulnerable groups, three examples might be given of what shall be called the *indirect* mechanisms of power's third dimension.

In the first instance, the conceptions of the powerless may alter as an adaptive response to continual defeat. If the victories of A over B in the first dimension of power lead to non-challenge of B due to the anticipation of the reactions of A, as in the second-dimensional case, then, over time, the calculated withdrawal by B may lead to an unconscious pat-

1966); and critique by Richard Lichtmann, 'Symbolic Interaction and Social Reality: Some Marxist Queries', *Berkeley Journal of Sociology*, 15 (1970) 75–94.

[48] Lukes, op. cit., p. 23.

[49] Karl W. Deutsch and Leroy Rieselbach, 'Recent Trends in Political Theory and Political Philosophy', *The Annals of the American Political and Social Science*, 360 (1965), 151.

[50] Michael Mann, 'The Social Cohesion of Liberal Democracy', *American Sociological Review*, 35 (1970). Frederick W. Frey, 'Comment: On Issues and Non-Issues in the Study of Power', *American Political Science Review*, 65 (1971), 1081–1101.

tern of withdrawal, maintained not by fear of power of A but by a sense of powerlessness within B, regardless of A's condition. A sense of powerlessness may manifest itself as extensive fatalism, self-deprecation, or undue apathy about one's situation. Katznelson has argued, for instance, in *Black Men, White Cities* that 'given the onus of choice, the powerless internalize their impossible situation and internalize their guilt . . . The slave often identified with his master and accepted society's estimate of himself as being without worth . . . The less complete but nonetheless pervasive powerlessness of blacks in America's northern ghettos . . . has had similar effects.'[51] Or, the powerless may act, but owing to the sense of their powerlessness, they may alter the level of their demands.[52] The sense of powerlessness may also lead to a greater susceptibility to the internalization of the values, beliefs, or rules of the game of the powerful as a further adaptive response—i.e. as a means of escaping the subjective sense of powerlessness, if not its objective condition.[53]

The sense of powerlessness may often be found with, though it is conceptually distinct from, a second example of the indirect mechanisms of power's third dimension. It has to do with the interrelationship of participation and consciousness. As has been seen in the pluralists' literature, it is sometimes argued that participation is a consequence of a high level of political awareness or knowledge, most often associated with those of a favourable socio-economic status. However, it might also be the case, as is argued by the classical democratic theorists, that it is participation itself which increases political consciousness—a reverse argument from the one given above.[54] Social psychology studies, for instance, have found that political learning is dependent at least to

[51] Ira Katznelson, *Black Men, White Cities* (Oxford University Press, 1973), p. 198.

[52] Walter Korpi, 'Conflict, Power and Relative Deprivation', *American Political Science Review*, 68 (1974). Korpi writes, 'in the long run the weaker actor will, through internal psychological processes, tend to adjust his aspiration level towards the going rates of exchange in the relationship'. (p. 1571).

[53] See discussion by Paulo Freire, *The Pedagogy of the Oppressed* (Penguin Books, Harmondsworth, Middx, 1972), pp. 1–39.

[54] e.g. Rousseau, John Stuart Mill, G.D.H. Cole. See discussion of this theme in Pateman, op. cit., Chap. 3.

some degree of political participation within and mastery upon one's environment.[55] And, as Pizzorno points out, there is a 'singular relationship, well known by all organizers of parties and political movements: class consciousness promotes political participation, and in its turn, political participation increases class consciousness'.[56] If this second understanding of the relationship to participation and consciousness is the case, then it should also be the case that those denied participation—unable to engage actively with others in the determination of their own affairs—also might not develop political consciousness of their own situation or of broader political inequalities.

This relationship of non-participation to non-consciousness of deprived groups is developed by Paulo Freire, one of the few writers to have considered the topic in depth. 'Consciousness', he writes, 'is constituted in the dialectic of man's *objectification* and *action* upon the world.'[57] In situations of highly unequal power relationships, which he terms 'closed societies', the powerless are highly dependent. They are prevented from either self-determined action or reflection upon their actions. Denied this dialectic process, and denied the democratic experience out of which the 'critical consciousness' grows, they develop a 'culture of silence'. 'The dependent society is by definition a silent society.' The culture of silence may preclude the development of consciousness amongst the powerless thus lending to the dominant order an air of legitimacy. As in the sense of powerlessness, it may also encourage a susceptibility among the dependent society to internalization of the values of the dominant themselves. 'Its voice is not an authentic voice, but merely an echo of the metropolis. In every way the metropolis speaks, the dependent society listens.'[58] Mueller similarly writes about groups which 'cannot articulate their interests or perceive social conflict. Since they have been socialized into compliance, so to speak, they accept the definitions of political reality as offered by dominant groups, classes or government institutions.'[59]

[55] Melvin Seeman, 'Alienation, Membership, and Political Knowledge: A Comparative Study', *Public Opinion Quarterly*, 30 (1966), 353–67.
[56] Allesandro Pizzorno, 'An Introduction to the Theory of Political Participation', *Social Science Information*, 9 (1970), 45.
[57] Paulo Freire, *Cultural Action for Freedom* (Penguin Books, Harmondsworth, Middx, 1972), p. 52.
[58] ibid., pp. 58–9.   [59] Mueller, op. cit., p. 9.

Even as the 'silence' is broken, the initial demands of the dominated may be vague, ambiguous, partially developed. This might help to explain the phenomenon of the 'multiple' or 'split' consciousness[60] often cited in the literature for poor or working-class groups. As long as elements of the sense of powerlessness or the assuming consciousness that grow from non-participation can be maintained, then although there may be a multitude of grievances, the 'unified' or 'critical' consciousness will likely remain precluded. And, in turn, the inconsistencies themselves may re-enforce the pattern of non-challenge. In Gramsci's terms, 'it can reach the point where the contradiction of conscience will not permit any decision, any choice, and produce a state of moral and political passivity'.[61]

This understanding gives rise to a final indirect means through which power's third dimension may work. Garson has described the 'multiple consciousness' as being characterized by 'ambiguity and overlays of consciousness; different and seemingly contradictory orientations will be evoked *depending upon the context'.*[62] If such is the case, then the consciousness of the relatively powerless, even as it emerges, may be malleable, i.e. especially vulnerable to the manipulation of the power field around it. Through the invocation of myths or symbols, the use of threat or rumours, or other mechanisms of power, the powerful may be able to ensure that certain beliefs and actions emerge in one context while apparently contradictory grievances may be expressed in others. From this perspective, a consistently expressed consensus is not required for the maintenance of dominant interests, only a consistency that certain potentially key issues remain latent issues and that certain interests remain unrecognized—at certain times more than at others.

These direct and indirect mechanisms of power's third dimension combine to suggest numerous possibilities of the means through which power may serve to shape conceptions

[60] David Garson, 'Automobile Workers and the American Dream', *Politics and Society,* 3 (1973), 163–179; Antonio Gramsci, trans. by Lewis Marks, *The Modern Prince and Other Writings* (International Publishers, New York, 1957), p. 66.
[61] Gramsci (1957), op. cit., p. 67.
[62] Garson, op. cit., p. 163.

of the necessities, possibilities, or strategies of conflict. Not only, as in the two-dimensional approach, might grievances be excluded from entering the political process, but they might be precluded from consideration altogether. Or, B, the relatively powerless, may recognize grievances against A, the relatively powerful, but desist from challenge because B's conceptions of self, group, or class may be such as to make actions against A seem inappropriate. Or, B may recognize grievances, be willing to act upon them, but not recognize A as the responsible agent towards which action should be directed—e.g. because of the mystifications or legitimations which surround A. Or, B may recognize grievances against A and be willing to act, but may not through viewing the order as immutable or through lacking conceptions of possible alternatives. Or, B may act, but do so on the basis of misconceived grievances, against the wrong target, or through an ineffective strategy. Any or all of these possibilities may serve the same purpose of protecting A's interests owing to B's shaped conceptions of potential conflict, to B's detriment.

But the indirect mechanisms of power's third dimension, seen as a consequence of the powerlessness experienced in the first two, have suggested yet a further consideration: the dimensions of power, each with its sundry mechanisms, must be seen as interrelated in the totality of their impact. In that simple idea lies the basis for developing a more coherent theory about the effects of power and powerlessness upon quiescence and rebellion in situations of great inequality.

1.3 POWER AND POWERLESSNESS: QUIESCENCE AND REBELLION—A TENTATIVE RELATIONSHIP

Power, it has been suggested, involves the capacity of A to prevail over B both in resolution of manifest conflict and through affecting B's actions and conceptions about conflict or potential conflict. Intuitively, if the interests of A and B are contrary, and if A (individual, group, class) exercises power for the protection of its interests, then it will also be to A's advantage if the power can be used to generate and maintain quiescence of B (individual, group, class) upon B's interests. In that process, the dimensions of power and

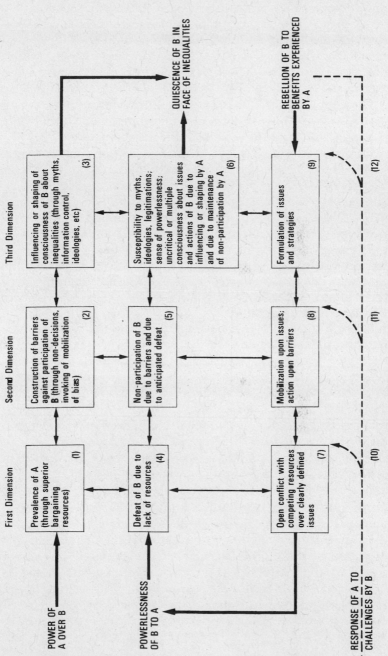

1.1 Power and Powerlessness: Quiescence and Rebellion — A Tentative Scheme

powerlessness may be viewed as interrelated and accumulative in nature, such that each dimension serves to re-enforce the strength of the other. The relationships may be schematized, as in Figure 1.1, and described as follows:[63]

As A develops power, A prevails over B in decision-making arenas in the allocation of resources and values within the political system [1]. If A prevails consistently, then A may accumulate surplus resources and values which may be allocated towards the construction of barriers around the decision-making arenas—i.e. towards the development of a mobilization of bias, as in the second dimension of power [2]. The consistent prevalence of A in the decision-making arenas plus the thwarting of challenges to that prevalence may allow A further power to invest in the development of dominant images, legitimations, or beliefs about A's power through control, for instance, of the media or other social-ization institutions [3]. The power of A to prevail in the first dimension increases the power to affect B's actions in the second dimension, and increases the power to affect B's conceptions in the third.

The power of A is also strengthened by the fact that the powerlessness of B is similarly accumulative, and that power and powerlessness may each re-enforce the other towards the generation of B's quiescence. In the decision-making arena, B suffers continual defeat at the hands of A [4]. Over time, B may cease to challenge A owing to the anticipation that A will prevail [5]. But B's non-challenge allows A more oppor-tunity to devote power to creating barriers to exclude partici-pation in the future [2, 5]. The inaction of B in the second-dimensional sense becomes a sum of the anticipation by B of defeat and the barriers maintained by A over B's entering the decision-making arena anyway, and the re-enforcing effect of one upon the other.

In turn, the second-dimensional relationship may re-enforce the sense of powerlessness, the maintained non-participation, the ambiguous consciousness, or other factors which comprise the indirect mechanisms of power's third dimension [5, 6]. Further withdrawal of B though, in turn, allows more security

[63] This is not meant to imply that in an empirical situation the relationships develop in this sequence, or in a linear fashion at all. However, it is analytically useful to describe them in this manner.

for A to develop further legitimations or ideologies which may be used indirectly to affect the conceptions of B [3, 6]. And, as has been seen, the powerlessness of B may also increase the susceptibility of B to introjection of A's values. In the third-dimensional sense, then, B's response becomes understood as the sum of B's powerlessness and A's power, and the re-enforcing effects of the one upon the other.

Once such power relationships are developed, their maintenance is self-propelled and attempts at their alteration are inevitably difficult. In order to remedy the inequalities, B must act, but to do so B must overcome A's power, and the accumulating effects of B's powerlessness. In order to benefit from the inequalities, A need not act, or if acting, may devote energies to strengthening the power relationships. Indeed, to the extent that A can maintain conflict within the second- or third-dimensional arenas, then A will continue to prevail simply through the inertia of the situation. Pocock describes what may have been such a relationship with reference to the maintenance of power by Ancient Chinese rulers:

Where A has the power and B has not, it is a sign of weakness for either to take initiative, but B must take it and A need not . . . Once acquired, it (power) is maintained not by exertion but by inaction; not by imposing norms, but by being prequisite to their imposition; not by the display of virtue, but by the characterless force of its own necessity. The ruler rules not by solving other's problems, but by having none of his own; others have problems—i.e. they desire the power he has—and by keeping these unsolved he retains the power over them.[64]

In such a situation, power relationships can be understood only with reference to their prior development and their impact comprehended only in the light of their own momentum.

Challenge, or rebellion, may develop if there is a shift in the power relationships—either owing to loss in the power of A or gain in the power of B. (The two need not be the same owing to the possibility of intervention by other actors, technological changes, external structural factors, etc.) But even as challenge emerges, several steps in overcoming power-

[64] J. G. A. Pocock, 'Ritual, Language and Power', in Pocock, *Politics, Language, and Time: Essays on Political Thought and History* (Methuen, London, 1970), p. 69.

lessness by B must occur before the conflict is on competitive ground.[65] B must go through a process of *issue and action formulation* by which B develops consciousness of the needs, possibilities, and strategies of challenge. That is, B must counter both the direct and indirect effects of power's third dimension [9]. And, B must carry out the process of *mobilization of action upon issues* to overcome the mobilization of bias of A against B's actions. B must develop its own resources —real and symbolic—to wage the conflict [8]. Only as the obstacles to challenge by B in the second and third dimensions are overcome can the conflict which emerges in the first dimension be said to reflect B's genuine participation—i.e. self-determined action with others similarly affected upon clearly conceived and articulated grievances [7].

This formulation of the steps in the emergence of effective challenge provides further understanding of the means by which A may prevail over the outcome of any latent or manifest conflict. In the first instance, A may simply remain aloof from B, for to intervene in a situation of potential conflict may be to introduce the notion of conflict itself. But, if conceptions or actions of challenge do arise on the part of B, A may respond at any point along the process of issue-emergence. That is, the powerless may face barriers to effective challenge in the processes of the formulation of issues, of the mobilization of action upon issues, or in the decision-making about issues—any or all of which may affect the outcome of the conflict [10, 11, 12 . . .]. What are for B barriers to change are for A options for the maintenance of the status quo.

But, by the same token, as the barriers are overcome, so, too, do A's options for control lessen. And, just as the dimensions of power are accumulative and re-enforcing for the maintenance of quiescence, so, too, does the emergence of challenge in one area of a power relationship weaken the power of the total to withstand further challenges by more than the loss of a single component. For example, the development of consciousness of an issue re-enforces the likelihood of attempted action upon it, in turn re-enforcing consciousness.

[65] Parenti, op. cit., calls this the problem of political capital accumulation: 'just as one needs capital to make capital, so one needs power to use power'. (p. 527).

A single victory helps to alter inaction owing to the anticipation of defeat, leading to more action, and so on. Once
patterns of quiescence are broken upon one set of grievances,
the accumulating resources of challenge—e.g. organization,
momentum, consciousness—may become transferable to other
issues and other targets.

For this reason, the development and maintenance of a
generalized pattern of quiescence of B by A in situations of
latent conflict will always be in A's interests. A will act to
thwart challenges by B regardless of whether they appear,
in the immediate sense, to be directed against A; for once the
patterns are broken, the likelihood of further action by B
increases and the options for control wielded by A decrease.
For this reason, too, A will support A' on matters of common interest *vis-à-vis* the behaviour and conceptions of B; and
B must ally with B' for the emergence of effective challenge
against A—giving rise over time to social grouping and social
classes of the relatively powerful and the relatively powerless.

1.4 METHODOLOGICAL CONSIDERATIONS

What may appear conceptually useful may not correspond
to actual circumstance. That which is analytically distinct
may in fact occur simultaneously. Thus, a primary task of
this study is to consider whether this model of power and
participation can be applied to an empirical situation and
whether that process in turn can lend further understanding
to the relationships so far put forward. That there are methodological difficulties to the task is recognized from the
outset. The suggestion of Bachrach and Baratz of even a
'second face' of power met vocal challenge on procedural
grounds: how can one find the 'hidden' aspects of power?
How can a non-decision be observed? Which non-events are
relevant?[66] The presentation of a 'third face' of power poses
yet further problems: how can one study what does not
happen? What about the problem of imputing interests and

[66] For example, Raymond E. Wolfinger, 'Nondecisions and the Study of
Local Politics', *American Political Science Review*, 65 (1971), 1063-1080; also,
'Rejoinder to Frey's Comment', *American Political Science Review*, 65 (1971),
1102-4; Richard M. Merelman, 'On the Neo-Elitist Critiques of Community
Power', *American Political Science Review*, 62 (1968), 451-60; Polsby (1963),
op. cit.

values? This book argues that these problems are surmountable. Broad guidelines used for the empirical study are presented here. Then, the telling test for the method, as for the model, will be the extent to which it helps to illuminate the empirical case itself.

In the first instance, the methodology assumes Frey's suggestion that 'we can expect non-issues when: 1) glaring inequalities occur in the distribution of things avowedly valued by actors in the system, and 2) those inequalities do not seem to occasion ameliorative influence attempts by those getting less of those values'.[67] Secondly, rather than assuming the inaction or inertia to be 'natural' in the mass and activism as the phenomenon to be explained (as is done in the pluralist methodolody), this approach initially assumes that remedial action upon inequalities by those affected would occur were it not for power relationships. The study of quiescence in a situation of potential conflict becomes the task, rather than the study of manifest conflict in a situation otherwise assumed to be conflict-free.

It is not adequate, however, merely to observe that inequalities exist and that such inequalities are met only by quiescence, to conclude that non-challenge is a product of power. As Lukes questions, 'Can we always assume that the victims of injustice and inequality would, but for the exercise of power, strive for justice and equality?'[68] On the contrary, he writes, 'we need to justify our expectation that B would have thought and acted differently, and we need to specify the means or mechanisms by which A has prevented, or else acted (or abstained from acting) in a manner sufficient to prevent B from doing so'.[69] From the model put forward, I suggest there are several means in an empirical study through which mechanisms can be identified and through which 'relevant counterfactuals' can be demonstrated to substantiate the expectation that B would have thought and acted differently, were it not for A's power.

[67] Frey, op. cit., p. 1097. This is essentially the approach used by Crenson, who objectively identifies varying levels in air pollution, assumes that people generally do not want to be poisoned, and asks why action upon pollution does not occur.

[68] Lukes, op. cit., p. 46.

[69] ibid., pp. 41–2.

In general, to do so requires going outside the decision-making arenas and carrying on extensive, time-consuming research in the community in question. There, non-actors and non-leaders become important, not as objects of scrutiny in themselves but to discover through their experiences, lives, conditions, and attitudes, whether and by what means power processes may serve to maintain non-conflict.

In pursuing the answer to the question more specifically, it may be necessary, first, to look at the historical development of an apparent 'consensus'. In so doing, it may be possible to determine whether that situation has been arrived at by 'choice' or whether it has been shaped by power relations. And, the background study may help to identify certain key symbols, cues, or routines that affect the maintenance of quiescence in a given situation but which may not be identifiable as part of the 'language of power' without knowledge of their antecedents.

Secondly, within a given situation of apparent non-challenge, processes of communication, socialization, acculturation, etc., can be studied to determine whether there is a specific relationship between the actions or ideologies of the power-holders and the action, inaction or beliefs of the powerless. In addition, it might be possible to determine whether the conditions do exist under which the actions and consciousness of B could develop, or whether identifiable power barriers serve to preclude their development, as in the indirect mechanisms of power.

Thirdly, it might be possible in a given or changing situation to posit or participate in ideas or actions which speculate about or attempt to develop challenges. The response of the quiescent population to such possibilities, and the response of the powerholders to the beginning formulation or raising of issues may help to show whether power mechanisms are at work to preclude challenge from emerging.

Even if the identification of specific processes of power is successful, it still does not satisfy the requirement of justifying the 'expectation that B would have thought and acted differently'. Several more types of evidence must be gathered. First, as Lukes suggests, it may be possible to observe what occurs on the part of B when the power of A over B weakens, i.e. in 'abnormal times . . . when the apparatus of power is removed or relaxed'.[70] Secondly, it may be possible to observe what occurs when alternative opportunities for action develop within B's field—through the intervention of third parties or new resources. If action or conceptions of action emerge upon previously existing conditions—whether due to alteration in the power of A or the powerlessness of B—then it may be possible to argue that the prior inaction or apparent consensus did not reflect real consensus. Finally, it may be possible to develop a comparative approach to the study of the problem: if similarly deprived groups are faced with observably differing degrees of power, and if one rebels while the other does not, then it should be possible to argue that the differing responses are related to differences in the power relationships.

If, after following such guidelines, no mechanisms of power can be identified and no relevant counterfactuals can be found, then the researcher must conclude that the quiescence of a given deprived group is, in fact, based upon consensus of that group to their condition, owing for instance, to differing values from those initially posited by the observer. In this sense, this approach allows the falsifiability of the hypothetical relationships being explored.[71] Moreover, the 'third-dimensional methodology' provides the possibility of reaching conclusions that power in a given situation is either three- or two- or one-dimensional in nature—a possibility not provided for in the other two approaches. Thus, the conclusions of this approach are less dependent upon the methodological assumptions than they might be in the approach of the pluralists' or of Bachrach and Baratz.

However, assumptions must be made in this, as in all studies of power, about the definitions of three key concepts: interests, consciousness and consensus.

For the observer to posit that B would act towards the attainment of a value X or would want X were it not for the power processes of A may involve avowing that X is in B's interest. However, to do so—unlike it is often alleged[72]—is

[70] ibid., p. 47.

[71] See, for instance, critique by Merelman, op. cit.

[72] See, for instance, Polsby (1963), op. cit., p. 96; Wolfinger 'Nondecisions and the Study of Local Politics', op. cit., p. 1066.

not necessarily to avow that X is in B's real interest, nor to give the observer the right to impose his interpretation of what is B's interest upon B. Rather, the observer's interpretation of what appears in a given context to be in B's interest may be used as a methodological tool for discovering whether power relationships are such as to have precluded the active and conscious choice by B about such interests, regardless of what the outcome of that choice actually would be. What B would choose (were B free from the power of A to do so) would be B's real interests—but they do not require identification for the study of power. That B is prevented from acting upon or conceiving certain posited interests is sufficient to show that the interests that are expressed by B are probably not B's real ones.[73]

The stance has ramifications for the consideration of consciousness. The unfortunate term 'false consciousness' must be avoided, for it is analytically confusing. Consciousness refers to a *state*, as in a state of being, and thus can only be falsified through negation of the state itself. If consciousness exists, it is real to its holders, and thus to the power situation. To discount it as 'false' may be to discount too simply the complexities or realities of the situation. What is far more accurate (and useful) is to describe the content, source, or nature of the consciousness—whether it reflects awareness of certain interests and not of others, whether it is critical or assuming, whether it has been developed through undue influence of A, and so on.

To argue that existing consciousness cannot be 'false' is not to argue the same for consensus. 'Real' consensus implies a prior process of agreement or choice, which in a situation of apparent consensus may or may not have been the case. The process may not have occurred; it could have been shaped or manipulated; the 'consensus' could be maintained by power processes, etc. In any event, what may appear consensus may not be what would appear were the real

[73] See discussion by William E. Connolly, 'On "Interests" in Politics', *Politics and Society*, 2 (1972), 459-77. This definition is similar to Connolly's that: 'Policy X is more in A's interest than policy Y if A, were he to *experience* the results of both X and Y, would *choose* X as the result he would rather have for himself.' (p. 472). However, less emphasis is put on the ability to experience the unforeseen consequences of a given choice; more on the process of making the choice itself.

process to take place. The investigation of the possibility that power processes have given rise to a 'false' consensus must be carried on to establish more accurately the nature of the first appearance.

Examples: The Closed and Colonial Societies.   Even with the help of these methodological guidelines, the identification of power processes may be easier in some situations than in others. For instance, in his pluralist critique of Bachrach and Baratz, Wolfinger readily accepts that power relationships may affect consciousness and action in closed societies, such as the plantation South. He writes, 'Some examples of false consciousness are indisputable, e.g. the long period of feeble protest by southern Negroes. Their reticence was due in part to repression, but much of it was based on myths and procedures.' Moreover, in making such conclusions, Wolfinger attributes to the Negro certain interests (as goals) assumed to be common: 'Almost any social scientist would agree that the blacks have been manipulated, because almost any social scientists' views of rational behaviour, irrespective of their specific character, would attribute certain goals to southern Negroes.'[74] What appears to be in question in this and other pluralists' critiques, then, is not whether the hidden faces of power exist, nor whether methodological assumptions can be made in certain situations for their identification, but whether such methods can be applied to consideration of the concepts in other situations—especially those of the more 'open' industrial democracies. There, the assumption is made in the pluralists' methodology that non-conflict represents social cohesion or integration, not, as others have argued, social control or hegemony.

It may be possible to develop an explanatory theory further, though, by looking not just at the example of the closed society but at situations where penetration (or integration) have not fully occurred and in which power processes, if they are at work, may be more readily self-evident. One example of such a case might be found in the colonial or neo-colonial relationship, involving, as it does, the power of a metropolis or developed industrial society over a less developed, more traditional society.

[74] Wolfinger, 'Nondecisions and the Study of Local Politics', op. cit., p. 1077.

In the first instance, the development of domination, or *the colonizing process*, involves the prevailing of the colonizer over the allocation of resources in the colony owing to superior resources of the former, such as capital, technology, or force. Secondly, however, the maintenance of that power involves the establishment of certain institutions and organizational forms. As Emerson describes:

Imperialism spread to the world at large the ideas, techniques, and institutions which had emerged from many centuries of European history. By its direct impact . . . it established many of the forms and methods of the West abroad, inevitably disrupting in greater or lesser degree the native societies on which it encroached in the process.[75]

The establishment of dominance includes the development of an administrative relationship by the dominant society over the dominated, either through the direct control of the representatives of the former, or through the development of collaborators or mediating élites amongst the latter. It includes a prevailing ideology through which the values of the metropolis are legitimated as superior and those of the colony as inferior. In short, the colonization process involves the development of a mobilization of bias—a set of predominant values, beliefs and institutional procedures that operate systematically to the benefit of the colonizer at the expense of the colonized. It is the development of a second-dimensional power relationship.

However, writers of and about the Third World insist that there is a further form of power that grows out of the effective colonizing process—one which serves to shape the legitimacy of the colonizers' dominance. Referring to the internalization of alien norms amongst dependent societies, Balandier wrote in 1951 of the *colonial situation* which 'not only conditioned the reaction of dependent peoples but is still responsible for certain reactions of people recently emancipated'.[76] Others, such as Freire, Fanon, and Memmi have since described further the means by which the consciousness of the colonized

[75] Rupert Emerson, *From Empire to Nation: The Rise to Self-Assertion of African and Asian Peoples* (Harvard University Press, Cambridge, Mass., 1960), p. 6.

[76] G. Balandier, 'The Colonial Situation: A Theoretical Approach', in Immanuel Wallerstein, ed., *Social Change: The Colonial Situation* (John Wiley and Sons, New York, 1966), pp. 34-61.

is affected by the values of the colonizer, as well as the extent to which the shaping is strengthened because of the sense of inadequacy or submissiveness amongst the dominated. Memmi, for instance, writes that as power develops its justifying ideology, so, too, must powerlessness:

There undoubtedly exists—at some point in its evolution—a certain adherence of the colonized to colonization. However, this adherence is the result of colonization not its cause. It arises after and not before colonial occupation. In order for the colonizer to be complete master, it is not enough for him to be so in actual fact, but he must believe in its legitimacy. In order for the legitimacy to be complete, it is not enough for the colonized to be a slave, he must also accept this role.[77]

In short, the development of the colonial situation involves the shaping of wants, values, roles, and beliefs of the colonized. It is a third-dimensional power relationship.

Do similar processes exist within developed societies? How can one tell? Admittedly, it may be more difficult to observe whether the second and third faces of power are behind apparent quiescence amongst inequalities in more open or homogenous societies. But the difficulties in observation should not alone refute the possibilities of the occurrence. Rather than avoid the problem, it might be preferable to attempt further to develop a theory of power relationships as well as a method for their study through an intermediary step: a focus upon the perhaps more visible processes that affect a dominated but relatively non-integrated sector within industrial democracy itself. The possibility for such an exploration lies in the study of the impact of power and powerlessness upon the actions and conceptions of the people of an under-developed region of the United States known as Central Appalachia.

[77] Albert Memmi, *The Colonizer and the Colonized* (Beacon Press, Boston, 1967), pp. 88-9.

2

THE CASE OF A
CENTRAL APPALACHIAN VALLEY

Stretching along a mountain range from western New York to northern Georgia is the region of the United States known as Appalachia. Within Appalachia is the rugged subregion known as Central Appalachia, covering some sixty counties of Kentucky, Tennessee, Virginia and West Virginia; and within coal-rich Central Appalachia is found the most highly concentrated rural non-farm population in the United States.[1]

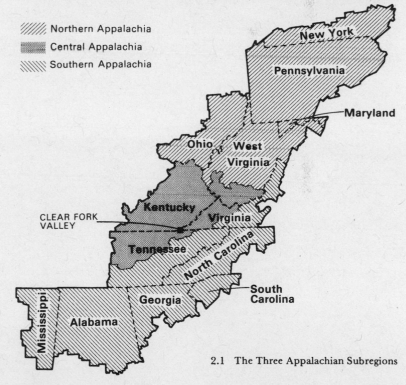

//// Northern Appalachia
▓▓ Central Appalachia
\\\\ Southern Appalachia

New York

Pennsylvania

Maryland

Ohio   West
        Virginia

Kentucky

CLEAR FORK
VALLEY   Virginia

Tennessee

North Carolina

South
Carolina

Mississippi

Alabama   Georgia

2.1 The Three Appalachian Subregions

[1] *Appalachia,* a publication of the Appalachian Regional Commission, (August 1968), p.1.

Often referred to as 'mountaineers', bound together by a distinctive blend of folk and mining culture, these people represent an often overlooked segment of the 'other America'—the primarily white and rural, lower and working class.[2]

Indeed, the images most often associated with Central Appalachia are those of poverty. It was there, in his campaign for the presidency in 1960, that John Kennedy encountered the depressed conditions that helped inspire his support for the War on Poverty of the later 1960s. Although by 1974 per capita income in Central Appalachia had risen to 65 per cent of the nation's average (up from 52 per cent in 1965), in 1970, 35 per cent of families lived below the poverty level, 72 per cent of the adult population had less than a high school education, and problems of unemployment and poor health care persisted.

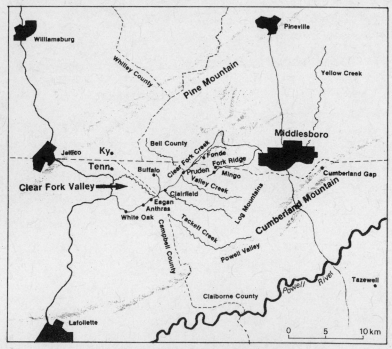

2.2   Clear Fork Valley and Vicinity

[2] Michael Harrington, *The Other America* (Penguin Books, Baltimore, Maryland, 1962), see especially, pp. 43–51.

Despite the images, Central Appalachia is not poor. Within its borders is tremendous wealth, in the form of natural resources, particularly the black gold of the energy era—coal. In 1974 Appalachia supplied 65 per cent of the coal produced in the United States. Within Central Appalachia alone there were 1,460 mineral industry establishments, 43 per cent of the country's total; and beneath the mountains lies enough coal to feed the national energy demand for 200 years to come.

Appalachia is not poor, then, but its people are. They rarely own and scarcely benefit from the area's wealth. Instead large, absentee, corporate land and coal owners do— increasingly multinational conglomerates which also own and deliver much of the rest of the energy of the nation and of the world.[3] In 1965, *Dun's Review of Modern Business* wrote, 'for all their small numbers . . . these coal royalists hold what may be one of the most lucrative investments in all of America',[4] while a government-sponsored study also pointed out that despite the War on Poverty, about twice as much capital flowed out of Central Appalachia as into it in 1967 and entered 'the financial markets centered around New York' and other metropolitan centres.[5] Not even in the energy boom of the 1970s, did the wealth produced from Appalachia go to its people.

In a word, Central Appalachia is a region of poverty amidst riches; a place of glaring inequalities. And yet, at

[3] For a more complete account, see my compilations in John Gaventa, 'In Appalachia, Property is Theft', *Southern Exposure*, vol. 1, no. 2, (Summer–Fall 1973), pp. 29–41; or John Gaventa, 'The Property Taxation of Coal in Central Appalachia', a report prepared for the Senate Committee for Inter-governmental Relations, from Save Our Cumberland Mountains (1973). Other accounts may be found, with reference to Kentucky, Richard Kirby, 'Kentucky Coal: Owners, Taxes, Profits', a study for the Appalachian Volunteers (unpublished, 11 March 1969); James C. Millstone, 'East Kentucky Coal Makes Profits for Owners, Not Region', in David S. Walls and John B. Stephenson, eds., *Appalachia in the Sixties* (University Press of Kentucky, Lexington, 1972), pp. 69–75; with reference to West Virginia, J. Davitt McAteer, *Coal Mine Health and Safety: The Case of West Virginia* (Praeger Publishers, New York, 1973), pp. 140–80; and Tom Miller, 'Who Owns West Virginia?' reprints from the *Huntington Advertiser* and *Herald Dispatch* (1974).

[4] *Dun's Review of Modern Industry* (Apr. 1965), p. 40.

[5] *Capital Resources in the Central Appalachian Region*, report to Appalachian Regional Commission (Checchi and Co., Washington, 1969).

least on the basis of social science literature on the region, the inequalities do not appear to have prompted major challenges from those deprived. Moynihan, for instance, in recounting Kennedy's 1960 visit to West Virginia, wrote:

The American poor were not only invisible, in Michael Harrington's phrase, but they were also silent. Kennedy had ventured into West Virginia searching for Protestant votes, not for poverty. There he encountered the incredible pauperization of the mountain people, most particularly the soft-coal miners, an industrial workforce whose numbers had been reduced by nearly two-thirds in the course of the decade, but with hardly a sound of protest. The miners were desperately poor, shockingly unemployed, but neither radical nor in any significant way restive.[6]

The picture presented is one of quiescence amongst poverty and inequality, and this picture is not an unusual one. Whether as citizen, worker, or potential protestor, the Appalachian appears to illustrate the quiescence described in social science literature on lower and working classes in America generally.

As regards the Appalachian citizen, for instance, Thomas Ford wrote in the major study of the region in the early 1960s that of the 'adjustment problems' of the people 'perhaps the most serious . . . are those that stem from their failure to develop a strong sense of civic responsibility—this is evident in the shortage of effective community action'.[7] In a study of a coal-mining community in southern Illinois, Lantz wrote that 'although economic impoverishment was clearly manifest . . . there appeared to be a marked apathy and hopelessness about change and about making life different or better'.[8] Richard Ball refers to the 'widespread, apparently "irrational" recalcitrance among the people'.[9] Plunkett and Bowman, too, write of the problems of low participation at the grass roots level in the modernization

[6] Daniel P. Moynihan, *Maximum Feasible Misunderstanding* (Free Press, New York, 1969), pp. 24-5.

[7] Thomas R. Ford, 'The Passing of Provincialism', in Thomas R. Ford, ed., *The Southern Appalachian Region* (University Press of Kentucky, Lexington, 1962), p. 31.

[8] Herman R. Lantz, 'Resignation, Industrialization, and the Problem of Social Change: A Case History of a Mining Community', in Arthur B. Shostack and William Gomberg, *Blue Collar World* (Prentice-Hall, Englewood Cliffs, New Jersey, 1964), p. 258.

[9] Richard Ball, 'A Poverty Case: the Analgesic Subculture of the Southern Appalachias', *American Sociological Review*, 33 (1968), 885.

process of the region.[10] And, even outside the region, as in the case of Appalachian migrants, Griffin finds in a study in Cincinnatti that 'the Southern Appalachians participate much less often in voluntary organizations, such as lodges, unions, neighbourhood clubs, and community center activities'.[11] The studies lack comparative focus, but given the high incidence of poverty in the region, the pattern might be considered as a persuasive example of the generally accepted political science lesson, that socio-economic status greatly affects participation in the United States. More so, Verba and Nie find, than in all but one of nine other major countries for which data are available.[12]

One might expect, on the other hand, more challenge to social deprivation from the Appalachian worker. The Ford study, for instance, found that 41 per cent of the wage earners surveyed in the region were members of a union or had had some union experience,[13] a figure significantly higher than in many parts of the South or the nation as a whole. Moreover, several studies have suggested that mining communities—as occupational communities, or as 'isolated masses'—are likely to be more militant than are other segments of the working population.[14] And, in Central Appalachia 11 per cent of the population are miners, five times the concentration found in Appalachia as a whole and sixteen

[10] H. Dudley Plunkett and Mary Jean Bowman, *Elites and Change in the Kentucky Mountains* (University Press of Kentucky, Lexington, 1973).

[11] Roscoe Griffin, 'Appalachian Newcomers in Cincinnatti', in Ford, ed., op. cit., p. 84.

[12] Verba and Nie, *Participation in America*, op. cit., p. 340. The other countries in which the relationship was lower than in the U.S. were the United Kingdom, Italy, Mexico, Germany, Nigeria, Netherlands, Austria, and Japan.

[13] Ford, op. cit., p. 15.

[14] The 'isolated mass' concept is developed by Clark Kerr and Abraham Siegal, 'The Interindustry Propensity to Strike—an International Comparison', in Arthur Kornhauser, Robert Dubin, Arthur M. Ross, *Industrial Conflict* (McGraw-Hill, New York, 1954), pp. 189–212; and Gaston V. Rimlinger, 'International Differences in the Strike Propensity of Coal Miners: Experience in Four Countries', *Industrial and Labour Relations Review*, 12 (1958-9), 389–405. The occupational community concept is also considered by Lipset, *Political Man*, op. cit.; and Robert Blauner, 'Work Satisfaction and Industrial Trends in Modern Society', in Galenson and Lipset eds., *Labor and Trade Unionism* (John Wiley and Sons, New York, 1960), pp. 339–60. For a general discussion of approaches to mining communities, see M.I.A. Bulmer, 'Sociological Models of the Mining Community', *The Sociological Review*, 23 (Feb. 1975), 61–92.

times higher than the national average.[15]

Yet, the communities in the heart of Central Appalachia have a higher percentage of non-union or 'company union' miners than any other district of the national United Mine Workers of America in the eastern United States. And, though there unquestionably has been widespread labour militancy, there has not developed the class organization or class consciousness found in mining communities in many other parts of the world.[16] Historically, in fact, the miners of the region in comparison with other American miners have had the image of the 'docile diggers'.[17] Similarly, in 1934 a comparative study of the miners of South Wales and Appalachia found 'both to be splendid fellows in their own way' but added, 'one cannot help but be impressed by the contrast', noting:

The American miner is clever in tinkering with an automobile or radio and can talk knowledgeably about the house property, insurance, or other investments; if he belongs to the union he may occasionally discuss it but his criticism will probably be in terms of personalities rather than principles . . . The British miner, more particularly the Welsh miner, is not interested personally in investments or house property . . . You will find him eagerly interested in economic and political theories and problems . . .[18]

Since the days of John L. Lewis, the American miner has come, of course, to be commonly associated with labour unrest, but even so, the consciousness often remains a 'conflict consciousness',[19] reflective of that more generally in the United States described by Aronowitz as:

working class consciousness . . . industry oriented, if not always job oriented. Workers will fight their unions and companies through wildcat

[15] Based on 1970 census as reported in 'The Appalachian Labour Force and Its Work', *Appalachia,* vol. 7, no. 6, (June–July 1974), pp. 11–28.

[16] See discussion by John H.M. Laslett, *Labor and the Left: A Study of Socialist and Radical Influences in the American Labor Movement, 1881–1924* (Basic Books, New York, 1970), pp. 192–240; also Laslett, 'Why Some Do and Some Don't : Some Determinants of Radicalism Among British and American Coal Miners, 1872–1924' (unpublished paper, 1973).

[17] McCalister Coleman, *Men and Coal* (Farrar and Rinehart, New York, 1943), p. 122.

[18] Harold Watkins, *Coal and Men* (George Allen and Unwin, London, 1934), p. 83.

[19] A distinction from 'revolutionary consciousness'; see, for instance, Giddens, *The Class Structure of Advanced Societies,* op. cit., pp. 112–17, 202.

strikes and other means outside the established framework of collective bargaining. But they are ideologically and culturally tied to the prevailing system of power . . .[20]

Rather than being different from, the Appalachian worker, like the Appalachian citizen, tends to reflect broader patterns in the United States.

The 1960s and the 1970s, however, have been decades in which challenges to social inequalities in America have been expressed less through the traditional modes of civic or union action than through protest movements of relatively powerless groups or ethnic minorities. Yet, amidst the literature of community unrest or the rise of ethnic power, there is little reference to the development of protest or consciousness of the Appalachian miner-mountaineers. Nor does their poverty receive the attention that has been given to urban poverty by the upheavals in the cities. When compared to their urban counterparts, the Appalachian poor, as the rural poor more generally in America, are 'unorganized, dispersed and less visible'; though numerically there are almost as many rural poor as there are in urban areas.[21]

While there may be found in Central Appalachia examples of the starkest deprivations in American society, these deprivations do not appear to have been met with extraordinary challenges from the deprived. The pattern is not unique to the Appalachias; it is found in the country more generally. It is a fundamental problem for American democracy, for it calls into question the 'relationship of political participation and social and economic equality'. Verba and Nie describe further:

Through political participation, deprived groups can obtain beneficial government output—welfare legislation, anti-discrimination legislation, specific allocations—that may, over time, make them equal in social and economic ways . . . However, there is one thing wrong with this approach to overcoming deprivation: those social and economic deprivations—lower levels of education, lower status occupations, inadequate income—that political participation is supposed to be used to overcome, impede political participation . . . Those who need the beneficial

[20] Stanley Aronowitz, *False Promises: The Shaping of American Working Class Consciousness* (McGraw-Hill, New York, 1973), pp. 259-60; see pp. 257-63 generally for a discussion of worker quiescence.

[21] Peter Dorner, 'Fourteen Million Rural Poor', *Yale Review*, 63 (1969), 283.

outcomes of participation the least—who are already advantaged in social and economic terms—participate the most.[22]

Scholars more on the left similarly point to the gap between their theory of social change 'from below' and the fact of working-class quiescence.[23] But though the problem may be widely recognized, its reasons, its implications, and to some degree, its very extent depend strongly upon the role assigned to power as a possible mediator between the conditions of inequality and the response they evoke.

Perhaps the dominant school of Appalachian studies has adopted the pluralists' approach to the problem. In separating the study of non-participation from the study of power, this approach has placed the explanation for inaction in the culture or circumstance of the deprived themselves. Thus, Ford argues that the 'lack of civic responsibility' represents a 'deficiency' within the culture which (in terms similar to those Banfield used in southern Italy) is 'a logical consequence of the traditional social organization of Appalachian society based on family and the culture of individualism as a value'. The problem is not whether the institutions that affect the people are open and responsive, but whether the people are 'willing to accept and sustain the fundamental premise that furtherance of the commonweal in a democratic society requires a common effort'.[24] Other studies focus upon a fatalism or backwardness of the culture, allowing conclusions such as 'What needs to be developed is not the Region but the Region's people . . .'[25] Similarly, in his study of the work attitudes of the miners of 'Coal Town', Lantz finds a predominant 'resignation'. 'Because they are unable to concern themselves', Lantz writes, such groups 'constitute a serious economic burden for the country.'[26] They do not conform to the view of the 'economic rational, self-seeking man'.[27]

The application of the pluralists' methodology to the

[22] Verba and Nie, op. cit., p. 150.

[23] For instance, Christopher Lasch, *The Agony of the American Left* (Penguin Books, Harmondsworth, Middx, 1973).

[24] Ford, op. cit., p. 32.

[25] James S. Brown and George A. Hillery, Jr., 'The Great Migration, 1940–1960', in Ford, ed., op. cit., p. 78.

[26] Lantz, op. cit., p. 257.

[27] ibid., p. 268.

the Appalachian region can be criticized on the same basis as it has been elsewhere. By assuming an open system in which people could participate and would if they had grievances, the view must place explanation for non-participation in value-laden allegations about the non-participants themselves. Terms such as 'the people left behind' or 'yesterday's people',[28] connote that if people were to participate they would choose the same values as those being ascribed to them by the dominant order. Integration not reform becomes the strategy for change, and the appearance of apathy justifies the dominance of an élite in the integrative process. As one study put it, 'successful adaptation of the regional culture and social structure must depend very heavily on the persistence and persuasion of a minority of local men who are motivated and equipped to play cultural bridge roles'.[29]

Within Appalachian studies, though, this approach to the region has been challenged by alternative views which may be said to illustrate second- and third-dimensional approaches to the study of power.

From a second-dimensional view, the region is seen as a victim of 'neglect' or of 'broken promises' by the institutions which affect it. Expression of politically latent grievances is found to be blocked by institutional practices, control of élites, a wielding of a 'mobilization of bias'.[30] From this perspective, the 'maximum feasible participation' components of the War on Poverty may be seen as unparalleled efforts to remove political barriers to effective voice, and the conflict which emerged as indicative of the previously latent conflict.[31] The work of Robert Coles, which uses open-ended tape recording techniques (much as Bachrach and Baratz might have done on the streetcorners of Philadelphia), also documents the often unexpressed grievances of

---

[28] National Advisory Commission on Rural Poverty, *The People Left Behind* (Government Printing Office, Washington, 1967); and Jack E. Weller, *Yesterday's People*, (University Press of Kentucky, Lexington, 1966).

[29] Plunkett and Bowman, op. cit., p. 46.

[30] See, for instance, the work of Harry Caudill, *Night Comes to the Cumberlands* (Little, Brown and Co., Boston, 1962). Also, David S. Walls and John B. Stephenson, *Appalachia in the Sixties* (University Press of Kentucky, Lexington, 1972).

[31] To be discussed further in Chapter 6. For a good account of the War in Appalachia, see Huey Perry, *They'll Cut Off Your Project* (Praeger Publishers, New York, 1972).

the poor, the miners, the rural people in the region.[32] Couto's study of how the liberal myths about poverty in America have been used by the medical profession to discourage substantive action on health care in Floyd County, Kentucky, well exemplifies the political importance of being able to invoke prevailing norms and beliefs for the protection of certain interests over others.[33] If the barriers to the expression of grievances lead to powerlessness, it can be remedied, in this view, primarily by reform of the political institutions to allow widespread participation by the deprived themselves.

In the third approach, contradictory interests, often those of the local non-élite with an absentee élite, are seen as the basis of Appalachian under-development. Power serves to maintain prevailing order of inequality not only through institutional barriers but also through the shaping of beliefs about the order's legitimacy or immutability.[34] In Appalachia, this is seen primarily in the impact of the values of the dominant interests upon those of the dominated. Gish, for instance, has described the government development programmes in Appalachia as 'an attempt to do away with the mountain man and all he represents . . . they are out to change us into something else—the homogenized all—American model American'.[35] Branscome similarly writes of the power of technological society to 'annihilate the hillbilly', while exploiting the region's resources.[36] And Couto suggests that not only are myths used to defer grievances about health care but they also may affect the beliefs of the non-élite about their roles in relationship to the medical professionals: 'acceptance of attributed identity instills myth with its

[32] See particularly, Robert Coles, 'Rural Upheaval: Conflict and Accommodation', in James Sundquist, *On Fighting Poverty* (Basic Books, New York, 1969), pp. 103–26; and Robert Coles, *Migrants, Sharecroppers, Mountaineers (Children of Crisis,* vol. II) (Little, Brown and Co., Boston, 1967).

[33] Richard Couto, *Poverty, Politics and Health Care: An Appalachian Experience* (Praeger Publishers, New York, 1975).

[34] See, for instance, Helen M. Lewis and Edward E. Knipe, 'The Colonialism Model: the Appalachian Case', in Edward Storey, ed., *An Uncertain America: Anthropological Approaches to Domestic Crisis* (Little, Brown and Co., Boston, 1971); and Roger Lesser, *et al.,* in *Peoples' Appalachia,* 1 (1970), among others.

[35] Tom Gish, *Mountain Life and Work,* 69 (May 1963), 14–16, quoted by Couto, op. cit., p. 512.

[36] James Branscome, 'Annihilating the Hillbilly: the Appalachians' Struggle with America's Institutions', pamphlet by Appalachian Movement Press, Huntington, West Virginia, 1971.

greatest power, the power to go unquestioned'.[37]

In this third approach, Central Appalachia itself is often compared to a colony, affected by the processes of colonization similar to the processes through which a metropolis develops and maintains dominance over hinterlands in other parts of the world.[38] Such a power relationship, as has been suggested, may mean not only that the local political and economic institutions are controlled by those of the metropolis—either directly or through collaborators—but also that the conceptions of the colonized communities are affected in a variety of ways. Much as Memmi has suggested, there may be a tendency among the colonized, especially the local élite, to adopt the prevailing values of the powerholders more readily—i.e. to give up their culture in favour of the 'homogenized all-American model American'. A more recent study has argued that Appalachia's cultural domination should be seen not as a function of 'colonization' but as the class hegemony and legitimation of a peripheral region within an advanced capitalist nation.[39]

While these various studies indicate the nature of the problem, there has yet to be a specific, empirical development of the means and extent to which the multiple faces of power affect the politics of a single area, over time, in a variety of aspects of community life. What might be offered by such a study would be not only a better understanding of the

[37] Couto, op. cit., p. 471.

[38] In addition to Lewis and Knipe, op. cit., and Lewis, *et. al., The Colony of Appalachia* (forthcoming, Appalachian Consortium Press), the analogy has been widely used in reference to the Appalachian region by Branscome, op. cit.; Caudill, op. cit.; Emil Malizia, 'Economic Imperialism: An Interpretation of Appalachian Under-development', *Appalachian Journal*, vol. 1, no. 2, (Spring 1973), pp. 130-37; *Peoples' Appalachia*; Jack Weller, 'Appalachia: America's Mineral Colony', *Vantage Point*, 2 (1972), among others. The concept of 'internal colonialism' has been widely developed in the Third World countries, for instance, by Pablo Gonzalez-Casanova, 'Internal Colonialism and National Development', in Irving Louis Horowitz, *et. al.*, eds., *Latin American Radicalism* (Vintage Books, New York, 1969), pp. 118-40. The analogy is used in reference to other under-developed parts of the United States by Robert Blauner, 'Internal Colonialism and Ghetto Revolts', *Social Problems* 16, no. 4 (1969), pp. 393-408; Andre Gorz, 'Colonialism at Home and Abroad', *Liberation* 16, no. 6, (Nov. 1971), pp. 22-9; Joe Persky, 'The South: A Colony at Home', *Southern Exposure* (Summer-Fall 1973), 14-22, among others.

[39] David S. Walls, 'Central Appalachia: A Peripheral Region Within an Advance Capitalist Society', *Journal of Sociology and Social Welfare*, 4 (1976).

politics of inequality within the Appalachian region but also, through the example, an understanding of the processes of power which may be involved in the quiescence phenomenon in industrial society more generally. In fact, what may be distinctive about the Central Appalachian case is not a difference in the nature of power compared to the rest of the country, but in the extent to which the power processes may be revealed, because of the starkness of the inequalities, the exaggeration of the quiescent patterns, and the relative non-integration of the region into the nation's political, social or cultural mainstreams. It is with that possibility in mind that I turn to the case of the Clear Fork Valley.

PART II

THE HISTORICAL FORMATION OF POWER RELATIONSHIPS

3

THE IMPACT OF INDUSTRIAL POWER: THE SHAPING OF A COMPANY VALLEY

In the latter part of the nineteenth century, in and around the Cumberland Gap, the historic passageway of the Appalachias, an unprecedented economic boom created the industrial and mining centre of Middlesboro—'Magic City of the South'. (The original spelling 'Middlesborough' has been modernized to 'Middlesboro'.) Founded by a single company, the American Association, Ltd., of London, boosted by over twenty million dollars of British capital, and masterminded under the energetic leadership of a Scotsman, Alexander Arthur, this 'Anglo-American enterprise' rapidly acquired 80,000 acres of coal and mineral-rich land. As counterpart to the Middlesborough in the industrial coalfields of northern England, this city was to feed the resources of iron, coal, and steel to the rapidly industrializing American South. Speaking to a group of dignitaries visiting his city in 1890, founding father Arthur proclaimed, 'I would say that America needs this place and our Anglo-American money, experience and push.'[1] The London Stock Exchange concurred by valuing a single share in the enterprise only three years after the Company's founding at over £40 sterling.

One suspects, though, that the initial encounter of the industrial metropolitan and agricultural Appalachian societies involved rather more than what Arthur called 'but a transfer of British business to American soil'.[2] Arthur's secretary may have been more accurate:

Thus it happened that almost a hundred years after England lost her colonies, "conquistadores" from Albion came out to a still crude and settled quarter of the United States for the purpose of further colonization.[3]

[1] Alexander Arthur, speech delivered in the hall of the Middlesborough Hotel, 11 November 1890 (mimeo, Middlesboro Public Library).

[2] ibid.

[3] Papers of C. B. Roberts, 'The Building of Middlesborough', referred to hereafter as *Roberts Papers*, used by kind permission of the Filson Club, Louisville, Kentucky.

A review of the period from 1887 to 1895 may provide useful insights into the nature of industrial power and the means by which it established its hegemony within the rural Central Appalachian region.

3.1   PRE-INDUSTRIAL APPALACHIAN SOCIETY

To understand the 'colonization' of Appalachia, one has to look first at the nature of its pre-industrial society. Briefly, it was founded upon a determination for independence, based upon a relationship to nature and to the land; and it developed a particular culture quite different from that of the industrial society developing around it.

Perhaps more than any other region of the frontier, the Southern Highlands were settled by the rebels of industrialization—those who cherished their own independence enough to leave both the Old World, and the initial developments in the east of the New World. Most of these early settlers were Scotsmen, Englishmen and Welshmen. In 1772, in what is now eastern Tennessee, they formed one of the first independent local governments, the Watauga Association, of which Theodore Roosevelt wrote, 'It is this fact of the early independence of the settlers along the headwaters of the Tennessee that gives to their history its particular importance. They were the first men of American birth to establish a free and independent community on the Continent'.[4] In a similar expression of self-determination, an assembly of these frontier backwoodsmen, meeting in Mecklenburg County, North Carolina in May 1775, passed the first American 'Resolution of Separation' from the Crown—more than a year before the Continental Congress approved Thomas Jefferson's Declaration of Independence.

These Appalachian mountains attracted not only the more independent westward migrants, but also those seeking a rural lifestyle. In 1842, for instance, a publication of the East Tennessee Land Company argued that the industrialization of Britain was threatening the livelihood of the small

[4] Theodore Roosevelt, *The Winning of the West* G. Putnam's Sons, New York, 1900), p. 231. Quoted by John C. Campbell, *The Southern Highlander and his Homeland* (University Press of Kentucky, Lexington, 1969), p. 29.

[5] J. Gray Smith, 'A Brief Historical and Statistical Descriptive Review of East Tennessee' (East Tennessee Land Co., London, 1842), p. xi.

entrepreneur and that the solution to his confines of poverty
was migration to the beautiful valleys of East Tennessee—to
'the peaceful solitude, the clear blue sky, the song of the
mocking bird, the note of the dove, the hum of the humming-
bird, the silence of nature, where all is echo'.[5] Similarly, on
the Cumberland Plateau as late as 1880, Thomas Hughes
(author of *Tom Brown's School Days*) founded a utopian
colony for agrarian-inclined intellectuals, naming it Rugby,
after the school in Britain.[6] More generally, the isolation and
ruggedness of the Appalachian mountains attracted a breed
of American frontiersmen whose 'absorbing passion was not
for religious discussion'. Rather, it was, wrote one early
visitor to the Cumberland Gap area, 'for the possession of
land, for the organization and diversions of rural life'.[7]

Located beneath the Cumberland Gap, the valleys of Bell
County, Kentucky and Claiborne County, Tennessee provide
examples of the sort of life that developed throughout the
Central Appalachias. The area had long been a hunting
ground for Indians: the Cherokees, Creeks and Catawbas
from the South; the Delawares, Shawnee and Wyando from
the North. The first recorded discovery of the Gap by a
white man was in 1750 by Dr Thomas Walker, an agent of
the Loyal Land Company, who had been authorized by the
Province of Virginia to survey and claim some 800,000 acres
to pre-empt claims by the French. A trail was blazed in
1775 by Daniel Boone and others (Boone's son was killed in
a skirmish in Powell Valley, near the Cumberland Gap), and
by 1795 the first white settlement had been founded along
the Yellow Creek.

In the early 1800s, the new road and railways bypassed
the difficult country around the Cumberland Gap, which
for decades had served as a gateway to the west. For almost
a century the rural communities within Central Appalachia
developed slowly, in relative isolation, and scarcely influenced
by the rapid industrialization to the east, north and west.

By the mid-nineteenth century there were still only sixty
families living in the Yellow Creek Valley of Bell County,
Kentucky. To the south of the Gap, in Claiborne County,

[6] Thomas Hughes, *Rugby, Tennessee* (Macmillan, London, 1881).
[7] Thomas Shaler, quoted in H.H. Fuson, *History of Bell County* (Hobson
Book Press, New York, 1947), vol. II, p. 73.

Tennessee, the population was scattered throughout the county in small settlements like those along the Yellow Creek. The communities were identified by the names of their natural or geographical markings—Laurel Fork, Pleasant and Little Gap, Buffalo, or South America (because of its remoteness). The economy was agricultural, sparse in the mountain hollows, richer in the river valleys. Families settled next to each other. Kinship became a key to social organization. Though some families were more prosperous than others, land resources were abundant and more or less equally divided. As in many such frontier communities, labour was often co-operatively shared at 'corn-huskin's', log-rollings, or house-raisings.[8] Other than the courthouse in the county seat, there was little formal governmental organization, nor was there much desire for any. In Claiborne County only one school existed, but the county (which had a population of 9,321 by 1870) refused to levy a tax for further educational purposes. A survey of all the counties in Tennessee in 1874 wrote:

The farmers of Claiborne County are said to be the best contented in the State. They are not ambitious of wealth or distinctions, but make what they live upon and live upon what they make. They work for a competency and are satisfied with it. No visions of princely wealth in the future beguile them into a neglect of the enjoyment of the present. Life to them is a thing to be enjoyed, not merely to endure.[9]

In a nearby county, Thomas Hughes wrote at about the same time of an Englishman who had to come to the area to found some 'manufactures' but who had 'left in sheer despair and disgust, saying he had found at last a place where no one seemed to care for money'.[10]

3.2 THE ECONOMIC DEMANDS OF THE METROPOLIS

Towards the end of the nineteenth century, forces were developing outside these Central Appalachian enclaves that would transform the rather independent, peasant-like communities within them. The forces were basically the same as

---

[8] For further discussion, see Fuson, ibid., p. 325.
[9] M. Killebrew, *Resources of Tennessee* (Tavel, Eastman and Howel, Nashville, Tennessee, 1874), p. 481.
[10] Hughes, op. cit., pp. 63–4.

those which gave rise to imperialism in under-developed areas
of the world generally. Hobson, like Lenin, thought of imperialism as brought about by the need for the export of
surplus capital. As investment opportunities declined in metropolitan centres, capitalist financial institutions had to create
new opportunities for investment in the under-developed
regions. Other writers, such as Magdoff, focus on the necessity
of the industrial powers to control raw material sources and
markets.[11] Both factors were neatly juxtaposed in the founding of Middlesboro in the Yellow Creek Valley of Kentucky.

On the one hand, excess capital in Britain was clearly a
factor. Between roughly 1870 and 1914, Britain invested
abroad about as much as the value of her entire industrial
and commercial capital at home (excluding land).[12] The
investments were not confined to the Third World. In fact,
'by far the greatest part of British capital export went to
independent countries. Only about 20 per cent was invested
in British colonies, including India, and another 20 per cent
in Latin America. The main investment was in other capitalist
countries.'[13]

On the other hand, while the metropolitan centres in
Britain faced the need for capital export, those in the United
States faced the need for resources. These centres were not
just those in the North; they included the rapidly developing
cities of the South such as Atlanta, Chattanooga and Birming-
ham. An industry publication in 1875 wrote that, 'The
proximity of iron and coal has been the secret of England's
mercantile success, and History will repeat itself in the
Southern States.'[14] Quoting a speech by Sir Isaac Lothian
Bell at Britain's Iron and Steel Institute, it continued, 'the
great advantage possessed by the mineral fields of the South
is exemplified by the cost for transport in the State of
Alabama, which compares favorably with the best of those
in Great Britain. Localities in Tennessee possess powers
superior, if anything, to Alabama.' In this search for cheap

[11] Harry Magdoff, 'Imperialism Without Colonies', in Roger Owen and Bob
Sutcliffe, *Theories of Imperialism* (Longman, London, 1972), pp. 143–69.

[12] A. K. Cairncross, *Home and Foreign Investment, 1879–1913*, (Cambridge
University Press, 1953), p. 3.

[13] Owen and Sutcliffe, op. cit., p. 54.

[14] 'Cumberland Gap: Its Geographical and Commerical Features and Importance as a Railroad Center' (Fleming, Brewster and Alley, New York, 1888), p. 13.

resources, the Southern Appalachias—bypassed by the forces of expansion for almost 100 years—began to be viewed with a new eye.

Particularly attractive was the area around the Cumberland Gap. In 1887 the Inspector of the Mines in Kentucky reported:

The territory around and about, and tributary to, the town on the Kentucky side is phenomenally rich in stores of coal of the best quality; just beyond the border, on the other side of the Cumberland range, are great deposits of the finest limenites and soft hematites, while the completion of the railroads to the north and the south brings the steel-making ores of Tennessee and North Carolina within easy reach of the Kentucky ironmaster, and opens the way to all the markets . . . The importance of the discovery of this coking coal, and its bearing upon the future industrial development of the state cannot be over-estimated.[15]

The economic demands of the metropolis destined these resources to be developed at any time. The catalyst was the visionary Alexander Arthur, described upon his death as 'the instrument which opened to man another of the waste places of the world'.[16]

Arthur first visited the area in 1886 to explore the possibility of a railroad development. The resources and their location gave him a grander plan. With financial help from five wealthy capitalists from New York and North Carolina, a company was formed known as the 'Gap Associates.' Immediately Arthur began to secure options on the land, but as more capital was needed, he hurried to London where other financiers would be able to back his plan. On 10 January 1887 a company called the American Association, Ltd. was incorporated under British law. Its purposes included:

1) to acquire certain coal and iron properties situated in the United States of America . . .
2) to carry on the trade and business of ironmasters, colliery proprietors, coke manufacturers, mineral smelters, engineers, steel conversions, and iron founders, in all their prospective branches . . .
3) to search for, get, work, raise, make marketable, sell and deal in iron, coal, ironstone, brick earth, bricks and

[15] State of Kentucky, *Report of Inspector of Mines,* 1887, pp. 52, 53.
[16] *Roberts Papers,* letter to Mrs. Arthur, 11 March 1912.

other metals, minerals and substances, and products
(including oil, salt and natural gas) ...

4) to enter into any arrangements with any governments
or authorities—supreme, municipal, local or otherwise—
that may seem conducive to the company's objects ...

5) Generally to purchase, take on, or in exchange, hire or
otherwise acquire any real or personal property, and any
rights or privileges which the company may think necessary or convenient for the purpose of its business ...[17]

The industrial 'colonization' of the Yellow Creek, Clear Fork
and other valleys of the Cumberland Gap region had begun.

3.3 THE INITIAL ENCOUNTER: LAND ACQUISITION

In a rural area, particularly one from which minerals are to be
extracted, acquisition of land is the first step in the process
of economic development and the establishment of power.
In a process of internal colonialism the entry into an area
may be forced, i.e. involuntary on the part of the residents.[18]
Most of the written histories of the Cumberland Gap area say
that the American Association simply 'acquired' its 80,000
acres of land.[19] Courthouse records appear to give it legal
title, but today, one, two, or three generations later, histories
differing from the 'official' version of the acquisition of the
land abound among mountaineers.

The Company had an advantage over the mountaineers—a
knowledge of the value of the minerals to the industrial
centres. Thus the mountaineer often 'voluntarily' sold his
land, sometimes for as little as fifty cents or one dollar an
acre, more usually for about three dollars an acre;[20] for while
the agents wanted the land, the mountaineers were more
interested in maintaining community harmony. To them,
there seemed to be plenty of land for everybody. As one

[17] 'Memoranda of Association of the American Association Ltd.', 10 January
1887, (Public Records Office, London; Board of Trade Documents 31, Box 3795,
no. 23755).

[18] See, for instance, Blauner, 'Internal Colonialism and Ghetto Revolts',
op. cit., pp. 393–408.

[19] For example, R. L. Kincaid, *The Wilderness Road* (by Mrs. R. L. Kincaid,
Middlesboro, Kentucky, 1966, originally, Bobbs-Merrill Co., New York, 1947),
p. 322.

[20] Based on the study of Warranty Deed books in Bell County, Kentucky,
Campbell and Claiborne Counties, Tennessee,

resident described, 'since land was plentiful, folks would just take what money was offered and move on to the next mountain'. One mountaineer, the residents say, traded his mountain for a hog rifle—and today upon that mountain is located the largest mine in Tennessee, operated by a subsidiary of the Continental Oil Company, on land still owned by the British company.

However, where resistance did begin to develop, oral tradition suggests that the Company would use deceit or force to 'otherwise acquire the property'.[21] Residents recount, still with anger, how some of the mountaineers were burned out if they would not sell. One old miner presented the deed of sale from his father to the Company. The deed bore a signature of his father's name—but, said the miner, his father could not write and, as was common at the time, signed documents only with his special mark. Another resident at the headwaters of Rock Creek tells how his father was jailed, supposedly for fighting, and had to post the title to his land for bond in order to return to his farm and take care of his family. The title was never recovered, though the children until recently still lived in the house which their father built—as tenants to the American Association.

Court actions (or 'lawin') were strange to the people in and around Yellow Creek, but a series of actions involving the American Association and its property began to appear in the record books of Bell, Claiborne, and Campbell counties in the late 1800s and early 1900s. With only minor exceptions, the Company won. A common pattern, that extended into the 1930s, was for the Company to acquire the rights of a single heir on a piece of property left to several family heirs. When the other heirs refused to sell, the Company would go to court and ask for a judgment on whether the property could be 'fairly and impartially partitioned' and on whether the 'said property is of such a nature so that its sale could be of manifest interest to all parties'. Almost invariably, the court would rule that it could not be divided, and that it should be sold at a 'public auction to the highest bidder' — usually the American Association. At one such sale in 1889, 2,000 acres of land granted to its original settlers in 1839 were bought at

21 'Memoranda of Association', op. cit.

the auction for 200 dollars, and the clerk of the court recorded the order that the land be 'averted out of them (the heirs) and vested in the purchaser, the American Association, Ltd. of London, England'.[22] Even now it is not uncommon in the area to hear statements like 'see that mountain, the 'sociation stole it from my daddy'.

Today, ownership of the land and its resources is the basis of the distribution of wealth and power in the region. Significantly, although the land was perhaps acquired unjustly, its unequal distribution is often now accepted as a natural, ineradicable fact of the social situation. Although the mountaineers suggest that their forefathers were ignorant of the future value of the land to the Company, and that the land was stolen by the agents, they consider these matters to be examples not of exploitation but of their forefathers' 'ignorance', or 'poor doings'. The powerlessness reflected in the first key encounter of their society with industrial society has often been internalized as their fault. The means by which corporate power turned itself to the shaping of its own legitimacy is the question to be pursued.

3.4 THE ECONOMIC BOOM: THE STRUCTURING OF INEQUALITIES

After the acquisition of the land, Alexander Arthur and the American Association turned their energies and their capital to its development. Only thirteen months after Arthur first viewed the Yellow Creek Valley, the Knoxville, Cumberland Gap and Louisville Railway was begun, and using the labour of hundreds of men, a tunnel was constructed under the Gap. The Watts Steel Company of England announced plans to build two furnaces. The Middlesborough Town Company was formed to develop 5,500 acres of the Yellow Creek Valley into the 'Magic City of the South'. Tents and saloons sprang up, and a hotel for visiting industrialists. A coking furnace, iron works, four large planing mills, four brick works, a branch of the Standard Handle Company, a machine shop, two large dry kilns, eight lumber mills, more shops and hotels, the Vaughan Tannery, and an electric power company appeared. The Yellow Creek threatened to flood, and its

[22] *American Association Ltd., of England* v. *heirs of Cocke,* Claiborne County Quarterly Court Minute Book B, pp. 121, 171-2.

channel was moved. The Middlesborough Beltway Railroad circled the city. Coal leases were let and collieries established in the narrow valleys along the creek. In two years, twenty million dollars flowed into the transformation of this valley.

By the end of 1889, a city had grown up. Where three years before there had been sixty families in a hamlet along Yellow Creek, there were now some 5,000 people. Where there had been an economy of relatively self-sufficient agriculture, there were now sixteen operating industries (with forty-one more planned), and six banks. Where there had been little formal social organization, there were now seven churches, a town hall, a public library, an opera house, and a golf course. Where transportation had been by horseback, there were now streetcars in the city and 368·80 miles of railway connecting to other main railway lines.[23] Reported coal production in Claiborne county leapt from none in 1889 to 135,558 tons from five mines three years later, while in Bell county, Kentucky 26,623,171 bushels were mined in 1893.[24]

Booms have a habit of instilling reckless enthusiasm, and in Middlesboro there developed a spirit of excitement, almost drunkenness, often found in frontier expansion. Stories abounded of the money to be made. For a brief, critical juncture between the old way of life and the new, the social structure appeared fluid; it seemed everyone stood an equal chance of loss or gain in the new venture. Looking back on the rapidity of the change, a writer in 1911 observed, 'the labor-capital question was immediately solved, for everybody became a capitalist—carpenter, brick-layer, singing teacher, and preacher'.[25]

Yet beneath this legitimating, momentary *Zeitgeist,* there was quietly occurring the structuring of inequalities that was to have major long-term impact upon the political economy of the region, even up to the present. There were two key, interrelated factors in the process—the development of social stratification and the establishment of absentee, concentrated

[23] J. C. Tipton, *The Cumberland Coalfield and Its Creators* (Pinnacle Printery, Cumberland Gap, 1905). Quoted, too, in Fuson, op. cit., p. 378.

[24] State of Tennessee, *Annual Reports of Commissioner of Labour,* 1889 and 1892. State of Kentucky, *Report of Inspector of Mines,* 1894.

[25] John Fox Jr., 'The Days of the Big Boom', *Thousandsticks,* 22 April 1912.

economic control of the resources and the means of their extraction.

During the initial development of the Company one of its British directors remarked to another, 'We have got to buy that property but we have got to make sure that the Americans make money alongside with us.'[26] In retrospect, however, some were clearly intended to make more than others. The upper class of the city were its absentee owners who controlled the capital. In addition to those in the City of London, there were some in America—primarily the wealthy élites of the cities of the North. While these owners occasionally visited, their interests were represented on a day-to-day basis by the superintendents and managers of their enterprises, again primarily British or from the northern cities. Beneath these, another class developed in the city—a host of small entrepreneurs, merchants, and professionals who saw in this venture the chance to make a new start. At the bottom were the vast majority of the city's new population: labourers, ditch-diggers, construction workers, and miners. Few in this area were foreign immigrants; most were attracted from the farms and 'hollows' of the rural region, and some came from working backgrounds in other cities. There is no indication that the mobility here was the upward mobility for which frontier boom-towns enjoy a reputation. Rather, it was of a horizontal nature, the coming together in one area of various representatives of pre-existing strata from other areas.

The city, despite its apparent diversity of purpose, developed as a company town, unitary in the dependence of all within it upon the British owners. Other companies were encouraged and even subsidized to come to the city, but they did so on the American Association's terms, for it maintained control in key factors of production. It owned the land and minerals, which it would lease but would not sell; and also the railroads, upon which distribution of the products depended. More often than not the mines were owned by other interests. These had to pay royalty to the American Association (then at one cent per bushel) and a haulage fee

[26] H.F. Pollock, speech in Middlesborough, 14 March 1891, in *Roberts Papers*, File XIX.

to ship the minerals to the markets. A *Scribner's Magazine*
article in 1890 praised the monopoly control as 'benevolence'
and wrote, 'The care of the Association thus attends to the
staple of commerce from the raw state in the earth's bed
until the final and finished result is in the hands of the
consumer . . . To this parental character of the American
Association, and to the comprehensive protection with which
it pursues the course of industry is largely due the prosperity
of Middlesborough.'[27]

The spirit of the boom, then, was qualified only by its
long-term economic realities. From the beginning in this
'Magic City', some were to be more equal than others. While
there would be opportunities, they were by no means equal
opportunities. Beneath the boom was the structuring of the
inequalities that would draw the wealth from the region it
had conquered and the labour it had attracted. But while
the spirit of the boom lasted, the interests of the absentee
owners and the interests of the majority of the people of
the city—the small entrepreneurs, miners, and labourers—
would appear as one.

3.5 THE POLITICAL APPARATUS

Booms and their spirit do not last. To survive, the interests
behind them must develop more stable forms of self-protection, such as control over the political apparatus and the
shaping and instilling of supporting values.

There are several fairly clear indications of the development of political leverage by the new economic élite of
Middlesboro. The State Inspector of the Mines in Kentucky
set the stage in 1887. He wrote, 'as the assured position of
what will undoubtedly prove to be one of the great industrial
centers of the Union, and one of the most important in the
South, the region about Middlesborough demands special
consideration'.[28] The Kentucky State Legislature responded
in 1888 by passing an 'Act for the benefit of the company'.
'Be it enacted by the General Assembly of the Commonwealth of Kentucky', the Act began, and it continued by

[27] 'Southern Lands: Middlesborough, Ky.', *Scribner's Magazine* (Nov. 1890),
adv. 41.
[28] State of Kentucky, *Report of Inspector of Mines*, 1887, pp. 51-2.

granting the corporation rights to purchase land, railroads,
mines, etc.[29]

The local level of politics, with its powers of taxation and
law enforcement, was where control would be important, yet
where traditional political ties could be hardest to overcome.
The first Middlesboro City election featured 'The Yellow
Creek Valley men against the foreigners'.[30] Leading the
'natives' was a Colonel David G. Colson, whose father, known
as the 'Patriarch of Yellow Creek', was a long-time resident,
county judge of Bell County, lawyer, farmer, and preacher.[31]
In this election the son lost to the Company's candidate, a
Knoxville Civil War veteran brought into the city by Arthur.
The remaining four of the city's first councillors were similarly
recruited. According to one source: 'They were the men of
wealth, and fine backgrounds, and politics was not new for
them . . . there was little regard for what law there was and
money ruled the day. Arthur and his friends felt that their
interest could best be protected by their associates.'[32] In
time, the local leaders were incorporated into this élite:
Colonel Colson became an employee of the Company, began
a new political career that took him to the State Legislature,
and came to be known as the 'Greater Patriarch' of the
Valley.

What may appear to be merely the normal process of vested
interest politics must be set in the context of state laws
meant to control the behaviour of these new 'joint stock'
companies. The Tennessee State Legislature had passed in
1882 an Act 'to prevent joint stock companies from impair-
ing or infringing upon the rights, privileges and liberties of
their servants and employees'. The Act included a provision
making it unlawful to discharge any employees or to threaten
to discharge any employees 'from voting or not voting in any
election . . . for any person or measure'.[33] Another Act made

[29] State of Kentucky, *Acts of the General Assembly,* 1888, chap. 203, para 1.

[30] *Middlesboro Daily News,* 19 August 1965.

[31] Fuson op. cit., pp. 156, 162, 304.

[32] *Middlesboro Daily News,* 19 August 1965.

[33] State of Tennessee, chapter 208, Acts of 1882. Quoted in *Annual Report
of Commissioner of Labor and Inspector of Mines,* 1893, p. 27; for other Acts
cited, see chapter 155, Acts of 1887; chapter 259, Acts of 1889; chapter 70,
Acts of 1881; chapter 206, Acts of 1887; chapter 18, Acts of 1883; chapter 5,
Acts of 1891, respectively.

it illegal for a company 'to attempt to control their employees or labor in the purchase of store goods or supplies . . .' from the company store. Other legislation of particular importance for coal miners and their families provided for protection of employees in the selection of their family physician, for the ventilation of coal mines and collieries for 'the protection of human life therein', for the right of miners to employ a checkweighman ('as in no way to interfere with the working of the mines'), and for protection of workers against insolvency of corporations or defaulting by employers on payment of wages.

While these were the laws on the books, evidence suggests that they could be, and were, easily contravened. It was not until 1891 that the Tennessee State Legislature made any provision for the enforcement of laws relating to mines and even then it was for only one inspector with limited funds to protect the rights and conditions of 5,575 miners.[34] A miner in a mine near Middlesboro complained that there was no checkweighman and that 'it is time that if Tennessee has a mining inspector he ought to be doing his duty in this place'.[35] The letter continues:

If you say anything to the boss, he will give you no satisfaction but will merely say 'Oh, that's nothing.' Discrimination against anyone dealing elsewhere than the Company's store is the order of the day here, as was witnessed in a case a few days ago when a man was told he was not needed; they charge double on everything; such tyranny is an outrage, and these companies ought to have a dose of their own medicine.

Later, even the inspector's report complained, 'the mine operators look upon the inspector as a lawbreaker would look upon a police officer, giving but little if any assistance toward showing the true conditions existing in and around the mines, frequently resulting in important evasions of the mining laws being overlooked'.[36]

In the political arena, then, a pattern was quickly emerging: the influx of capital meant the establishment of certain controls and biases that clearly served to benefit the primarily absentee economic élite more than they did the mountaineers

[34] ibid., chapter 157, Acts of 1891.
[35] Letter to *UMWA Journal,* from miner in Hartranft, Tennessee, 31 March 1892.
[36] State of Tennessee, Inspector's report for 16 December 1891, in *Annual Report of Commissioner of Labor and Inspector of Mines,* 1892, p. 278.

or workers. If the model of the emergence of power relations put forward in Chapter 1 is accurate, then this economic and political hegemony should also have been accompanied by a supporting ideology.

3.6 THE IDEOLOGICAL APPARATUS

Industrialization assuredly brought values very different from those of the previous culture in and around the Cumberland Gap. Four aspects of the new ideology show its significance for the mountaineers and miners.

The first element has already been seen in the notion of a 'common purpose' in the growth of Middlesboro—a notion which served to disguise the less obvious inequalities which were also emerging. Middlesboro, according to Arthur, demonstrated, 'remarkable sturdiness, singular perseverance, and oneness of purpose, and promises to be indeed what its sponsors have declared—an Anglo-American metropolis'.[37]

The second element of the ideology often went with the first: the benefits were attainable by all, but only hard work would provide them. The ethic, expressed above in the idea of 'perseverance' is also expressed by Arthur in this statement:

Our mines, ovens, furnaces, and works you have seen: these comprise our plant. We have also the sinews of body and of money, and stand ready, clean-cut and vigorous for a generation of progress and success in manufacture and arts and sciences. Come and join hands with us in the great enterprise which is worthy of the noblest efforts of us all, native or foreign born though he may be.[38]

Yes, into the hills came a new way which, thirdly, justified itself as 'progress'. Like the ideology of colonialism in the Third World, it proclaimed the virtues of 'civilization', and would not pause to ask about the virtues of the culture there before. Arthur, as instrument of the new order, described its merits:

Think of it all for a moment—crafty Indian, sturdy pioneer, gallant, dusty iron worker, thrifty miller, half-starved squatter, peaceful trader, and last the forerunner of development and promise, bearing gold in his hand, having energy in his stride, the searching eye, the creating mind—Romance, History, Progress! That was Cumberland Gap . . .[39]

[37] Alexander Arthur, speech in Middlesborough, 11 November 1890.
[38] ibid.
[39] Alexander Arthur, *Roberts Papers,* File XX.

Each of these notions is a common one in American capitalist ideology—an open system, hard work, leading to progress. Yet, there was another element of the ideology that was perhaps to have more impact upon the mountaineers. It was embodied in a way that all could see in the moving of the Yellow Creek and the tunnelling under Cumberland Mountain. Whereas the culture of the mountaineer had been founded and shaped by its relationship to nature—its isolation, its struggle for survival, its harmony with streams and mountains —this new civilization would not be so bound; indeed, it would conquer:

A creek has to be straightened to improve drainage—they spend on it a hundred thousand dollars . . . The mountain is in their way—that mighty wall of the Cumberland Mountains which has been in the way of the whole United States for over a hundred years—they remove this mountain; that is, they dig through it a great union tunnel three thousand seven hundred and fifty feet long, beginning in Kentucky, running under a corner of Virginia, and coming out in Tennessee . . .[40]

When the tunnel was completed, through the work of hundreds of men, hundreds more cheered and Arthur himself reflected upon the new spirit: 'I realized as never before how powerful and dominant is man and that his mind could sway and use the giant force of nature.'[41]

In everything about the Middlesboro boom this new industrial, humanist ideology was symbolized. Where there had been a solidarity of family and farm there was now an industrial solidarity, witnessed as together men swung their axes, laid rail, raised capital, or weighed coal. Although life had involved work before, it had not been so glorified—nor bought as a mass product. Where there had been a sense of contentment, there was a progress that transformed. Where there had been a struggle to obtain a harmony with nature, this civilization would dominate nature and free the creating capacities of man. However, for the study of power it is not enough to say that this was a different ideology; one must look at the processes or mechanisms through which it was instilled. It is true that the situation so far portrayed resembles the notion of colonialism in traditional societies

[40] James Lane Allen, 'Mountain Passes of the Cumberlands', *Harpers New Monthly Magazine*, 81 (Sept. 1890), 568.

[41] Alexander Arthur, *Roberts Papers*, File XX.

given by the *International Encyclopedia of the Social Sciences*: 'contact between a machine-oriented civilization with Christian origins, a powerful economy and rapid rhythms of life, and a non-Christian civilization that lacks machines and is marked by a backward economy and slow rhythm'. But, the *IESS* also adds to the definition: 'And the imposition of the first upon the second'.[42] In what sense can the new ideology be said to have been imposed upon the people in and around the Yellow Creek Valley?

It could be argued that the coercion seen so far represents the imposition that the only option available to the mountaineer was submissive acceptance (slave analogy). Alternatively, it could be said that any rational man would have chosen the rewards of industrial society, and that there could be no question about the nature of the consensus (free man analogy). Both approaches, I suggest, are too simple: while coercion helps to shape consensus, when used to an extreme it can have negative effects (e.g. resistance). While rationality is important, it is itself a socially bound concept. The power which should be expected is more subtle. It is one which shapes the outcome of 'choice' while allowing the chooser to believe that, in fact, a choice has been made. The imposition of choice by conscious design or unconscious effect, was occurring in the boom of Middlesboro in at least four observable ways.

The first process of shaping wants involved a distortion of information: the industrial order was introduced to the mountaineers' society by conspicuous consumption, with an exaggerated demonstration of its benefits.

To the industrial world, the mountain valley became not just a place of capital investment and mineral development, but also a vacation ground for the wealthy, a health resort of fabulous proportions and mystique, comparable to the 'watering places of Vichy, Homburg and Baden-Baden'.[43] In addition to The Middlesborough and other more functional hotels, the fabulous 700-room Four Seasons Hotel was built, and upon a hill nearby a sanitorium was added. The furnishings of the hotel were of the best: 'with money being no

---

[42] Rupert Emerson, 'Colonialism: Political Aspects', *International Encyclopedia of the Social Sciences*, 3, 1.
[43] Kincaid, op. cit., p. 329.

consideration on its beautiful decorations and ornaments'.[44]
With the advice of a special physician-consultant, the Turkish
baths of the Rue de L'Etat Major in Algiers were duplicated
and the natural streams explored for their medicinal value.
To this great resort came the wealthy from industrial society:
four hundred New Yorkers chartered a train to attend the
opening night; from Britain came members of the aristocracy,
including the Duke and Duchess of Marlborough, and hundreds of others who spent weeks in the Cumberland Mountains. A permanent class of leisure developed who, 'having
no occupation, neither toiled nor spun, but passed the time
in riding and hunting wild deer, turkey, and fox and in
pretty heavy drinking'.[45]

Contrast this life of consumption and leisure with that of
the mountaineers and labouring classes all around. The
mountaineer had enjoyed nature, but these people from the
industrial world enjoyed it more luxuriously, and without
having to diversify it with work. To those who had not been
to the seat of the industrial world, here was the manifest
expression of its potential benefits, undifferentiated by the
thought that these representatives of that world were the
exception rather than the rule. How does the lifestyle of the
occupants of the Four Seasons appear to a miner who writes
to other miners as follows?

When you come here you will as a general thing be working in water,
without any pay for it, in rooms and they just take out the water to
suit the company's purpose. There is a good deal of bad roof and a
room-man has to cross timber his road and receives no pay for it either.
The man who occupies a house here has to carry a sack to the work
with him every day to carry coal with him as there is no road to haul it
and the houses are located in a place where there is no road but a foot
road.[46]

Surely the contrast must have had some impact on the
consciousness of the working man?

A clue to this impact is found in a description by Arthur's
secretary of the reactions of the mountaineers to the new
Four Seasons Hotel:

[44] *Roberts Papers,* File XX.
[45] *Roberts Papers,* op. cit.
[46] Letter to *UMWA Journal,* from miner in Hartranft, Tennessee, 31 March
1892.

As for the native . . . he dared advance only within good contemplative distance and halt in his tracks, daunted by the enormous proportions and inner magnificence of the fabulous pile, but more than these by the storied segars costing not less than twenty cents and the unimaginable whiskey at a quarter a drink. Although he may have itched to feast his eyes on the wonders of the walls enclosed, to him they remained as Carcassonne to the French peasant of Nadaud's famous ballad.[47]

The medieval city of Carcassonne, located in southern France, is renowned for the impregnable walls which surround it. The secretary's statement suggests that while desires for consumptive goods may have been instilled, there also developed clear social and economic boundaries which defined who could legitimately partake of the luxuries of the new order.

At the same time, the wants of the non-élite were at least partially accommodated, if for no other reason than to help ensure that the walls of Carcassonne were not stormed. Though the non-élite could not participate equally in the enjoyment of luxuries, they could replicate the pattern in a lesser style, and did so in extravagant purchase of goods and consumption of liquor in the stores and saloons of the booming town.

The exaggerated attractiveness of the industrial order, on the one hand, carried with it the degradation of the culture and society of the mountaineers, on the other. Students of colonialism observe that degradation by the colonizer of the colonized usually takes the form of racialism. While the mountaineer was not exactly of another race, he could be portrayed as a breed whose lifestyle represented a deficient way of existence. For instance, while the new Middlesboro was said to represent 'true social enjoyments', 'health', a 'fine climate, natural beauty', and 'good things', the older culture was said to consist of 'wilder mountaineers', who were 'usually not attractive', but were 'rather yellow and cadaverous looking, owing to their idle and shiftless ways, and the bad food upon which they subsist, and perhaps also to their considerable consumption of moonshine whiskey'.[48]

---

[47] *Roberts Papers,* op. cit.
[48] 'Southern Lands', *Harper's* Magazine (Jan. 1891).

Glorification of the one culture and degradation of the other could combine with the ideology of openness and hard work to help ensure a 'choice' by the mountaineers to pursue the new values. The coherent and shaping effect of the ideology can be seen, for instance, in the writing of one observer:

Creeping slowly across the Wilderness Road toward the ascent of Cumberland Gap came a mountain wagon, faded and old with its dirty, ragged canvas hanging motionless, and drawn by a yoke of mountain oxen which seemed to be moving in their sleep. On the seat in front . . . sat a faded, pinched and meagre mountain boy. . .

Thus the writer is using the appropriate images —sleeping oxen, dirty canvas, starved mountain child—to set the stage for the new ways. But the description continues; the child can make a choice:

His stained white face was kindled into an expression of passionate hunger and mental excitement. For in one dirty, claw-like hand he grasped a small paper bag into the mouth of which he had thrust the other hand, as a miser thrust his into a bag of gold . . . He had just bought with a few cents, he had perhaps saved no one knows how long, some sweetmeat of civilization which he was about for the first time to taste . . .[49]

Unlike the French peasants in the medieval city, the Appalachian native could enjoy the benefits of this new city. His 'deficiencies' precluded equal consumption, but with hard work and savings the 'sweetmeats of civilization' could at least be tasted. Degradation could be escaped by joining what Arthur called 'the enterprise of the Anglo-American race'.[50]

A third process of imposing values involved the more direct appropriation of local culture. Perhaps the best example of the process in Middlesboro was found in the replacement of names from the old order with those from the new. A striking pattern is found in the transformation of the Yellow Creek: while places of work, the mines (where labour was expropriated), retained Appalachian names, places of cultural development (town, school, countryside) were given names from foreign cultures. For instance, the mines were called by such names as Mingo Mountain, Fork Ridge, Bryson Mountain,

[49] Allen, op. cit., p. 569.

[50] Alexander Arthur, speech, 11 November 1890, in *Roberts Papers*, File XIX.

and Reliance; but the hamlet of Yellow Creek became
Middlesborough; areas that had been identified by the
owner of the homeplace (e.g. the Colson place) became
streets with the identities of cities in Britain: Ilchester,
Manchester, Exeter, Amesbury, etc. The hills of these Highlander people were renamed after symbols of urban development: Maxwelton Braes, Arthur Heights, and Queensbury
Heights. The mining camp at Fork Ridge was named Hartranft by its Pennsylvania developers, after a Pennsylvania
governor. Indeed a school in the area started by a missionary
to educate the mountain children was named 'Harrow School'
(at the suggestion of the wife of the visiting English ambassador). If one accepts that linguistic symbols are an expression
of and help in shaping consciousness,[51] then the names must
be considered more than mere words, and the patterns more
than a coincidence. By the imposition of one identity over
another in the cultural arena, and by allowing names to lend
the appearance of local possession in the workplace arena
(where there was none at all), the development of a counter-
hegemony was made less likely, and the belief in economic
oneness maintained.

The above processes were probably not conscious exercises
of control; nevertheless, they did have important consequences
for the development of the Company's power and legitimacy.
In addition, there were other, more direct means, by which
values could be shaped, such as control of the socializing
agencies of government, church and school. Arthur pointed
out in 1890, 'We saw at once that if we were to develop the
iron and coal we would have to control the territory here in
the valley to prevent little hells in our midst.'[52] Consequently,
as has been seen, the Company established its control over
the governmental authorities (police force, mayor, and
councillors). A minister, Revd. Myers, was encouraged to
help convert and civilize the mountaineers, gamblers and
moonshiners who were debasing the city. Harrow School,
later to become Lincoln Memorial University, was started by

[51] For a good summary of literature on language and legitimation, see Claus
Mueller, *The Politics of Communication*, op. cit. For discussion of appropriation
of working-class culture, see Stanley Aronowitz, *False Promises: The Shaping of
American Working Class Consciousness*, op. cit.

[52] Alexander Arthur, speech, 11 November 1890.

him. While the express purpose of this University was noble—
'to make education possible for the children of the common
people of America among whom Lincoln was born'[53]—the
effect applauded by the Company was to socialize the
mountain youth away from their beginnings. Arthur's secretary was later to write:

The customs and social code of the native have been . . . in process of
gradual relinquishment in favor of those of the other inhabitants, which
supposedly reflect the standard. At Lincoln Memorial University, the
young mountaineer is moulded more or less to this form, but the result
is largely achieved by what he sees independently . . . A sharp observer,
he notes for himself the conduct, manners, and techniques of the 'city
man' and, as a rule deeming them superior becomes, in general, con-
formist, or, as the Bourbons among the stock regard him, a deserter,
an 'apostate' to his kind.[54]

Whether by 'moulding' in the socialization institutions, or by
'choice' from amongst the alternatives presented to him in
the power situation, the effect upon the mountaineer was the
same: a shaping and influencing away from his 'stock' to
participation in the ways and values of the new order.

3.7 THE CONSENSUS

The theory of power put forward suggests that the effective
development of a mobilization of bias (as in the second
dimension of power) and the shaping of wants and values (as
in the third dimension) should lead to a felt consensus about
the new order amongst the people (much as in a colonial or
neo-colonial situation). What was the nature and extent of
the consensus in the city of Middlesboro?

On 14 March 1891 a three-hour mass meeting was attended
by hundreds of Middlesboro citizens to express appreciation
to the officers of the American Association and the Middlesborough Town Company. Held at the newly resplendent
Opera House, it was the 'largest and most enthusiastic meeting ever witnessed'[55] in the city. A report from the Committee
on Resolutions was read, 'interrupted many times . . . by
loud cheers and vociferous applause'.[56] The resolution reads

[53] Quoted in Kincaid, op. cit., p. 243.
[54] *Roberts Papers*, File VII.
[55] *Middlesboro Daily News*, 19 August 1965.
[56] Minutes of the Meeting, 4 March 1891, from *Roberts Papers*, File XIX.
(Emphases supplied in the following quotations).

strikingly like a creed or statement of belief used in religious services. It began with an expression of the authenticity of the statement about to be heard, as if to defend itself from accusations of undue company influence:

We deem it but appropriate as a preamble . . . to express as a people to the world, and by our voices as citizens, *independent of any land company or other organization of like nature*, what we have found to be the true situation here, as well as a statement concerning the advantages of, and the phenomenal growth of, a city not yet two years old.

It continued with an endorsement of the greatness of the Company and its new creation:

We realize that the far-seeing eye of the American Association, Ltd., three or four years ago made the discovery of the great industrial age . . . that time designated by months instead of years would show to the world that *whether it were the will of the people or not the establishment here of a city of importance was inevitable.*

We realize that the great work inaugurated by the American Association, Ltd. and the Middlesborough Town Company is the most deliberate and gigantic in the history of American city building and that not a stone has been left unturned, not a line stinted, and each department, being under the same head, have together rounded out the most magnificent enterprise of the kind in the world. . .

The statement continued by devoting a paragraph of praise to the vast resources, the magnificent scenery, the healthy environment and the miles of railroads associated with the city. It continued:

Instead of a boom or mushroom city, many of which we discover in glancing over the giant and industrial South, we have in Middlesborough a model city, built upon the most modern and substantial plans and ideas, and a city designed more as a metropolis as aught else . . . we venture the assertion that in no young city in the Union is there such a class of buildings, erected at such cost, or which are returning more handsome revenues, than those of Middlesborough.

The praise of the material, metropolitan greatness of Middlesboro was followed by an endorsement of the concepts of cultural progress it brought and an apologetic for the ways of the people before its coming:

We realize with deep sense of gratitude and pride the remarkable state of order that exists here, and the strict regard of the people for the law, and their interest in, or devotion to religious and educational affairs. But two years ago this section was the scene of bitter feuds, and the revolver and the rifle were considered the only adequate settlement of differences of opinion. But a determination of law-abiding people who came here to live, together with the refining influence of civilization, and the earnest endeavour of the officers, *have combined to thoroughly convince the 'native element' of the error of their ways* . . .

Though it had begun with a statement of independence from the Company, the resolution ended with a note of deference, a recognition of the dependence of the people upon the American Association's wealth and power:

While we recognize strongly all of these . . . very material points and the fact that the people as a whole have been a great factor in these grand results, we can but confess that but for the grand efforts and liberal expenditures of the American Association, Limited, and the Middlesborough Town Company this great city could not have been, as *they are the fountain head where the stream had its rise and from which it continually flows and drives the great wheels of our progress* . . .

For such things, thanks were given to the officers of the Company and of the city. The resolutions were adopted by a unanimous vote, and then there were calls to Alexander Arthur who arose 'amid deafening applause'.

As an endorsement to the new order, there could have been few more powerful. It was an expression of unquestioning loyalty to city and to corporation. Time and again in the city's future, people would be remined of this thanksgiving ritual. But was this consensus expressed by all in Middlesboro?

Evidence suggests not—that it was primarily the statement of the smaller capitalists, owners and managers who had been attracted to the city. A list of names and occupations of a 'permanent organization' of Middlesboro appointed at the meeting shows that the president was a real estate dealer, while the 140 vice-presidents included 44 small merchants or proprietors, 14 contractors, 12 real estate men, 12 lawyers, 9 bankers, capitalists, or insurance agents, 4 top city officials, 2 coal operators, 2 railroad officials, and 16 persons whose occupations were not identified. All these were the local élite, whose interests depended entirely upon the maintenance and growth of the new order.

What of the hundreds of labourers in the city—the railway-men, miners, ditch-diggers, and construction workers? What was their opinion of the city and the Company? It is difficult to tell. The history of the common people of Middlesboro is largely unrecorded. But, looking particularly at the miners, the available evidence suggests that they too granted a 'consensus', though perhaps more latently. The Kentucky Inspector of the Mines reported in 1889 that the area 'continued to be uncommonly free from disturbances due to strikes'.[57] Organizers for the United Mine Workers reported that they were having more difficulty starting a union there than they were elsewhere.[58] One report, entitled 'A Sad Tale from Mingo Mine—the Boss Heaven', says that the miners would not attend union meeting for 'fear the scarecrow of Tom Pruden [an English mine boss] would appear to see who was at the meeting'.[59]

Though organized opposition to the new order was not apparent, unorganized conflict was. The city came to be known for its violence. 'Pistols were carried openly by large numbers, while the native, according to immemorial habit, seldom went abroad unaccompanied by his rifle.'[60] The violence seemed primarily horizontal, that is, among the non-élite:

Killings were not uncommon, and infrequently several men would fall in a single fight. Not always were the victims feudists: sometimes they were mountaineers or 'Yellow Creekers', sometimes from the ranks of the newcomers, among whom was the usual rate of brawlers, criminals, and shady characters.[61]

Another report wrote of an impression widespread throughout the State and the country that 'when one enters Bell County he or she is in great danger of being killed by a "mountaineer"'.[62] This violence reflects one of two possibilities, or a combination of both. It could have been participation by the workers in the reckless spirit of a boom town, or it could have reflected an expression of frustrations which, blocked from relief through attack against the major powerholders in the situation, took the form of attack on

[57] State of Kentucky, *Report of Inspector of Mines,* 1889, p. 36.
[58] *UMWA Journal* (21 May 1891; 31 Mar., 3 Sep. 1892).
[59] From a miner in Mingo, *UMWA Journal* (4 March 1893).
[60] *Roberts Papers,* op. cit.
[61] ibid.
[62] State of Kentucky, *Report of the Bureau of Agriculture,* 1897, p. 8.

one another, or on the weakest of the outsiders.[63] Whatever
the reason, the net effect left an impression of latent consensus to their situation among the mountaineers and the
miners.

Compared to the overt endorsement given to the new
order by the local élite, the 'consensus' of the non-élite
appeared primarily as a silence, i.e. a lack of either endorsement or opposition. Yet, compared to the behaviour and
conceptions of miners and mountaineers in the immediately
surrounding region, where the power lacked the unified
nature or symbolic garnishes of that in Middlesboro, the
silence of the non-élite in the 'Magic City' becomes notable.

While the conditions of the Yellow Creek miners were
apparently worse than the conditions of these other miners,
the Yellow Creek miners were more quiescent about them.
For instance, a major grievance of miners at the time concerned the weighing of coal. Miners were paid for production,
not for the amount of time worked. The work system was
highly competitive, and the weighing of what the miner
produced was the key factor in determining what he earned.
In the Yellow Creek area, several sources report that the
companies would not weigh the coal properly.[64] For instance,
a miner in one of the mines wrote:

The company has got a dead-head standing on the tip. All that he does
is to dock the poor miners' cars if they don't come out from 3 to 4
inches over the tips of the bed. The cars contain 65½ cubic feet level
full; but if a car comes out not more than level it is docked 500 pounds;
that is, 10 cents off the car. The company is only paying the men sixty
cents for digging these gondolas full. The car is 9 by 4 by 2 feet. What
do you think of that for a ton and a half car?[65]

[63] Freire, for instance, writes of the oppressed in 'closed societies', 'Chafing
at the restrictions of that order, they strike out at their comrades.' To support
his point he refers to Fanon's notion of horizontal violence within oppressed
communities. 'While the settler or the policeman has the right the livelong day to
strike the native . . . you will see the native reaching for his knife at the slightest
hostile or aggressive glance cast upon him by another native; for the last resort
of the native is to defend his personality *vis-à-vis* his brother.' Quoted by Freire,
Pedagogy of the Oppressed op. cit., p. 38. Campbell makes a similar point about
the high homicide rates in the Appalachias being, potentially, a reflection of the
poor social conditions, though he was referring to the period in the early 1900s
(see Campbell, op. cit.).

[64] *UMWA Journal* (31 Mar. 1892), and State of Tennessee, *Annual Report of
the Commissioner of Labour,* 1892, p. 273.

[65] *UMWA Journal* (4 May 1893).

When requests were made for scales, the bosses refused. Grievances were expressed, but there is no sign that the miners in Yellow Creek took the grievances beyond that and organized action or further developed consciousness of the situation.

On the other hand, in the nearby Jellico area (in the adjoining county, about 30 miles away), the miners facing a similar problem responded with militant, collective organization, including an effort to discourage any other labour from coming into the area until checkweighmen were allowed.[66] They succeeded in winning the Jellico Agreement of 1893, one of the most advanced agreements of any miners in the country. Not only did the agreement provide for uniform standards in the scaling of coal, but it also allowed a miner to refuse to work if he thought the mine was dangerous through failure of the bosses to supply enough support timber. The Jellico Agreement grew out of the joint union organization of miners in at least eight mines in the region; but miners in the Middlesboro area did not participate in these efforts to develop unionization, though they were encouraged by organizers to do so. This difference in behaviour under similar conditions, I suggest, arose from the more effective use of power in Yellow Creek to encourage and maintain quiescence, through the processes that have been described.

Comparison with behaviour of other miners in the region illustrates a second important point: unlike much of what the literature and ideology suggests about the individualism, apathy, and inability to organize of the Appalachian 'natives', these miner-mountaineers were not incapable of organized rebellion, indeed insurrection. Contrast the reports already quoted about the Middlesboro workers with reports at the same time about a little-known struggle in American labour history occurring just fifty miles south-west of the Cumberland Gap:

July 23, 1891: at 10 o'clock this morning, 2,000 miners, farmers and other natives who have no occupation at all took possession of the hills around the Briceville Camp. Fifteen hundred of those were armed with rifles, the rest with shotguns, and pistols. They came from all the mines

[66] *UMWA Journal* (10 Nov. 1892).

in a radius of 50 miles. The organization was complete and their leaders placed them along the hillsides with military precision.

The miners called a parley and were met on neutral ground by Colonel Sevier. They stated that they had sufficient force to overwhelm the soldiers but did not care to shed blood . . .[67]

Or another report on 5 November 1891:

. . . for days there has been a tacit understanding among the miners of Tennessee and Kentucky that something had to be done to secure the needed relief of this portion of the South . . . quietly, but in a systematic manner . . . 1,000 armed men . . . formed themselves into an irresistable body.[68]

Here the issue was the use of convict labour which was leased out by the State to the companies for mining coal, in direct competition with other labour. Suffering the resulting loss of jobs, the miners of Coal Creek and Briceville, Tennessee organized a strike. When that failed, hundreds of miners from throughout the region came to their support and seized and burned the stockades in four insurrections against the state militia. The freed prisoners, most of whom were black, were given civilian clothes by the miners and sanctuary in the mining camps and mountaineers' cabins. While the insurrections arose out of somewhat different grievances from those lying latent in Middlesboro, the point remains: the miners and mountaineers of Appalachia were entirely capable under certain conditions of banding together in collective action upon their perceived interests.

The insurrections and other actions at the time carried with them the expression of a consciousness different from that found in the Middlesboro workers—a consciousness that looked at systematic roots of exploitation and identified other miners and mountaineers as having common class interests. Following the second Coal Creek insurrection, a miner's letter read, 'through every ravine and every hill in East Tennessee and Eastern Kentucky the song of freedom for the oppressed miner is being sung not only in the humble log cabins but in the palatial farm residences as well . . .'.[69] For a time, at least, the 'song of freedom' was crushed by the force of the state militia, causing in these Appalachian

[67] *UMWA Journal* (23 July 1891).
[68] *UMWA Journal* (5 Nov. 1891).   [69] ibid.

coalfields further, more radical, expressions about the 'oppression' of the working man. The newly-elected president of District 19, S.P. Herron, wrote to the miners at the time:

> If the militia are the tools of the corporations to overcome and keep in subjection the labouring people—and it seems that they are—we must learn the facts and prepare ourselves for the coming dangers.
>
> The taxpayers—the poor men—go around with their hand in their pockets, thinking, I suppose, of the lords who thieve: 'Who toileth not, neither do they spin; yet Solomon in all his glory was not arrayed like one of these.' Then again they must think of the poor convict—driven to crime by the cash of the taskmasters to double the work that they are able to do. They ought and must think of the crimes against the criminals and the crimes against the citizens perpetrated by the State.
>
> Besides these evils, you can step into the company store and price the articles sold and you see $6.80 per barrel for common flour and 25 cents per pound for lard and $7 for house rent; yet, the earnings of the men do not average more than $10 per month. How do they live?[70]

It is a powerful political statement of an alternative conception of the new order. It moves from the force used by the State and experienced by the miners, to a suggestion of the power of the corporation developing over the State; from a suggestion that the basis of theft for the criminals may be their enforced poverty, to the thought that that was not dissimilar to what the miners themselves daily experienced in their own coal camps. It represents a conception of interests that fuses together those of the corporation with those of the State, and those of the miner with those of the (primarily black) criminals.

Thus there were alternatives in the coalfield to the apparent quiescence of the workers in Middlesboro. They took the form of actions upon work conditions; widespread, organized class rebellion in support of a strike of workers at a particular set of mines; and the beginning of expression of an ideology alternative to that instilled by the capitalist order. The comparative focus supports the thesis that the 'consensus' of the miners in Yellow Creek was inherent neither in their conditions nor in their nature, but grew from the effective wielding of power—in all its dimensions—by the new 'instruments' of civilization.

[70] ibid. (8 December 1892).

3.8 THE COLLAPSE

Not only can one look at the shaping of consensus and the behaviour of other groups in similar conditions to tell something of the roots of quiescence, but one can also observe what happens when the power of the élite weakens. As the power at the top begins to recede, if the non-élite begin to assert latent challenges, then one is provided with the demonstration of a 'relevant counter-factual'. This would suggest that the prior situation had not been based on consensus, but on something else, such as control.[71]

In Middlesboro, the student of power would not have had to wait long to test this 'collapse' theorem. The 'boom' of the city was matched only by its 'bust'. The first sign of a problem came late in 1890 when the 'fountainhead' began to dry up. The Bank of Baring Brothers in London, through which had flowed some $20,000,000 of capital to the city, was closing.[72] Frightened bondholders in Britain began to wonder about the security of their American investment. An auditor's report revealed that the apparent profits were only 'paper' profits—capitalizations had far exceeded for years to come the amount the developments would realistically support.[73] The value of American Association shares tumbled in less than six months from £40 to £1.5 per share.[74] Criticized by his associates in London for extravagance and mismanagement, Arthur was replaced. The oneness of purpose of the Anglo-American enterprise began to show signs of fray. The English chairman of the Middlesborough Town Company reminded angry shareholders that, 'as English shareholders in an American company, they must admit that they had been prepared to have their affairs managed rather by the light of American ideas than those which prevailed in London'.[75] Meanwhile in America, an author wrote, 'nobody saw why a hurt to the Lion should make the Eagle soar, and so the American spirit held faithful—dauntless—for a while'.[76]

[71] See prior discussion, Chapter 1, Section 1.4.
[72] *Middlesboro Daily News,* 19 August 1965.
[73] Tipton, op. cit. (quoted in Fuson, op. cit., p. 378).
[74] Kincaid, op. cit., p. 334.
[75] *The Times* (London), 13 October 1891, p. 8.
[76] Fox, op. cit.

The American financial panic of 1893 succeeded in bring-
ing about the final collapse of Middlesboro. The city's banks
failed; liquidations and receiverships were common. The
Town Company had to auction off all its properties, while
70,000 acres of American Association land were mortgaged
to a New York bank. At an extraordinary General Meeting of
shareholders in London on 27 October 1893, just six years
after the formation of the American Association, Ltd., a
resolution was passed declaring bankruptcy.

It was upon the Company that the city had depended.
Without its organization and capital, Middlesboro was nothing.
Thousands of small investors, working immigrants, and
mountaineers had lost their savings, their jobs, their land.
In retrospect in 1911, a new Middlesboro newspaper, *Thousandsticks*, wrote, 'It may be doubted if ever in the history
of "boom" towns there had been so complete a collapse.'[77]

What was the response to the collapse? In the first stage of
the weakening of the Company, the reaction of the towns-
people was not rebellion but even more overt expressions of
loyalty. While questions of the competence and possible
fraud of Arthur's management led to his dismissal in London,
the relatively powerless, those in Middlesboro, greeted him
upon his return with enthusiastic celebration, and refused to
believe that they had been misled. Only as the effects of the
crash became more apparent, did challenges develop. Creditors
demanded repayment. Law suits were filed. For instance, one
suit claimed that the Company had 'falsely and fraudulently
advertised that a large and prosperous City would be built',
that its industries would employ 12,000 men, that there was
'unlimited capital' and that $18,503,500 was 'already invested
and secured'. Its performance, however, had broken the
guarantee 'in every respect'.[78] After initial re-utterances of
loyalty in the face of the weakened Company, the actions of
the citizens began to suggest that the prior consensus had
been a manipulated one.

As challenges emerged, another pattern indicated something

[77] Charles T. Rogers, ' "Magic City" Arises From the Wreckage of Panic',
Thousandsticks, 9 November 1911.
[78] *J. M. Rains* v. *Middlesborough Town and Land Co., and American Association*, Bell County, Kentucky, Circuit Court, Docket L, no. 1, case 245.

more about the power situation. Though the third dimension
of power was weakening, the power in the other two dimensions remained strong. The political institutions did not back
the challengers, but maintained their support of Arthur and
the weakened Company. Law suits and other expressions of
grievances were soundly defeated. For instance, in 1894 a
strange transaction took place. A Federal Court ordered a
public auction of what had been the crux of the corporation's
developments, the 70,000 acres of mineral-rich, mountain
land mortgaged to the New York bank. A Mr. J. H. Bartlett
was appointed receiver and auctioneer. A 'new' company,
American Association, Inc., was formed as an American
company with essentially the same British backers as the
'old'. It then bought back at the sheriff's auction for $15,000
the property that had been mortgaged for $1,500,000 only a
few months before. Bartlett, the court-appointed auctioneer,
himself became general manager of the 'new' company, and
the London capitalists retained their control.[79]

This apparently manipulative transaction did not go unnoticed, as it might have in the earlier days of consensus. A
Bell County commissioner, on behalf of creditors of the
original company, American Association, Ltd., filed suit
claiming fraud, rigging of the Federal Court, etc., and demanding that depositions be taken from Bartlett and the
others involved. The case was dropped when the commissioner
died.[80]

It was pursued anew, however, by his successor. At this
point the Company argued and was upheld by the local court,
that it bore no responsibility for any of the claims, as it was
legally a different corporation, American Association, Inc.
Arthur, in whose name the debts had been drawn, had been
agent for another corporation, American Association, Ltd.
An appelate court disagreed with this argument, however,
and remanded the case back to the local courts for a re-
hearing.[81] Despite the collapse and the subsequent challenge,

[79] Reconstructed from courthouse records. See especially, *American Association, Inc.* v. *E. Hurst,* Bell County Circuit Court 20, Civil orders 549, Box 144,
Docket 738½.

[80] ibid.

[81] *American Association* v. *H. Steel,* Bell County Circuit Court 20, Civil
Order 528, Box 205, Docket 3267, (1901). The records were apparently destroyed in a courthouse fire in Claiborne County. Although they were on index

the American Association retained control and continued to rebuild its empire.

A similar pattern is found in the behaviour of the miners in the Mingo region, located primarily upon the Company's property around Middlesboro. In 1894, in an attempt to win a uniform national agreement, a national convention of the four-year-old United Mine Workers, headed by its president John McBride, called for the first general strike of coal miners in the history of the country. Although their prior quiescence in the boom period might have led one to expect non-participation by the miners of Mingo, in fact they joined with 150,000 others in walking out of the mines on 21 April 1894. Coming at a time of national depression, the strike was almost a total failure nationally, as it was in Middlesboro. There, however, the significant point was that the miners stayed out on strike for a shorter period than did the other miners in the Tennessee region, declaring that a strike was off and returning to work on the old scale almost two months before the neighbouring miners in Jellico and Coal Creek.[82] Little is known of the reasons for the short-lived nature of the Mingo strike, but the pattern remains: despite the weakened state of the élite of Middlesboro, challenges which emerged from the non-élite neither succeeded nor survived.

With the erosion of felt consensus (as in the third dimension of power), other dimensions of power may be able to 'hold the line' until quiescence is re-established. So it happened in the reconstruction of Middlesboro. The process was not as spectacular, perhaps, as in the first round, but it was just as thorough. The primary factors of production in the rural mining areas—the land and the minerals beneath it—were re-acquired by the 'new' company. The American Association, Inc. turned its energies principally to the development of mines upon its property. By 1905 fourteen mines were operating under its leases in Claiborne County alone, employing 1,299 men—four times as many as a decade before.[83] The Company's interests continued to be well protected in the political apparatus, as one of its mine

in Bell County, the files could not be found.

[82] State of Tennessee, *Annual Report of Bureau of Labor, Statistics and Mines for 1894*, pp. 1–54.

[83] State of Tennessee, *Annual Report of the Mining Department*, 1905.

officers rose to the State Legislature, and as actions which
challenged its interests (particularly questions of land or
taxation) continued to be defeated in the local courthouse.[84]
By 1911, the new newspaper *Thousandsticks* could add
Horatio Alger heroism to the myths that today still legitimate
the city's original founding. It described the recovery as 'the
grimmest battle ever fought by an community in the United
States . . . a battle fought against overwhelming odds by men
who had faith in the possibilities of East Tennessee, and the
ultimate destiny of the city they had chosen to make their
home'.[85]

3.9 CONCLUSIONS

In the initial encounter of industrial forces with the rural
Appalachias is found the shaping of patterns of quiescence
and rebellion which continue in the contemporary situation.
The absentee, monopoly economic control of the area with
its forms of legitimation and protection remains essentially
unchanged. What were the key elements of this encounter?

We have seen the establishment of the hegemony of
industrial economic interests over a particularly independent,
roughly equal, and relatively content enclave society of the
American frontier. The forces which propelled the development of a capital-intensive, resource-extractive centre in
Yellow Creek and the surrounding valleys lay not in Appalachia but in the economic and energy demands of the British
and American metropolises. The agents and institutions of
that world possessed the power to prevail which manifested
itself in multiple ways. Its several faces were first seen in the
initial crucial stage of 'colonization'—the acquisition of these
rural peoples' land and minerals, their major bargaining
resources. A boom was created, a period of rapid economic
and social change, a time of flux and apparent fluidity.
Within that boom, economic inequalities and monopoly
control were also created, though the *Zeitgeist* of the era

---

[84] *Re* non-partitionable land cases, see Claiborne County Quarterly Court,
American Association, Inc. v. *Henry Hamblin* (1909) and *American Association,
Inc.* v. *Robert Hall* (1909) Minute Book G, pp. 248, 276. *Re* taxation, see *Ameri-
can Association, Inc.* v. *B.F. Creech,* Bell County Circuit Court (1906) 24 Civic
Orders 435, Box 237, Docket 4952.
[85] Rogers, op. cit.

may not have brought them into the focus of the thousands of small entrepreneurs, workers and mountaineers who had been attracted to the city. Control of the political apparatus was developed through the election of sympathetic local officials and through non-decisions that ensured certain laws were not enforced. The establishment of power meant more: it meant the instillation of an ideology that would more permanently serve to shroud the inequalities and help to ensure non-challenging participation by the non-élite in the new order.

Despite the fact that the coming of industrialization to Yellow Creek was rooted in imperial forces, there appeared in a very short time a 'consensus' to the system of industrial inequalities. But the basis of the 'consensus', I have argued, was not 'choice', but the effective use of power by the élite to obtain it. Several factors provide support for this assertion. First, at least for the mountaineers, the presence of the new economic élite had never been a matter of their own determination—conflict was present, though latent. Secondly, the small businessman and professional people in the city were almost totally economically dependent upon the absentee élite, giving rise to expressions of their loyalties not autonomously but as reflections of their relative powerlessness within the situation. Thirdly, the miners and labourers, unlike the city's emerging middle class, did not give overt endorsement to the new order, though neither did they challenge it. However, their silence cannot be assumed to be consensus, nor inherent in their nature as peasant-like mountaineers or members of a working class. Comparison with adjoining minefields shows that there was a capacity for collective action and, indeed, a consciousness of class interests expressed by similar populations nearby. That these did not develop in the 'Magic City', where the conditions of the miners were apparently worse than elsewhere, reflected the capacity of greater power in Middlesboro, in its multiple dimensions, for encouraging the acquiescence of the miners in this new social order.

When the field of power shifted, in the collapse of Middlesboro, further evidence was found to show that the prior quiescence may have been a function of powerlessness. At first, the loyalties of the middle class, who had been dependent upon the stability upon the absentee economic élite, expressed themselves all the more fervently. But with time, challenges emerged which claimed manipulation to have been the basis of the prior 'consensus'. Similarly, the miners began to voice challenges where they had not before, becoming more on a par with the miners elsewhere in the region. Yet, this test of the 'counterfactual' reveals a qualifier: even with the weakening of the power élite and the emergence of conflict in one dimension, other dimensions of power, including the internalization of the roles of powerlessness, may serve to repudiate effective challenge until the strength of the prior powerholders is re-established. Indeed, though it was not precisely the case here, one can deduce a hypothesis for future consideration: the most insidious use of power is that which maintains non-challenge of the powerless even after the powerful have fallen. In Middlesboro the collapse meant only that some challenges emerged, but not that they were successful or that they survived. Though not as dramatically as before, the inequalities were re-established and re-legitimated. The people in and around the Cumberland Gap had lost, while their new absentee landlords had gained.

In time, perhaps, the industrialization of Yellow Creek would inevitably have occurred, and the people of Yellow Creek would inevitably have lost to its power. But why did the encounter of apparently different interests and values occur with such little apparent conflict? I have argued that the answer lies in the powers of the industrial society for establishing control and for breeding consensus. The process was like a colonizing process; the development of dominance of one set of values and procedures over another, out of which there emerges a colonial situation, in which the dominant set of values and procedures is accepted by the colonized. In fact, the colonial analogy was made at the time of Alexander Arthur's death by his secretary, who wrote, as Arthur was buried on Cumberland Mountain:

I have often thought of him as a type of Cecil Rhodes; and as the great empire builder's dust lies amongst the Matopos Hills of South Africa, so it is meet that the remains of Alexander Arthur, the instrument which opened to man another of the waste places of the world, should rest amid the theatre of his achievement . . .[86]

As the examination of the nature of industrial power in an Appalachian Valley is continued perhaps more significantly recalled are the words of Arthur himself in 1890 in a speech in Middlesboro. 'In conclusion . . . I simply wish to say that what we have done is but the beginning of what we shall do. . .'[87]

[86] *Roberts Papers,* letter to Mrs. Arthur, 11 March 1912.
[87] Alexander Arthur, speech, 11 November 1890.

4

THE IMPACT OF UNIONISM: THE RISE AND QUELLING OF PROTEST, 1923-1933

In 1933, Lester Cohen, a member of the Dreiser Committee investigating conditions in the Kentucky coalfields, wrote of the Central Appalachian people: 'The great change that came upon them did not come through war or the law . . . A free primitive people had become the vassals of modern industrialism.' He continued, 'Today Harlan and Bell Counties have heard the rattle of machine guns, the roar of dynamite, the curse of thugs, and the multitudinous voices of industrial warfare. And, the mountain men, once more Union, Republican, and revolutionary, are leaving their blood upon the ground . . . For the pioneer people have become the rebellious protestants of His Majesty, King Coal.'[1]

The period 1929-33 was not one of quiescence in the Central Appalachian area around the city of Middlesboro. In the wave of the Depression, rebellion against the conditions of industrialization emerged as these miner-mountaineers sought to unionize, first in the United Mine Workers of America (UMWA), then in the Communist-backed National Miners' Union (NMU), then again, in the UMWA. Their rebellion was dramatically quelled, but the patterns of power witnessed during this period have continued to shape conflicts to this day.[2]

[1] Lester Cohen, 'Bloody Ground', in Theodore Dreiser, *Harlan Miners Speak* (Da Capo Press, New York, 1970).

[2] Except where otherwise indicated, sources from this chapter are primarily from the period, including oral history interviews, UMWA documents, local newspaper accounts, and descriptive works of the time. Numerous oral history interviews were carried out personally. In addition, I am very grateful for being allowed to transcribe and use materials from the Model Valley Oral History Videotape Project, funded by the National Endowment for the Humanities and carried out by local students in 1973. I am also grateful to the UMWA Research Department, Washington, D.C., for use of correspondence files and other documents in its archives, to be cited as *UMWA Files*.

4.1 POWER IN THE COAL CAMP

The importance of South Central Appalachian coal to the national economy increased during the 1920s, though on a national level the coal market was generally down. The lack of uniform wage standards, the general lack of unionization in the Appalachian region, and the favourable long-distance haulage rates given by the railroads, allowed the southern operators of Kentucky, Tennessee, West Virginia and Virginia essentially to corner the coal market.[3] In 1922, for instance, these non-union fields provided about 22 per cent of the total bituminous coal output; by 1930 they were providing 80 per cent.[4] Though production was increasing, the miners' demands were not; in fact, union strength was on the decline. While the coal companies were benefiting immensely from their favourable position, for some reason, as Coleman pointed out in 1943, 'the non-union operators were finding *docile diggers*' in the newly-important Central Appalachian fields.[5]

Who were these 'docile diggers' of the Southern Appalachias? As in the 1890s they continued to be primarily rural, Anglo-Saxon mountaineers. A professor of Fisk University in Nashville, Tennessee reported in a 1933 study that of 359 miners interviewed in the fields in eastern Kentucky, 24 per cent were born in the county in which they lived, an additional 21 per cent were born in the adjacent county, and a further 43 per cent were born within other parts of Kentucky, West Virginia, or Tennessee—an 88 per cent Southern Appalachian work force.[6]

In contrast, the mines in which the men worked continued to be owned by large, absentee, metropolitan interests. In Claiborne County, for instance, on the London-owned American Association's 44,000 acres of property, some ten mines were operating, almost all controlled by British, Pennsylvania, Illinois or Knoxville capital.[7] In Tennessee's

[3] E. E. Hurt, G. T. Tyron, J. W. Wilts, eds., *What the Coal Commission Found* (Williams and Wilkins Co., Baltimore, 1925), p. 234.
[4] Homer Lawrence Morris, *The Plight of the Bituminous Coal Miner* (University of Pennsylvania Press, Philadelphia, 1934), p. 14.
[5] Coleman, *Men and Coal,* op. cit., p. 122.
[6] Morris, op. cit., pp. 36-7.
[7] State of Tennessee, Dept. of Labor, Division of Mines *Annual Reports,* 1928, 1933.

Campbell County, Mellon interests had taken hold through the Koppers' Land Company; and in Kentucky's Bell and Harlan counties were found Morgan interests through International Harvester and the Louisville and Nashville Railroad, Insull interests through the Black Mountain Coal Company, Ford interests along Wallins Creek, Detroit Edison interests through the King Harlan Company, and those of an ambassador to Germany through the Black Star Coal Company—to name just a few.[8]

Why this reputation of docility amongst miners enduring low wages and poor conditions? One approach argues that the isolated, rural nature of the work force provides sufficient explanation. The Coal Commission found in 1923 that 88 per cent of the communities were more than 'five miles from the resources of community life and the institutions of civil liberty' that characterized the 'ordinary urban center'.[9] However, different behaviour has been observed in other 'isolated mass' communities, where the concentration of a single occupational group has led to militant actions and beliefs.[10] A more fruitful hypothesis might be drawn from other data of the Coal Commission: two-thirds to four-fifths of these miners of the Southern Appalachias lived in 'company-controlled communities'. Perhaps isolation is not a sufficient condition for the maintenance of quiescence, but it allows the development of a system of controls over miners and their families.

The first factor of control, external to the mining community, is often overlooked in studies of American rural labour. Although theoretically the miners might have objected to conditions in the mines by migrating, they had no desire to go to industrial occupations in the cities, and were not able to migrate easily to other occupations in the countryside. Many of these miners were essentially rural in character and would have preferred to be hillside farmers than coal diggers. Of 956 unemployed miners in Kentucky and West Virginia interviewed by Morris in 1932, only 11 per cent said they wanted to return to mining; 18 per cent wanted to enter

[8] Anna Rochester, 'Who Owns the Mines?', in Dreiser, op. cit., pp. 50–8.
[9] Hurt, Tyron, Wilts, op. cit., pp. 139–40.
[10] Kerr and Siegel, op. cit., (and see discussion, Chapter 2).

industrial occupations (e.g. mechanics, railroads, factories), while 48 per cent wanted to return to farming.[11]

However, the exit to farming, even in the rural Appalachias, was blocked: for in the case of the American Association, the corporations throughout the region owned not just the mines but also the land. Ross wrote in 1933 about miners who 'would desire to return to cultivation of the land: the trouble is that they no longer have any claim to it. The coal companies own the land. For the use of it the mountaineers cannot pay rent, since they raise no money crops. Nor can they remain for long in dependence on another man's soil.'[12] Watkins, a British visitor, wrote that for the attainment of independent communities in Appalachia 'a necessary step . . . would seem to be much larger and stricter social control over the ownership of land, for in many cases the operating companies own all the land within convenient reach of the mines'.[13] Even if some miners wanted to escape to the cities, they often lacked the resources or occupational skills to do so.

Thus a fundamental discrepancy existed between what the miners might want to do (escape) but could not (no exit), and so another elaborate set of controls was required to maintain their acquiescence. These took the form of the coal camp, a unitary and exploitative system of power that affected all aspects of the lives of the miners and their families.[14]

The key to control was the workplace—the mines. It only requires talking to miners, often coughing with 'black lung' from coal dust or gesturing with gnarled limbs from accidents, to know that conditions in the mines were rough. But these men were dependent upon their jobs, and the threat of losing them was the key to ensuring their acceptance of the conditions. Some older miners describe:

[11] Morris, op. cit., pp. 186-90.

[12] Malcolm Ross, *Machine Age in the Hills* (MacMillan, New York, 1933), p. 84.

[13] Watkins, *Coal and Men*, op. cit., p. 258.

[14] This concept is well developed by A.L. Epstein, *Politics in an Urban African Community* (University of Manchester Press, Manchester, 1958). He writes, 'The structure of mine society is essentially unitary. The African employees of the mining company are thus linked together not only through their work situation, but in almost every other aspect of their daily existence by a complex nexus of ties which has its basis largely in the mine organization itself.' (p. 147).

The operators treated you pretty rough, they did . . . if they got it in for you in any way. Before the union you didn't have any backin's at all. And they just drove ya'. They told ya' just to get your tools—they called 'em rusts, they called the tools rusts—they'd just say to load your rusts and t'get out. And that's what 'ya done.

. . . Before the union came into this holler, they worked 'em however they wanted to . . . They'd give you a place, no matter how big it was, you went and cleaned it up. Didn't make any difference what time it was. If you didn't you got your tools.

Why they took better care of a mule than they did a human. If you complained or kicked on it, you were discharged.

Often, not just an individual would be threatened with discharge but so would all the members of his family. Blacklists would make it difficult to get work elsewhere. A miner told the story:

They got me after my brother brought a suit against the company, the Wills company fired all four of us brothers . . . They didn't have any right to fire us. If the fact of the matter is looked into, they didn't have the right to fire the one that got hurt, because they wouldn't pay off without a suit and when he brought the suit they fired us all.

Upon losing his job this particular miner went to his brother-in-law who operated a timber mill. He told him he was in a 'close place' and needed work. But even the brother-in-law refused to hire him, because he had been told that if he hired any of the brothers he would lose his business selling timber to the mine.

In such a system of unitary power, powerlessness increased as various points of vulnerability were brought into play. The industrial operators were able to manipulate the prevailing values of the rural miner-mountaineers, such as values of kinship. The relationship was somewhat exponential: it multiplied in magnitude according to the number of workers in the family and the number of employers in the area (most of whom were lessees on the same land company's property). The power of the coal hollow was not just that of a single boss over a single worker; it was that of collective interests against collective groups of potential actors.

Yet the workplace experience of the underground miner also bred a certain dignity and collective pride, still apparent today as retired miners describe their work. The relative freedom from supervision of the boss at the coal face encouraged the development of self-reliance and interdependence. Because of this countervailing force against compliance, other controls were needed to ensure quiescence. They were found in the nexus between the job and the community.

A worker in the coal camp was reminded of that nexus every two weeks when he received his pay slip, for from his wages were docked rent, services, goods purchased at the store, medical bills, even funeral expenses—all by the same employer. The slip symbolically fused the miner's dependence as worker, tenant, consumer, and citizen. This unitary structure meant that power exercised in one part of the system could evoke a response in another: misbehaviour in the job could cause the loss of a home; failure to shop at the company store (where prices were often higher) could mean the loss of work; disobedience of a single rule could mean eviction from the game all together. It is interesting to note how the theme is expressed in the oral history:

. . . some places, if you didn't use the scrip, you would get a house notice.

. . . just another little Watergate, 'cept there wasn't anything you could do about it. You had to buy your food whether you wanted to or not

. . . but if you went in and out, you'd better not buy food and let the company know about it, because you might not have a job too long.

Well, now them coal camps . . . they were pretty rough . . . kind of like a family, you had to obey the rules.

The unitary power not only served to defer action upon grievances by the miners inside the coal camp; it also helped to maintain non-intervention by third parties. In 1930, John L. Lewis, president of the United Mine Workers, wrote to William Turnblazer, president of the district, 'We have been quite well aware for a considerable period of time that we can organize the mineworkers. . . and they would be glad to join the organization now as heretofore. The difficulty comes in attempting to care for them after they are organized; they are promptly discharged, evicted from their homes, and subjected to every manner of personal abuse.'[15]

It is not sufficient for the study of power in the coal camp simply to look at the controls over action upon grievances.

[15] Letter from John L. Lewis to Wm. Turnblazer, 3 February 1930, *UMWA Files.*

We must also ask whether the power situation served to
affect the miners' conceptions of those potential grievances.
As within the Magic City, there were clearly observable
processes at work which suggest that power did help, directly
or indirectly, to shape values and wants.

For instance, the dependency or powerlessness of the
miner served to shape a value of short-term individual interests, at the expense of concern for long-term, collective
interests. The uncertainties of the job (safety, tenure) combined with the costs of action upon the uncertainties, encouraged a value of one's own immediate situation rather
than upon one's long-term situation as member of a social
class. The same phenomenon appeared in the miner's life
as consumer and as citizen.

Despite the relatively low wages, for instance, there
developed in the mining camps an exaggerated consumptive
desire. A miner put it this way:

The coal mines have always been rough on the workin' man. The way
it was, the biggest majority, they made good money . . . but the coal
miner, he didn't live like other people—the coal miner, if he made
twenty dollars a day, he'd spend it; he lived high, if he made it: if he
didn't, he didn't.

A social worker for the Federal Employment Relief Administration reported in 1935 about the Tennessee coal camps
that 'Miners are victims of high pressure salesmen with
expensive wares. For instance, one day just before a strike
broke out, a salesman for $22.00 Bibles sold eighteen in one
miners' camp.'[16] Malcolm Ross wrote in the *New York Times*,
'The bait was too glittering for the hill people . . . they
bought automobiles, silk sheets, radios and washing machines
and generally behaved as backwoods people do when suddenly
showered with money.'[17] Like much of the contemporary
literature on high consumption amongst poverty groups,
these analyses failed to consider the circumstances of dependence which shaped the consumptive desire: with the monopoly ownership of long-term investment opportunities such
as land and housing, the uncertainties of long-term income,

[16] Memo from regional social worker to Mr. Aubrey Williams, Asst. Admin.,
FERA, 2 November 1935, *UMWA Files.*
[17] *New York Times,* 3 April 1932.

and the availability of company store scrip, it was only rational to 'want' that which 'glittered' while it could be had.

A similar phenomenon is found in the miner as citizen, particularly in the value he put on his vote. It was common practice for votes to be bought and sold as a commodity.

. . . you'd go to vote and the official of the election would take a yellow paper and punch a hole if you voted right; you'd go back to a certain man, and he'd give you three dollars if you voted right.

. . . Cause came back then, they'd give so much a vote. Had to have a poll tax receipt to vote. Why candidates would get a bunch of 'em and just write 'em out. Some of these fellows, they'd have em vote in Valley Creek, then they'd go to Clairfield and vote, and they'd give 'em so much. They'd just bought their way into office. They weren't exactly elected back then . . . 'cause I've helped hold the elections. Never seen an honest one yet.

A pluralist might ask, 'Why if they were exploited, did the miners and their families not try to use their voice to try to change the system?'. The question ignores the power field in which the miner found himself. In his position, he had little reason to value the vote: if he did not play by the rules of the game, or if he sought to oppose them, the sanctions were severe. The county rarely intervened in the coal camp, which was, in principle, a law unto itself; and the vote was like a franchise in a foreign election. On the other hand, the political stakes in certain outcomes were high for the owners of the coal camps, particularly in the elections of the sheriff and the tax commissioner. The owners were willing buyers of votes and the miners willing sellers—and the 'willingness' was rooted in the power situation.

While the coal camp thus served to shape certain individualistic values, it also served to shape certain collective values, while excluding others. Other than the workplace, the only organizations or institutions in the camp which brought the community together were the schools and churches. Both were encouraged and controlled by the same interests which controlled the workplace. As for the schools, the teachers were usually hired and the buildings usually financed by the companies, with 'docks' from the miners' wages. For adults, the churches were the only places where community solidarity could be expressed. Rather than being prevented like other collective organizations (e.g. the union), the development of churches was encouraged through leasing of land and even docking of wages to finance the building. A coal company official testified to the Costigan Senate Committee about the 'civic-mindedness' reflected in the practice:

> *Mr. Eavenson*: In the case of the churches, the universal practice in the country is, after the town is built, if the members of any particular denomination number enough, they will go to the company and say 'We want a church,' and the coal company will say invariably, 'We will donate the ground in fee for such a purpose.' In some cases they will build the church, but the usual practice is that you raise the money for the building and we will contribute half the cost.
> *The Chairman*: The companies seldom, if ever, part with title except in the case of churches?
> *Mr. Eavenson*: And schools.[18]

Within the churches there continued the development of an intensely felt, other wordly, fundamentalist religion which served as an outlet for community expression and an important agent of socialization. Morris wrote at the time that 'there are probably few sections in the United States where religion is called upon to bear so many of the burdens of life . . . If a minister should become imbued with a passion for social justice, it is doubtful if he could remain in a company-owned parish.'[19]

There was, finally, another process of shaping consciousness which grew from the power relations of the coal camp. Where plausibility of exit and effectiveness of voice are minimal, acceptance of a state of powerlessness may occur as an adaptive response to the exploitative situation.[20] The response in the coal camp took several forms. That most commonly noted was the internalization of the quiescent role. Morris wrote, for instance, of the coal camp residents, 'their utter dependence . . . develops an attitude of submission and servitude which undermines their confidence and self-reliance'.[21] A sense of powerlessness was instilled

[18] *Conditions of Coal Fields in Harlan and Bell Counties,* Report of Subcommittee of Committee on Manufacturing on Senate Resolution 178, p. 4.

[19] Morris, op. cit., pp. 93, 132.

[20] This implies, therefore, a critique of Hirschman's economic, 'rational man' model of consensus or discontent, put forward in *Exit, Voice, and Loyalty* (Harvard University Press, Cambridge, Mass., 1970); also see discussion, Chapter 1, of third-dimensional mechanisms of power.

[21] Morris, op. cit., p. 96.

which could lead to an introjection of the values of the controller or a loyalty to the powerholders. A miner put it this way:

I think like any other company, they want to dominate the lives of their people . . . The way they accomplished this was in owning everything. And, naturally, if a man worked in a coal company, and he traded at a company store, and lived in a company house, then he felt like maybe politically and socially he ought to go along with exactly the way they felt.

A third adaptive response developed as the enforced lack of participation or challenge over time led to a fading of conception of action itself. This was expressed by one miner when asked why challenge in the community did not take place at a point when the control of the company weakened. He responded, 'Well, I guess we could have gotten power then, there were so many of us, but we just didn't think of it.'

A picture is thus painted of the development and maintenance of worker and community quiescence by a unitary system of power and powerlessness in the coal camp. The 'consensus' in the face of inequalities was described by one miner who said, 'There was more millionaires living in one street than in any other place in the State of Kentucky or Tennessee, or four or five other states. . . They was coal operators. They worked their men for a song—*and the men sung it themselves.*' Despite what may appear to be clear examples of the processes of power's second and third dimensions, two problems still must be considered: the problem of the counterfactual, and the problem of significance.

The problem of the counterfactual is this: how do we know that without the power of the coal lords the miners would have done otherwise? A comparative approach can be taken that will provide useful data on the question. How did similar populations behave and think where the power of the coal camp was not so strong?

Within the Clear Fork Valley itself was one area which the land company had never been able to acquire, which provided a place for free assembly, and in which developed more activities and attitudes of challenge than in the coal camps. Its relative autonomy and differing environment are still remembered by many local citizens. One resident said:

I'll say that I've been very proud that I was born in Morgan Hollow for Morgan Hollow was a place of independence. It set as sort of an island in the midst of the properties that was owned by the American Association company . . . And not all the time was there the best of relationships between the people of Morgan Hollow and the coal companies themselves . . because the rebels sort of lived in Morgan Hollow. And I'm not saying rebels in the sense that we were trouble makers but in the sense that there was a lot more liberty to do what you wanted to do. You weren't under the arm of anybody there.

With the independence came patterns of participation and collective organization other than those found in the coal camps. He continued, 'The union, as it was being organized in the coal fields, Morgan Hollow was one of the places where the union could meet . . . Another thing that I thought was exciting was the politics of the thing . . . Grandmother and Granddad were on the school board. . .'

Beyond the Clear Fork Valley, too, the factor of the independence of the community was an important one in determining patterns of participation. According to the Coal Commission data there were three types of coal communities in the United States. In Ohio and Pennsylvania, where miners were more militant, the communities were well settled before mining camps came in. One-fourth to one-half of the miners lived in company houses and 'numerous civically controlled communities flourished'. In Illinois, Indiana and some of the mid-western States, less than nine per cent of the miners lived in company-owned dwellings, and 'agriculture and industry have . . . brought into being centers of self-governing populations'. In the fields of the Southern Appalachias, as has been seen, two-thirds to four-fifths of the miners were company tenants living in 'company-controlled communities'.[22] And it is here that the highest rates of non-unionism and the most claims of quiescent populations were found. The comparative data would indicate that these patterns came not from the 'backwardness' of the old ways or 'consensus' to the new order, but were related to the higher level of industrial power in the mountain communities.

Finally, a comparative insight is also offered by the work of Watkins of the University of Cardiff who studied the British and American coalfields in the early 1930s. He was

[22] Hurt, Tyron, Wilts, op. cit., p. 139–40.

struck by the lack of political activity and consciousness of the miners in the United States. He found that, 'in general British miners living in colliery-owned houses enjoyed a much larger measure of freedom as tenants than do the mine-workers living in company-owned camps in the U.S.'. He asked, 'How long will it be before a home in an independent community will be as normal to an American miner as it is today to the British miner? . . . Obstacles there are undoubt-edly, but one may fully realize how formidable they are and yet be deeply impressed by the urgency of the necessity of getting rid of the whole institution—company houses, com-pany police, company land, the company store, the company cinemas, the company-supported schools, and church and all the other features of the American feudal, serf-like company-controlled mining community.'[23] These controls, he con-cluded, and the related factors such as lack of effective worker education and lack of labour-oriented political parties had failed to bring the social and political development of the American miner on a par with that of the British miner (though the Americans enjoyed a higher standard of living).

The example of the second and third faces of power found in the coal camp is perhaps theoretically not a difficult one; but empirically it is by no means of minor importance. In this particular community, as we shall see, the coal camp environment continues to be of significance for patterns of rebellion and control; and this experience was not unlike that faced by large proportions of the southern work force, in hundreds of coal camps, mill towns, cotton plantations, and other single industry communities. It is perhaps from the prior workings of a system of unitary power that places like Gary, Indiana experience the non-decisions involved in a 'reputation for power'.[24] One should also not forget that substantial numbers of the blue collar workers of the metro-politan centres of the North—car workers in Detroit, plant workers in Ohio, factory workers in Newark—are displaced Appalachians whose social background is still reflected in their industrial behaviour and attitudes.[25] The unitary power

[23] Watkins, op. cit., pp. 272, 258.

[24] Crenson, *The Un-Politics of Air Pollution*, op. cit.

[25] See, for example, discussion by Aronowitz, *False Promises*: op. cit., pp. 28–9; or William E. Powles, 'The Southern Appalachian Migrant: Country Boy

in the company town and the accompanying shaping of acquiescence are more than just isolated examples of the second and third dimensions of power. They must be included as well as factors in any general understanding of the attitudes and behaviour of the American worker.

4.2 THE EMERGENCE OF REBELLION

Beginning in 1930, the conditions of dependency of miners in the coal camp began to change. The favourable conditions of production for the Southern mines that had developed in the 1920s led to overproduction, particularly as overseas markets began to decline, other fields began to compete, and the national depression spread. The demand for coal dropped dramatically, and by early 1931, the industry had enough equipment to produce twice as much coal as was needed, and twice as many miners as were required to run the machines.[26] Lay-offs and cut-backs began to occur. In February 1931, wage cuts were made in the fields of Harlan, Bell and Claiborne Counties. Work became sporadic. About one-fifth of the population were unemployed, and those who were employed were making as little as eighty cents a day and working only a few days a month.[27] The *Middlesboro Daily News* in 1931 reported about 5,000 people in the coal hollows to be 'facing starvation'.[28] Another coal boom in the Southern Appalachias had ended.

With this change in conditions, the nexus of control (the wage in the coal camp and the unitary set of controls surrounding it) was being severed. The paternalistic care in the coal camp began to show its limits. A mood of rebellion developed, expressed by one miner who said, 'If you are a slave workin' for nothin' it finally gets old.'

The events and non-events of the next year's rebellion (May 1931–May 1932) in the south-eastern Kentucky and north-eastern Tennessee coalfields are numerous and complicated. As quickly as it emerged, the rebellion subsided. In

Turned Blue-Collarite', in Shostak and Gomberg, *Blue Collar World,* op. cit., pp. 270–82.

[26] Louis Stark, *New York Times,* 11 October 1931, 3 April 1932.

[27] Charles Rumford Walker, 'Organizing a Union in Kentucky', in Dreiser, op. cit., p. 43.

[28] *Middlesboro Daily News,* 7 May 1931.

treating its rise and demise, a brief chronological review of what occurred will be given. The question can then be asked, 'Why the failure?', and an attempt made to answer by looking more extensively at the factors of power and powerlessness that were brought into play.

The United Mine Workers Union in the Southern Appalachias at the time was little more than a skeleton organization. Its leader, John L. Lewis, had been more concerned about quelling internal opposition of dissatisfied miners than about non-unionism. In December 1930, William Turnblazer, the Lewis-appointed president of District 19, had just written to 'John L.', mentioning prospects of organizing in the spring, but he had added more adamantly his assurance 'of my every good wish of cleaning out those who wish to destroy our union'.[29] However, when a few miners from the earlier organizing drives of the 1920s approached Turnblazer demanding assistance in a new drive, Turnblazer responded. By February 1931, circulars were being distributed and mass meetings were being planned. Turnblazer could write to Philip Murray, vice-president of the UMWA and later president of the Congress of Industrial Organizations (CIO), 'these miners are getting it through their stomach and about to bring the blood . . . They are going wild.'[30]

On 1 March 1931 over 2,000 miners gathered in Pineville, the county seat of Bell County, to hear Murray pledge support to the rebirth of the UMWA in the southern fields. 'Miners . . . need to organize,' he said. 'But we do not intend to precipitate strikes or create industrial catastrophe . . . the operators and the workers must meet their problems in a spirit of co-operation.'[31] A second mass meeting was held three weeks later in Lafollette, in Campbell County, Tennessee, addressed by Turnblazer and Congressman Will Taylor. Again, the UMWA promised support: 'If you will form a union with 10,000 dues-paying members, we will give you food and money for a strike.'[32] As a result of the mass meetings, hundreds of miners and their families were evicted

---

[29] *UMWA Files*, December 1930.
[30] *UMWA Files*, February 1931.
[31] *Knoxville News Sentinel*, 2 March 1931.
[32] Walker, op. cit., p. 43.

from their homes. Yet, they continued to fight. Lawrence (Peggy) Dwyer, an organizer for District 19, wrote to president Lewis on 10 April 1931 about the grass-roots drive for organization:

The spirit and determination that is being displayed by these men to belong to the union in the face of discharge, blacklisting, and eviction is wonderful. In one section of Harlan there is 1400 discharged and blacklisted men practically all of them with large families and at the time of their discharge several weeks ago, they didn't have a nickel and they have not whimpered about it to me. . . Any way I have never seen such a spirit in all of my life. My position to the men and to the public is that the men have a right to belong to a Labor Union and that they should insist on exercising that right, and by gravy the poor fellows is going the limit to do so.[33]

The newly-expressed militance of the miners was not generally to be encouraged by Turnblazer and Lewis, however. Turnblazer's response to the mass evictions was to send a telegram to President Hoover asking the President 'in the name of humanity, right and justice and as one who has been active on your behalf' to use his influence to get the companies to moderate their behaviour and to encourage the Red Cross to provide relief for the strikers. 'They have appealed to that great American Mother, that wonderful angel of mercy, the American Red Cross. They asked for bread and were given stone,' Turnblazer complained.[34]

Meanwhile, in Harlan, 2,800 men, women and children took matters into their own hands, marched into the county seat and demanded food from the merchants. Violence increased as the companies brought in strike breakers. On 5 May, the famous 'Battle of Evarts' occurred in which some 100 armed miners fought with several car loads of deputies. The conflict left 1 miner and 3 deputies dead. As a result of the shooting, 44 miners were arrested and jailed, and 400 Kentucky State troopers arrived on the scene. A general protest strike developed in the mines throughout the region, and this led to more evictions and shootings.

Over 11,000 miners joined the United Mine Workers of America in that spring organization drive. However, faced with widespread militance, with exorbitant legal costs and

[33] *UMWA Files,* 10 April 1931.
[34] *UMWA Journal* (15 April 1931).

with men needing the relief that had been promised, the UMWA backed down. The officials declared the strike to be a 'wildcat' and urged the men back to work. In response to appeals for financial help from the organizers, John L. Lewis made his position clear: 'We are not in a position to spend money in Harlan and Bell County for relief purposes. Our representatives and members will have to carry on in that territory under their own power.'[35] Having been dormant for almost a decade, the district had no resources or power, and offered the miners no support. The miners declared that they had been 'sold out', and that Turnblazer had actually encouraged the governor to bring in the troops to break the strike.[36] As a miner later reported to the Senate Committee, 'the strike was broke, the way we call it, because the men did not get anything to eat from the organization. They could not stay out. They were starved back in.'[37]

The militance of the miners continued. A few of the men formed an independent organization, the All Workers Union;[38] some joined a small chapter in Harlan of the International Workers of the World (IWW or 'Wobblies'). Most turned for leadership, however, to the National Miners' Union (NMU), a Communist-backed organization, under the Trade Union Unity League. Again, events moved rapidly. On 19 June Dan Brooks, the first organizer for the NMU, entered the area. On 30 June, Jesse Wakefield of the International Labor Defense Fund (ILD) began relief and defence work, taking up the cases of the arrested miners. A delegation of twenty-eight miners was elected to attend the NMU convention in Pittsburgh. Within a few weeks there were some 4,000 NMU members in the area.[39] Mr. Elsy Smith, one of the members, later testified about the development of the organization in his mine: 'we sent a delegation to the convention to find out what kind of organization the National Miners' Union was.

[35] Letter to Ben Williams from John L. Lewis, 6 August, 1931, *UMWA Files.*

[36] For a god account of these perceptions of the men see, 'A Harlan Miner Speaks', videotape of Tilman Cadle (Broadside TV, Johnson City, Tenn); Tilman Cadle interviewed by Jim Branscome, *'Hell in Harlan, a Review'*, *Mountain Eagle* (7 June 1973).

[37] Testimony of James C. Garland, Pineville, Ky., *Conditions in Harlan and Bell Counties,* op. cit., p. 3.

[38] Sterling D. Spero and Jacob Aronoff, 'War in the Kentucky Mountains', *The American Mercury*, 25 (1932), 230.

[39] Walker, op. cit., p. 46.

Our committee came back at midnight and made a report and we miners had taken the application blanks and started to work, and we wrote up 98 per cent of the workers within two weeks, and we were holding meetings secretly for practically a month.[40]

With assistance from the NMU, the organizing continued, matched by increased repression. More local chapters, women's auxiliaries, and a soup kitchen were set up. On 20 July, the home of one of the delegates to the NMU convention was raided. On 23 July, an ILD organizer, Jesse Wakefield, found his home destroyed by dynamite. On 25 July, there were reportedly sixty-five hired thugs in Harlan County area alone. On 26 July, 2,000 men, women and children held a support picnic, while armed men kept deputies at bay. On 3 August, in similar conditions, an NMU convention was held at Wallins Creek in Bell County, attended by 500 men and women, black and white. On 10 August, one of the seven soup kitchens was destroyed by dynamite. Mass arrests and widespread harassment of miners continued.

The repression was somewhat successful in cutting off relief and in preventing local meetings from taking place, but the militance of the miners continued at a level amazing even to the experienced Communist organizers. Some 125 miners attended a conference in Lexington, Kentucky on 13 September, and an ILD representative wrote a confidential report to the party secretariat in New York that read in part, 'When we consider the fact that the conference itself had to be organized secretly because of the terrors and that the men who attended knew they were risking their lives, we can get some idea of the determination that pervades the miners and their willingness to put up a fight . . . They will fight with or without our leadership.' A later report in October urgently requested permission from the secretariat for a strike, saying 'this is a situation certainly new in our history where workers demand a mass strike and we hold them back for weeks waiting for center to take action'.[41]

[40] Testimony of Mr. Elsy Smith, *Conditions in Harlan and Bell Counties,* op. cit., pp. 3–4.

[41] Quoted in Theodore Draper, 'Communists and Miners, 1928-1933' *Dissent,* 20 (1973), 383.

Meanwhile the repression in the area attracted national attention. The writer, Theodore Dreiser, and a committee of twelve others called the National Committee for the Denfense of Political Prisoners, went to Bell and Harlan Counties for an independent investigation on 'terrorism in the Kentucky coalfields'.[42] Dreiser himself was framed in a charge of adultery in the Continental Hotel in Pineville.[43] He and nine others were also indicted for criminal syndicalism, a felony at that time under Kentucky law.

During the weekend of 13 December 1931, following the decision of the party secretariat that a 'truly representative' conference should be held to decide a strike strategy,[44] 250 miners met at Pineville in Bell County. They voted for a strike to begin on 1 January; organizers promised that food and relief would be provided; and the party leaders announced that 'we realize that the overwhelming mass of the miners throughout the Kentucky and Tennessee fields are for the demands set forth by the convention'.[45]

It is difficult to assess accurately the extent of the strike, but by all accounts, it was less than what might have been expected by the previous miners' militance. In the first week the operators claimed the strike to be less than 10 per cent effective, while the NMU claimed that there were many more men out, particularly at the Pruden and Clear Fork mines. On 16 and 17 January rallies were held at Middlesboro, Lafollette, Wallins Creek, Straight Creek and Short Creek, with estimates of the number involved in the strike ranging from a mere handful to 7,000 workers involving 30–40,000 people.[46]

For a strike that was supposedly a failure, the level of

[42] See Dreiser, 'Why I Went to Kentucky', introduction to *Harlan Miners Speak,* op. cit., pp. 3-16.

[43] Dreiser was caught by the famous 'toothpick trick'. The management of the hotel reported that he had gone into his hotel room at night with an unidentified woman. The management had then leaned toothpicks against the door, which were still there in the morning, indicating that 'adultery' had occurred inside. See descriptions, for instance, in *Middlesboro Daily News,* 10 November 1931.

[43] Draper op. cit., p. 383.

[45] *Knoxville News Sentinel,* 30 December 1931.

[46] Compiled from *Knoxville News Sentinel,* 2- 4, 17–18 January 1932; *New York Times,* 15 February 1932; and *Middlesboro Daily News,* 15 February 1932.

repression, aimed especially at the organizers and leaders, continued to be high. Two miners were killed in Harlan on the eve of the strike. On 3 January, the second day of the strike, the NMU's headquarters in Pineville were raided by deputies. Nine organizers were jailed for criminal syndicalism, while 750 miners and supporters marched to the jailhouse on their behalf. On 4 January, Alan Taub, the ILD lawyer sent in to defend them, was himself arrested within two hours of his arrival in Pineville and jailed for eight days. Meanwhile, there was a rumour of six people killed in Gatliff, and ten more persons were arrested for criminal syndicalism in Bell County on 7 January. In the second week of the strike, Gil Greene, a black organizer, was arrested in Middlesboro; the two key organizers, Weber and Duncan, were picked up by the Claiborne County sheriff, were severely beaten, and barely escaped with their lives. On 14 January, a nineteen-year-old organizer, Harry Simms, was shot and killed by thugs near Barbourville, Kentucky. His body was taken to New York, where over 2,000 mourners marched behind it in a dramatic funeral procession from Penn Station to Union Square. Meanwhile, in the Cumberlands, the town of Middlesboro barred any meetings of the NMU, and as late as 20 March, fifteen more of the leaders were arrested in a secret meeting in the nearby Powell Valley in Claiborne County. The local sheriff, Frank Riley, announced that he had been called in to break up an 'all night party'.

The struggle of the miners and the resulting repression brought in more 'help' from the outside, in turn leading to more repression aimed at the 'outsiders'. Following the Dreiser example, writer Waldo Frank led the 'Independent Miners Relief Committee' into the coalfields to distribute truck loads of food and to 'establish the right to do so'. Though allowed to do so near Lafollette, Tennessee, they were arrested in Pineville, escorted to the State line at Cumberland Gap by a 'vigilante committee' of fifty to seventy-five businessmen, beaten, and ejected from the State. In March, during their spring vacations, bus loads of students from north-eastern universities attempted to enter Bell County to make an 'impartial survey' (in a twenty-four hour visit) of the conditions and troubles of the area. The

County Attorney of Bell County, Walter B. Smith, announced that they would be given the 'freedom of the county' but, he continued, the 'moment they identify themselves with the Red movement they will be filed with the other exhibits we have in jail here'. On 25 March, the group was met by Smith and other Bell County officials as they crossed the Cumberland Gap. They were interrogated, roughed up, and evicted, while a crowd of 2,000 on the hillsides yelled that they should be lynched. The next day, another bus load of students attempted to sneak into Bell County through the Clear Fork Valley and over the Fonde Mountain. Trailed by over 100 cars, Smith raced to meet them, and was able to stop them at the State line. On 10 April, Lucien Koch, president of the experimental workers' institution Commonwealth College, and four of his students were beaten up and also evicted from the county as they sought to inspect the strike area, hand out food and relief, and distribute copies of the Bill of Rights. On 4 May 1932, Arthur Garfield Hayes, head of the American Civil Liberties Union (ACLU), and a group of lawyers were refused entrance into Bell County on the road from London, Kentucky when they came to test their rights of freedom of speech and assembly.[47]

But while these forms of support were coming from outside, the miners' own militance and organization in the area was rapidly deteriorating. By 28 January, Frank Borich, National General Secretary of the NMU, wrote a confidential report that 'it is obvious now that the expectations of the Party in connection with the strike were not fulfilled. We were not able to organize a solid strike in the Kentucky fields and then spread it to other southern coal fields as was expected at the time it was prepared.[48] Officially the strike went on until the end of March, but after the first few weeks there was no evidence of the continuation of militant action. Following the strike, on 1 April, the UMWA's district president reappeared, announcing, 'if the operators of Harlan and Bell will sign up with the UMW, we will take care of the Reds'.[49] By the end of the year, the NMU nationally had

[47] Compiled from *Middlesboro Daily News, Knoxville New Sentinel* and *New York Times* reports.

[48] Quoted in Draper, op. cit., p. 387.

[49] *Knoxville News Sentinel,* 2 April 1932.

folded, the Communist Party had given up the dual unionism approach and had returned to the strategy of 'boring from within'. In the Cumberland Mountains, the widespread spirit and actions of challenge from below were no longer visible. As quickly as the great rebellion of 1931–2 had sprung up, it had withered away. Why?

4.3 THE QUELLING OF REBELLION: AREA AND SCOPE

At the very least, the rebellion of 1931–2 in Campbell, Claiborne, Bell and Harlan Counties succeeded in doing one thing — it smashed the image of the 'docile digger' of Southern Appalachia that had prevailed regarding the miners during the coal camp era of the 1920s. Yet the militance dramatically faltered at a crucial moment. The spirit of the men that had surprised both the NMU and the UMWA organizers throughout 1931 did not translate itself into widespread solidarity when the strike was called for 1 January 1932. What had happened? A range of possible answers lies within the various dimensions of power.

Arena. As the rebellion got under way, the unitary nature of the power of the élite all to clearly revealed itself throughout the coal-dependent area. Issues emerged but decisions in the local government arenas were singular in their protection of certain interests over others. At least two of the judges responsible for jailing the dozens of miners and organizers themselves had direct coal interests: Judge D.C. 'Baby' Jones of Harlan County, and Judge Van Bebber of Bell County, the latter being the manager of Log Mountain Coal Company, lessee from the largest landholder in the area, the American Association.[50] The County Attorney of Bell County, Walter Smith, and the sheriffs of Harlan and Claiborne Counties, J. H. Blair and Frank Riley, seemed to be striving to outdo each other in their apprehension of the rebels. Even the Red Cross, whose local officers included coal operators, was not impartial. The *New York Times* wrote, 'Feeding a hungry miners' family, or one who is in the bad graces of operators, is considered meddling in an industrial dispute. Miners

---

[50] Vern Smith, 'From Behind Kentucky's Bars', reprinted from *The Labour Defender . . . in the National Miner's Union as Reported at the Time* (Appalachian Movement Press, Huntington, West Virgina, 1972).

considered loyal to the company will be fed by the operators.'[51]

The control inside local government was matched by the reign of terror outside the formal decision-making structures. Hired thugs, machine guns, dynamiting, beatings and killings of organizers and sympathizers, raids, evictions, burnings, harassment, and arrests seemed everyday occurrences. However, the massive repression alone does not explain the breaking of the strike. As a Scripps Howard reporter wrote at the time, 'Let no one interpret the decay of the union as a decay of the spirit of resentment and bitterness. . . Not withstanding all the arrests that have been made, and all the measures that have been taken to make Harlan County obey orders and ask no questions, its people are still armed in strict accordance with their tradition, still in a mood to settle any issue with the rifle and still irritated by the hardships and distress which not only go with widespread poverty but with arbitary rule.'[52]

Scope. If repression was not sufficient for the control of the conflict, were there other perhaps more subtle processes of power which served the same purpose? Various means of manipulating messages seemed to contribute significantly to the outcome of the strike.

The 'gatekeeping' of information in this rural region was the prerogative of the local élites. Because of their centralized position in the county seats and their interaction from that position with the outlying areas, they were often local brokers of information. And, because of their status and visibility, they were often the mediators between the local situation and the outside world. The importance to the local élites of the monopoly over communication flows may be judged by the repression used to prevent or discourage alternative interpretations of the strike. At least two outside reporters who were sympathetic to the miners were shot, while numerous others were threatened.[53] The *Knoxville News Sentinel* was banned from the courtroom for its 'yellow

---

[51] *New York Times,* 28 September 1931.

[52] Tracy, *Knoxville News Sentinel,* 6 January 1932.

[53] Boris Israel of the Federated Press, and Bruce Crawford of *Crawford's Weekly.* See reports in Dreiser, op. cit., pp. 75–82.

journalism' in reporting the trial of the forty-four Harlan miners involved in the Battle of Evarts.[54] The *Daily Worker* reporter was jailed, and the sale or distribution of certain papers and literature was banned.[55] By shaping certain information into the communication flows and shaping other information out, the gatekeeping capacity could combine with the repressive capacity to *isolate, contain* and *redirect* the conflict. It is possible to understand how this was done in the 1931 conflict by comparing the coverage of the *Middlesboro Daily News* (which was very much aligned with the local élites) to that of the less aligned press, such as the *New York Times* and the *Knoxville News Sentinel* (Table 4.1).

An attempt to isolate the conflict sought to minimize knowledge of the extent of the strike and its support, both inside and outside the coalfields. Within the area, several patterns are found in the political communication of the élite, as reflected in the *Middlesboro Daily News*. First, the information tended to isolate leaders from workers, the former being described as manipulating or misleading the miners. Reports in other newspapers and other sources have shown that it was, in fact, initial rank and file demands which precipitated the entrance of the outside leaders. Secondly, the information tended to report only isolated instances of conflict. The extent of the strike was played down. Meetings that were prevented from occurring or which, according to outside sources, did occur, were reported locally as not having occurred or as having been 'called off' for lack of support. Some rallies and skirmishes were reported; others were ignored. Thirdly, the local information minimized the extent of support for the strike from elsewhere. Perhaps the best example of this was shown at Harry Simms's murder. The Middlesboro paper wrote, 'the outside leaders hoodwinked our leaders into believing that they were part of a movement to better labor conditions'. No mention was made of the story, reported by the *New York Times,* of 2,000 mourners, marching behind Simms's body in the streets of New York in a show of solidarity with the Kentucky miners.

[54] *Knoxville News Sentinel,* 3 January 1932.
[55] Accounts in the *Labor Defender,* op. cit.

TABLE 4.1

Political Communication: The Isolation of Conflict

	Middlesboro Daily News	*New York Times (NYT)* and *Knoxville News Sentinel (KNS)*
ROLE OF LEADERS	*19 Dec. 1931.* Editorial comment titled 'Poor Dupes' says that Foster, head of the Communist Party in the U.S., is using the strike as 'an entering wedge to bring about the revolution'; the poor miners are but 'dupes and pawns in the hands of Foster and his crowd'.	*30 Dec. 1931. (KNS)* reports NMU leaders statement, 'we realize that the overwhelming masses of the miners throughout the Kentucky and Tennessee fields are for the demands set forth by the convention'.
EXTENT OF LOCAL DISCON- TENT	*2 Jan. 1932.* 'NMU strike seems to be a Flop.' *4 Jan.* 'Strike's Back Broken This Morning.' *5 Jan.* 'Strike Seen Collapsing as Third Day Dawns.' *18 Jan.* 'All Quiet as Union Meetings Do Not Materialize', after law warns against. *15 Feb.* NMU meeting in Barbourville, home of Simms, 'called off'.	*2 Jan. 1932 (KNS)* 'Strike claimed to be less than 10% effective by operators.' *4 Jan. (KNS)* 'NMU Claims 300 men at Pruden and Clear Fork Creek Coal Co.' *5 Jan. (NYT)* '5 women and 3 men arrested in raid on NMU headquarters.' *18 Jan. (KNS)* 'NMU Claims Victory; Meetings Held Despite Machine Guns.' *15 Feb. (NYT)* Armed guards and force of special police prevent striking miners from entering county where Simms was shot for NMU meeting.
EXTENT OF OUTSIDE SUPPORT	No report No report *17 Feb.* Editorial. 'The out- side leaders hoodwinked our poor people into believing that they were part of a movement to better labor conditions.' No report of New York demonstration.	*7 Jan. (NYT)* Members of 100 labour bodies pledge support to jailed miners in Harlan. *22 Jan. (KNS)* Large crowd gathers in Knoxville in support rally for NMU. *18-20 Feb. (NYT)* Simms's body lies in rest in New York while hundreds of sympathizers file by. A parade from Penn Station through the 'strike grappled' garment district to Union Square consists of fifty girls wearing khaki shirts and bandanas of of young Communist league, followed by men in miners' caps, including many Negroes, followed by over 2,000 mourners.

Middlesboro Daily News	*New York Times (NYT)* and *Knoxville News Sentinel (KNS)*
EXTENT OF RELIEF	*12 Feb.* Editorial. 'The Crusading Uplifters from New York City have come and gone . . . Coming into Southeastern Kentucky, heralded by headline blasts, flanked by grinding cameras and self-appointed press agents, prepared to lift fallen humanity out of its misery in the mountains, the Uplifters met a cold, sullen ominous hostility on the part of the Kentucky mountaineers.'	*10 Feb. (NYT)* Writers distribute food on mountain near Lafollette to hundreds of hungry families. *11 Feb. (NYT)* 'Kentucky Ejects New York Writers': 'they had brought three truck loads of food for miners but were told they were not wanted.' *21 Feb. (KNS)* Fifteen miners, members of the NMU, arrested in relief-organizing meeting in Powell's Valley.

These attempts to control perceptions about the extent of the conflict combined with the repression to suggest that the opposition had been contained. It was one thing to imply that repression by the élite was responsible for the failure of the strike; it was even more effective to give the impression that the counter-organization had failed to give adequate support. A miner said of the NMU, 'They didn't do what they said they would do . . . At Pruden, they promised they'd feed 'em, and furnish 'em all the groceries they'd need—they came out on strike—and they didn't furnish 'em nothin', so they wouldn't have nothin' to do with it.' The organizers reported that the miners were ready to strike but when the relief failed to materialize they went back to work. And the newspapers made the most out of the fact that the NMU could not provide what it had promised, without reporting the extent to which force was being used to make certain that this remained the case, e.g. such incidents as the dynamiting of soup kitchens, the blocking of relief wagons from entering the area, and raids on relief-organizing meetings. Not all the fault lay in the effective use of local power to stop relief; the NMU itself was not effectively organized at a national level. By preventing the development of the resources (food and leaders) necessary for building a counter-organization, the prevailing organization could claim that the failures of challenge lay in the false promises of the opposition.

While thus attempting to isolate and contain the conflict, the final ploy was to attempt to redirect its emphasis away from the original grievances by providing alternative information of little consequence to the issue at hand. For example, when Dreiser came to hold hearings on terrorism and conditions, he was indicted for adultery and then for criminal syndicalism. Both incidents received far more public attention than the original purpose or findings of his investigation. When the NMU strike began, a raid on the organization's headquarters disclosed communist literature, the 'subversive' contents of which hit the headlines, rather than the demands of local miners. When Frank and Taub were beaten up, they were accused of fighting each other. In every instance, the disclosure of the redirective information came at a time of potentially escalating challenge. The effect of the new information was to shift the emphasis of conflict from relatively costly issues of unemployment, unionization or civil rights to other highly emotive but less costly issues, such as moral behaviour, patriotism and religion.

Each of these devices of power relating to the control of information about the conflict provides insights into why the strike did not succeed, in addition to those found simply by looking at the unitary power in the decision-making arena, or at the use of force. The processes are examples of both the second and third dimensions of power. They are of the second dimension in that they organized certain recognized grievances into the conflict arena while excluding others as non-issues; but they are of the third dimension in that they served to control the perceptions of the extent, substance and possibilities of the success of challenge. In both dimensions, power affected the choice of participation or non-participation in the emerging struggle.

4.4 THE QUELLING OF PROTEST: IDEOLOGY AND CONSCIOUSNESS

The dimensions of power were also seen as more coherent bodies of information—ideologies—served to shape actions and perceptions in the conflict. The intervention of the ideologies of the local élites, the liberal supporters and the NMU leaders had a major impact upon the emerging consciousness of the local miners.

Since the initial period of industrialization, the interests of the local middle-class élite had continued to be vested in protecting those of the larger, absentee financial concerns which owned the region. Dreiser wrote after his visit, '. . . I found the same line-up of petty officials and business interests on the side of coal operators and as against the miners as I have discovered in almost every other labor war or controversy that I have had the opportunity to observe'. In 1931–2, this local élite was facing new social phenomena upon its previously quiescent turf—rebellion (with communist involvement) and outside attention. An ideology had to be developed for the interpretation of these phenomena: new myths and symbols had to be created. The ideology which emerged appealed to the forces of law and order, respectability, and patriotism as opposed to the forces of disorder, anti-religion, and anti-government brought in by the outsider. 'Communism', as interpreted to the population by ministers and government officials, meant belief in the principles of:

1) hatred of god, 2) destruction of property, 3) social and racial equality and class hatred, 4) revolutionary propaganda leading to the stirring up of class hatred, advocating of violence, strikes, riots, etc. . . 5) destruction of all forms of representative and democratic government and the rights of liberty guaranteed under the American Constitution—the right of free speech, free press, and the freedom of worship; 6) worldwide revolution overthrowing all capitalist government and the reestablishment of the dictatorship of the Soviet proletariat, with headquarters in Moscow and with the red flag as the only flag.[56]

It was an evil brought in by the foreign organizers ('some from Russia, some from Pittsburgh, and some from the slums of foreign populated cities')[57] and by self-interested outsiders ('Communists disguised as writers whose purpose was to obtain publicity for their doctrines and for the books they intended to write').[58] Such invasions demanded the response of militant loyalty to one's nation and one's culture. 'One drop of pure Kentucky blood is worth more and is more sacred than an entire river of Communist blood.'[59] 'Mountain men and women with their boasted independence and pure

---

[56] *Middlesboro Daily News,* summary of lecture to Kiwanis Club by local minister, 18 November 1931.

[57] *Middlesboro Daily News,* ed., reprinted in *Knoxville News Sentinel* 16 January 1932.

[58] Letter from Pineville citizens in *New York Times,* 13 February 1932.

[59] County Attorney Smith in *Knoxville New Sentinel,* 6 April 1932.

heritage' *v.* 'powers which would crush the American they have always dearly loved and which their forefathers died to establish.'[60] The local élite assumed a special responsibility for paternalistic protection of the lower-class miners ('those poor dupes and pawns') who join the strike ('the entering wedge' of the revolution) for 'they know not what they do'.[61] Themselves faced with economic uncertainties and challenges from below, the local élite found in this ideology some means for interpreting their situation.

The liberal ideology was expressed primarily by the miners' sympathizers from the metropolitan centres of Washington and New York. Attention was first attracted by Dreiser's visit, which in turn spawned numerous other demonstrations of support: The Independent Relief Committee sought to 'establish the right to distribute relief'; 175 New York educators signed a protest that 'the constituted authorities' were 'clearly taking sides'; Commonwealth College students distributed copies of the Bill of Rights, and even read them aloud while they were being beaten for so doing,[62] and the American Civil Liberties Union (ACLU) sought to establish its rights to hold a public meeting in the area. The concern for the civil rights of the mountaineer carried with it a certain unexpressed hypocrisy. 'Rights' had long been ignored in the Appalachian coal camps, but never before had their lack evoked such attention. And this new attention from the city dwellers carried with it a certain paternalism similar to that felt by the local élite towards the miner-mountaineers. The feature stories by Malcolm Ross printed in the *New York Times* reflected this attitude. He considered these people as 'tragically helpless', 'a patient people who know so little that they suppose the present hard times are temporary . . . years of poverty have sapped their initiative'. The residents of the Southern Appalachias, were 'ignorant, and usually owned a personal charm matched only by irresponsibility'.[63] Little focus was given by this view to the industrial forces which had created and allowed the conditions to continue. Nor did the liberals' attention last.

---

[60] *Middlesboro Daily News,* 19 December 1931.   [61] ibid.
[62] *New York Times,* 9 February 1932, 2 March 1932, 11 April 1932.
[63] *New York Times,* 3 April 1932.

To understand the ideology and strategy of the National Miners Union, a bit more background is needed. In 1928, under the influence of the Stalinist line, the prior Leninist policy of boring from within the trade union movement was altered. In the face of what Stalin called 'capitalist stabilization', 'dual unions' were to be formed, aimed at destroying and replacing the reformist American Federation of Labor (AFL) through a new 'revolutionary upsurge'. The Trade Union Unity League (TUUL) was set up with its affiliate unions, including the National Miners Union.[64] Meeting at their first conference in Pittsburgh in September 1928, rank and file miners from eleven states adopted a constitution whose preamble said, in part, 'Our organization declares that the interests of the employers and those of the workers have nothing in common but are diametrically opposed to one another. The history of the Coal Miners, as well as all the workers of the country is that of the incessant struggle between these two classes—the class struggle.' Declaring the need for the education of workers, the need for 'independent working-class political action' and the need for solidarity among all the workers of the various industries, the preamble concluded, 'Our organization shall ever remain class conscious . . . It shall by the use of all the power at its command, vigorously carry out its mission to secure for its members shorter hours, higher wages, and better working conditions, and proceed as an organization of the class struggle for the abolition of capitalistic exploitation.'[65]

In the midst of these ideologies, what was that of the miner-mountaineer? Perhaps some of the mood was captured by John Dos Passos as he described the hearings at Wallins Creek, which took place as miners guarded the doors from thugs:

The hollow was completely black. To get to the Glendon Baptist church, where the meeting was to be held, we had to cross a high swinging bridge above the creek bed . . . The low frame hall was packed with miners and their wives; all the faces were out of early American history. Stepping into the hall was going back a hundred years (or

[64] See discussion of this background in Draper, op. cit.; and in Bernstein, *The Lean Years* (Houghton Mifflin Co., Boston, 1960).
[65] Quoted from Watkins, op. cit., p. 231.

perhaps forward a hundred years). These were the gaunt faces, the slow elaboration of talk and courtesy, of the frontiersmen who voted for Jefferson and Jackson, and whose terms of speech were formed on the oratory of Patrick Henry. I never felt the actuality of the American revolution so intensely as sitting in that church listening to these mountaineers with their old time phrases, getting upon their feet and explaining why the time to fight for freedom had come.[66]

This was a determined expression of opposition to years of subjection. The miners wanted revenge. But as a necessary consequence of the powerlessness of the coal camp, their consciousness was that of an oppressed group first emerging from quiescence. It was a-ideological, with its demands and grievances growing in an immediate sense from felt experiences.

So, in the first instance, the miners' consciousness, as that of the local élites, had to develop a meaning for those new phenomena—such as the symbol 'communist'. Looking back, a miner's wife described:

They called 'em commúnists (as in com-mún-al-ists), which was cómmunist, but they didn't know the pronunciation of it. They called em commúnists, where it should have been cómmunists . . . I don't know what they was . . . just, kind of like the union now, they was trying to get something started, to have an organization, so that people could have something to live on, you know, wouldn't be so badly mistreated . . . They even gave 'em clothes . . . like the Church of Christ . . . like when they started the Church here. They wasn't but a very few who took up with it. Everybody was scared.

Another miner, a boy at the time, described sneaking up to the 'Russian Red truck giving out food', only to be surprised. 'I didn't see no animal or any kind of ghost, it was supposed to be scary, a Russian Red.' The meaning of the symbol was not always one of fear, as the early participation in the NMU and the testimonies taken by Dreiser show. But the symbol was usually interpreted in terms of the local culture, such as family or church. For instance, at one of the hearings, Finley Donaldson, a Holiness preacher, 'who stalked up and down the platform pounding the table with his fist like an old time hell roaring evangelist' said:

The coal operators say the Russian Red has been down in this county. A man that won't support and stand by his children is ten times worse

[66] John Dos Passos, 'The Free Speech Speakin's', in Dreiser, op. cit., pp. 295–6.

than an infidel. There is no place for a capitalist sympathizer but Hell
. . . I love the flag of United States of America but I hate the men who
handle this country; these men have taken away our privileges so that
it is impossible to live . . . I love my children ten thousand times better
than I love Hoover or the coal operators . . . The thing I say is the
National Miners' Union is ready to handle it, to give you the same
livin' conditions you had before the government put in all these laws
that were unjust.[67]

While the miners sought in their struggle to give meaning
from their experience to this thing 'communism', that their
local élite told them was so frightening, it was the ideologies
of those who sought to support the miners that was to
help to undermine the fight.

The liberal northerners sought in good faith to help the
miners. But, through their efforts, the emphasis of the conflict shifted from the miners' conditions to the outsiders'
civil rights. A careful study of the chronology of conflict
shows that the miners' own internal organization and level
of challenge diminished as the groups of investigators came
in. With the 'invasions', the local élites were able, apparently
with some success, to shift the perceptions of the conflict
from that of an emerging class struggle to a more 'national-
istic' cleavage of 'mountaineers v. outsiders'. The consequences of this shift are well evidenced in the special congressional hearing convened to investigate conditions in
Harlan and Bell Counties. Held in Washington, its major
cast of witnesses was the outside delegations and the coal
operators; its major focus was not upon the conditions of
the miners but upon the treatment received by the investigators.[68] The conflict had thus become one amongst élites
on a stage foreign to the coalfields. The play which the
miners had put on no longer had a part for them, unless it
was to transfer their anger to this new symbol—the decoy of
their struggle—the outsider, concerned, for the moment,
about the mountaineers' rights.

The other major points of faltering came in the encounter

[67] Described and quoted by Dos Passos in Dreiser, op. cit., pp. 294-6.
[68] *Conditions in Harlan and Bell Counties,* op. cit. The thirty-page summary
report devotes two pages to the testimony of the two miners who appeared, nine
pages to the testimony of a National Guardsman and local professionals, and
nineteen pages to the testimony of five delegations of outside observers.

of aspects of communist ideology with that of the miners. Its timing, too, was important. Between the December convention and the end of February, the miners discovered that the Party did not believe in God. Not only were the local élite saying so, but several of the miners' leaders, taken to northern cities for training, returned disillusioned 'enemies of the union cause'.[69] In early February, several of them swore affidavits, publicly filed in the Bell County courthouse and widely publicized in the local press, dissociating themselves from the NMU. The statement of Donaldson, the Holiness preacher who had given the speech at Wallins Creek only three months before, was an example:

The teachings of the Communist party would destroy our religious beliefs, our government and our homes. We were misled into joining such an organization, and we here and now denounce it as a movement which derives its power from Soviet Russia . . .

In the teachings they demanded their members to teach their children there is no God; no Jesus; no hereafter; no resurrection of the dead; all there is for anybody is what they get in this world . . . I saw them who were believers in the Communist party with great applause give honor to Soviet Russia by honoring and saluting the Red Flag . . . I heard several men who was active in this communist work make the remarks, 'Damn the stars and stripes of our American flag' . . .[70]

Evidently the remarks of these leaders had some effect on breaking the emerging struggle. Donaldson himself claimed, 'more than a thousand members in Bell and Harlan Counties quit after I made my statement'.[71]

The new union had assumed that the militant workers' response to conditions would carry with it an equally militant rejection of aspects of their culture. They failed to recognize the differences in meaning ascribed by their ideology and by the local culture to the same symbols—differences that at least in part grew out of the value-shaping effects of power relationships in the past. While for communists the church was the 'opium of the masses', to the miners of the coal camps, as has been seen, it had been the only form of collective organization allowed. The contrasts in interpretation were dramatically portrayed early in the strike as 750-1000

[69] Morris, op. cit., p. 118.
[70] *Middlesboro Daily News,* 13 February 1932.
[71] Morris, op. cit., p. 118.

miners marched around the Pineville courthouse expressing protest and solidarity with the nine jailed revolutionaries as they knew how—singing hymns, carrying American flags, led by a fundamentalist preacher. Meanwhile, inside the courthouse in her trial for criminal syndicalism, Doris Parks, secretary of the NMU relief organization, testified in response to interrogation by County Attorney Smith:

Smith: Do you believe in any form of religion?
Parks: I believe in the religion of the workers.
Smith: Do you believe the Bible and that Christ was crucified?
Parks: I affirmed, didn't I, that I believe in the working class and their right to organize and to teach them they can be led out of this oppression by the Communist party.[72]

In this context, the denunciation of religion by Parks did not imply liberation to the miners but a denunciation of the religious forms through which they expressed solidarity and collective action.

Those who sought to alter the oppression of the miner—the northern liberal and the Marxist radical—failed partly because they did not understand fully the power situation they sought to change. The northern liberal sought to allow freedom of expression for the miners by challenging the barriers to the exercise of his civil rights; yet the consequence was the transformation of the substance and arenas of the issues away from those originally expressed and felt by the miners. The radical sought to develop a revolutionary class consciousness, but he misunderstood the prior role of power in shaping the consciousness which he encountered. It was the local mountain élite, who knew best the uses of power for control within their culture, who effectively capitalized on the mistakes of the others. The toll can be measured by the effects upon the miners, who faced the loss of control and ultimate failure of the rebellion, with a consequent increase of a sense of powerlessness. For them newly-shaped symbols—'communist', 'outsiders', 'dual unions'—had been added as resources to the prevailing mobilization of bias, to be used to re-instil labour acquiescence again in the future.

---

[72] *Middlesboro Daily News*, 17 February 1932.

4.5 PROTEST AND POWER WITHIN THE UNION

The quiescence of the miners after the failure of the 1931 rebellion was only short-lived. In 1933, their power situation again changed, this time through federal intervention. Labour was given certain rights to organize by the Norris LaGuardia Act and the National Industrial Recovery Act. New organization under the United Mine Workers occurred rapidly and with little conflict; yet its style was very different from that of the rebellion of the year before, and its effects upon the patterns of powerlessness of the miners remain problematic.

Section 7(a) of the National Industrial Recovery Act sent to Congress on 17 May 1933 by the newly-elected Franklin Roosevelt was heralded as the 'charter of liberty', the 'Magna Charta' of organized labour. In District 19 of the UMWA, William Turnblazer, district president, announced 'The President's Industrial Recovery Bill . . . is the "Declaration of Independence" of the coal miners and their families.'[73] As the Bill was passed in Congress, Lewis sent representatives throughout the coalfields. 'The President wants you to join the United Mine Workers', they proclaimed, always remaining vague as to whether the 'President' to whom they referred was Lewis or Roosevelt.

Men joined by the hundreds. Within two months the mines of the Clear Fork Valley were 100 per cent organized, as were those throughout the area. The *Middlesboro Daily News* described one of the organizing meetings: 'From before daylight until 1.30 Saturday afternoon, when the meeting was called, miners and wives and children, poured into the city . . . They came on foot, on mules, on trucks . . . 4,000 miners pledged all to the UMWA at the courthouse . . . The coal operators are standing by in silence.'[74] By June 1933 Turnblazer estimated he had signed up 13,000 new members in the district. Nationally, membership in the Union jumped from between 100,000 and 150,000 in 1932 to 541,000 by 1935.[75]

Where there was resistance, either on the part of the

[73] Copy of the leaflet, *UMWA Files.*
[74] *Middlesboro Daily News,* 11 April 1933.
[75] Walter Galenson, *The CIO Challenge to the AFL* Harvard University Press, Cambridge, Mass., 1960), p. 193–4.

operators or the men themselves, the miners responded with
renewed collective action. In the Clear Fork Valley sprang up
the legendary 'Jones boys'—a band of roving pickets who
assumed the name of the roving Wobbly organizer, Mother
(Ma) Jones. A miner described in oral history how the name
developed:

The mine superintendent came out and asked the boy his name. He
said, "My name's Jones"—cause he wasn't going to tell the right name.
He asked the next one; he said, "My name's Jones," too. . . . And they
all took it up. Then they connected it with Ma Jones, they called her,
she was out of West Virginia. She'd take the boys out on the picket
line with rifles . . . They first called 'em the wreckin' crew, until that
day . . . And, then, from that day, everywhere they'd go and they'd
ask 'em their name—"Jones," they'd say.

Where 'scabs' were found, they were marched with bells
tolling around their necks to the Clear Fork Creek, where
they were 'baptized' in the name of 'John L.' as other miners
on the bank strummed their guitars and sang the hymn
'Shall We Gather At The River'.

By the autumn of 1933, the first contract had been
negotiated with the Appalachian Joint Conference—a collective bargaining mechanism representing over 70 per cent of
the bituminous coal tonnage, including eastern Kentucky and
north-eastern Tennessee. As the specifics of the agreement
were about to be negotiated for each district, Turnblazer
wrote to his men, 'I am confident that our people are about
to enjoy the New Day and the New Deal which means so
much for the coal miner, his wife, and children.'[76]

But the miners of District 19 had learned an important
lesson from the earlier rebellion: if this was to be *their* union,
they wanted rank and file control. Since 1922, District 19,
like many other districts in the UMWA, had been under the
direct control of Lewis. Turnblazer, a loyal Lewis supporter
from outside the area, had been installed as district president
without the approval of the men. In the autumn of 1933,
this system of unilateral power was challenged. Upset with
the terms of the first Southern Appalachian contract negotiated for them by Turnblazer in Knoxville, the miners
charged that he had again 'sold out', i.e. that Turnblazer
had failed to gain the maximum benefits attainable. Turnblazer

[76] *UMWA Files,* August 1933.

called a meeting to explain his actions for 29 October 1933. Some 2,000 miners came. But apparently disturbed by the show of opposition, Turnblazer himself failed to appear.

In an orderly but angry fashion, the miners took business into their own hands. They voted for the dismissal of Turnblazer, and they elected a temporary committee of four men to see to the affairs of the district. They dispatched a delagation to Washington to meet with Lewis, and to urge him to appoint either John White, former president of the UMWA, as district chief or to allow elections to be held. They returned to their newly-formed local branches to ask the other miners to endorse their autonomous actions. A spontaneous parliament of 2,000 miners at Jellico, Tennessee had taken over their own affairs.

Hundreds of letters and telegrams from the locals poured into Lewis's office endorsing the assembly's actions and protesting Turnblazer's leadership. Often hastily phrased and poorly scrawled, they came from places like Eagen, Anthras, Westbourne, Pruden, Clairfield, Petros, Lafollette, Fork Ridge, Morley, Packard, Gatliff, Chevrolet, Wallins Creek, Middlesboro. A miner in the American Association camp of Fonde wrote, 'Dear Sir and Brother: . . . The men want to be loyal, make most any sacrifice to hold and have their union . . . but soldiers doesn't follow a captain in whom they mistrust.'[77] Another affirmed, 'John L. we have faith in you . . . and that you will listen to the voice of your members . . . The voice of the men is they are through with Bill Turnblazer for ever.'[78]

Lewis was placed in a difficult position. Either he sided with the leadership of his provisional government or he listened to the men in a key newly-organized district. His quick response demonstrated his absolute authority over the union and his contempt for dissent within it. Lewis firmly backed Turnblazer and employed two power mechanisms to suppress the conflict.

The first was—like threat of eviction from jobs or home by the Company—the threat of eviction from the union. Lewis wrote to each of the leaders of the Jellico movement, 'if you

[77] ibid., miner in Fonde, 13 November 1933.
[78] ibid., from chairman of Coal Creek local, November 1933.

are a loyal member and expect to be the beneficiaries of the United Mine Workers in the future, please take advantage of this official warning and immediately desist' in carrying on a 'dual organization'.[79] Similarly, each local received a circular from Turnblazer saying any members participating in the meeting would 'jeopardize their membership in our Organization'.[80]

The second mechanism was to employ the symbols of the past rebellion to isolate the leadership and redirect the conflict. 'Beware of False Prophets: In their Selfish Desire to Rule They Would Destroy', began one circular from Turnblazer to the men.[81] Each of the leaders was accused: one for being involved in a 'DUAL UNION', another for having been a delegate to the first convention of the 'NATIONAL MINERS UNION', a third for being one of the 'COMMUNIST BUNCH'.[82] These 'Apostles . . . will stop at nothing to poison the minds of our people',[83] Turnblazer wrote, echoing Lewis's warning: 'If these men were paid by hostile coal companies they could not serve them better than by creating distrust and confusion in the ranks of the membership.'[84] The chairman of the Jellico Assembly responded to Lewis, 'If you were a man that had a single spark left in your breast, for the betterment and uplift of the men whose welfare you should hold dear and guard with scrupulous care, you would give heed to the voice of 30,000 miners.'[85]

Lewis was not one to listen. He demanded loyalty or exit. And to the miners who had desperately fought against the coal companies in 1931 and before to get any union at all, exit was not really an option. Letters of apology began pouring into the Washington office. 'It is far from us ever to create trouble within the organization', wrote one eastern Kentucky local.[86] 'President Turnblazer is Honest, Able and Competent', wrote others.[87]

[79] ibid., 4 November 1933.
[80] ibid., circular from Turnblazer titled 'Beware of False Prophets', 8 November 1933.
[81] ibid.   [82] ibid., correspondence from Turnblazer to Lewis, 11 November 1933.
[83] ibid., Turnblazer circular, 8 November 1933.
[84] ibid., Lewis to local miners in reply to their letters.
[85] ibid., letter from chairman of the meeting to Lewis, 18 November 1933.
[86] ibid., letter from Gatliff local, 17 November 1933.
[87] ibid., from Coal Creek local, 23 January 1934.

By the next convention of the district, in May 1943, the initial demands for autonomy had been converted into unquestioning loyalty in the leader, John L. The convention unanimously passed a resolution of praise strikingly similar to that given to the Company and the city in the 1890s (see Chapter 3). It exalted him 'as the greatest Labor Leader of all times . . . blessed by a higher and keener perception of the possibilities and needs of the coal miner and the coal industry than the ordinary man . . .; he has shown the way with the result that the vision and the dreams of the Old War Horses and Pioneers of the Coal Miners Union have come true'.[88]

The minutes of the International Executive Board of the UMWA record little about this movement among the miners of the Cumberlands to oust the Lewis-appointed provisional government in their district. Through masterful uses of power, Lewis was able to keep the conflict out of the formal decision-making arenas and to give the appearance of consent to his authority.

For the next thirty years, the pattern of pragmatic gains for the miners offset by their dependency on the autocratic power of Lewis continued. As the men gained job security, better wages, a pension plan, safer conditions, a hospitalization scheme and more, their unquestioning loyalty increased. Today, in many of the older miners' homes are found side by side on the wall the pictures of John Kennedy, John L. Lewis and Jesus Christ.

The full effects of the power of John L. began to be revealed only after the man had gone. Turnblazer continued for twenty years to preside over the affairs of District 19. He was replaced after a brief interim by his son, Wm. Turnblazer, Jr., who remained in authority until 1972—when he was convicted for conspiracy to murder Jock Yablonski, the man who had sought, as had the miners in 1933, to gain democracy within the union. To some extent, as will be seen in Chapter 7, the Yablonski murder and the turmoil surrounding it may be seen as the hidden costs of the relentlessly shaping power of 'John L.', the man still considered by many 'the salvation of the hollows'.

[88] ibid., copy of resolution, May 1934.

PART III

THE MAINTENANCE OF POWER RELATIONSHIPS

5
INEQUALITY AND CULTURE IN THE CONTEMPORARY VALLEY— AN INTERLUDE

The impact of industrial power in the late nineteenth century and the conflicts of the coal camp era in later years were forces formative to the coal valleys of the Central Appalachias. Between the 1930s and the 1950s, the patterns of dominance continued very much as they had then been established. There were changes, of course: fluctuating demands for coal, the impact of the Second World War, and the further development of unionism under the leadership of John L. Lewis. Yet, in and around the Middlesboro area there was little alteration in the fundamental relationships of power and inequality.

As the contemporary era is approached in this study, attention will be focused upon a rural valley lying westwardly across the Fonde mountain from the now established trading centre of Middlesboro.[1] From within that valley, the Clear Fork Valley, important and illustrative questions can be posed about the maintenance of quiescence and the emergence of challenge in more recent years.

Contemporary Inequalities. For a few years following the Second World War, the coal valleys of Central Appalachia enjoyed a prosperity that was to contrast sharply with the depression years to follow. In 1950, in the small Claiborne County portion of the Clear Fork Valley, there were ten underground mines, producing almost a million tons of coal, employing some 1,400 men, with each mine employing over fifty men, (see Table 5.1). In the mining communities around Clairfield, the major community of the Valley, there were some 10,000 residents, with approximately 30,000 in surrounding coal camps. There was 'a small business section, a theatre, a store, and a local doctor'.[2] For the people of

[1] The town still has about 20,000 people, roughly the same as in 1894.

[2] Paul Campbell, Marcia Donald, Theodore Webb, 'A Descriptive Study of Health and Related Socio-Economic Conditions' (unpublished study for University of Tennessee at Knoxville, 1970).

the densely-populated and booming coal towns, times were relatively good.

TABLE 5.1

COAL PRODUCTION, MINES AND MINERS IN THE CLEAR FORK VALLEY
1945-1972[a]

Year	Production (tons)	No. of men employed	No. of mines	Av. no. per mine	% of men in mines employing more than 20 men	% of tons from underground mines
1945	1,731,986	na	na	na	na	na
1950	716,986	1,388	10	139	99.9	100
1952	828,249	1,230	12	102	99.9	100
1955	574,960	410	39	11	61	nd
1957	626,563	230	49	6	35	65
1960	177,678	144	20	7	58	73
1962	579,891	222	35	6	49	31
1965	383,344	173	30	6	31	70
1967	672,395	247	18	14	63	50
1970[b]	1,843,000	503	15	34	83	83
1972	2,116,822	553	14	40	80	73

[a]Data compiled from *State of Tennessee, Department of Labor Annual Reports,* 1945-72.
[b]The large Consolidation Coal Mine began to operate.

In a few brief years the scene changed dramatically. Here, as throughout the Central Appalachias, the mines began to close. By 1957 there were only 230 mining jobs in the county, and by 1960 only 144: 90 per cent fewer than there had been a decade before. Communities were shut down as people were forced for work to the cities of the North, part of a flow of some one million migrants away from the Central Appalachian region during the decade.

For those who remained, the type of mining changed from the medium-sized, underground mines of previous days. Small truck or 'dog hole' mines appeared as men tried to carve a living from the hillsides by the crudest of methods. Then, with the new technology, strip (open cast) mining began to blast and bulldoze away the mountainsides to get at the coal beneath—a process requiring machines, not men. By 1969, Clairfield 'had only 2,000 people, and the population in the Clear Fork Valley had dwindled from forty thousand to twelve thousand. Clairfield now had no theatre, no doctor, no employment and about 95 per cent of the families were living below the poverty line.'[3]

During the 1960s, the poverty of the Central Appalachias came for a moment into the forefront of national attention. Following his 1960 visit to West Virginia, Kennedy appointed a presidential task force to study the matter. Its recommendations led to the establishment of a multi-billion dollar Appalachian Regional Commission. A War on Poverty, with its special branch of Appalachian Volunteers, was announced in 1964. In 1967 a National Advisory Committee on Rural Poverty headed by Governor Breathitt of Kentucky included a section on Appalachia in its report *The People Left Behind*. 'For all practical purposes', it said, 'most of the 14 million poor in our poverty areas are outside our market economy . . . They are on the outside looking in, and they need our help.'[4]

'Help' adopted the strategy of attempting to integrate the poverty areas into the national economy, i.e. trying to find ways for the rural poor to 'catch up' with the metropolitan areas. In the view of at least one influential study, the outmigration of the previous decade was taken to reflect amongst the Appalachian people 'an increased awareness of the opportunities and benefits offered by urban-industrial society'.[5] Government policy focused not upon rural reform but upon building highways to connect rural regions with urban centres and on establishing 'growth centres' in which to encourage industrial development. By the early 1970s the Appalachian Regional Commission could announce that for the region as a whole economic conditions were 'improving' and that the migration flow had been reversed.

But in many rural hollows within the region, the conditions of under-development persisted. While Claiborne County as a whole made economic gains during the decade between 1960 and 1970, in the Clear Fork Valley outmigration continued at a 34·5 per cent rate; 52 per cent of the popu-

[3] ibid.
[4] National Advisory Commission on Rural Poverty, *The People Left Behind* (Government Printing Office, Washington, 1967); see, too, review by Dorner, 'Fourteen Million Rural Poor', *The Yale Review*, 68 (1969), 282–92.
[5] Brown and Hillery, 'The Great Migration, 1940–1960', op. cit., p. 61.

lation who stayed remained below the poverty line; 15 per cent were unemployed; 52 per cent were underemployed. The homes remained old-fashioned: 34 per cent were without piped water and 60 per cent without flush toilets. Other than the coal mines, there were no industries.

The development agencies sought to explain the persistent under-development of the Valley in terms of its isolation. In that area, they said, a 'poor transportation network and small population continue to handicap . . . improvement in economic condition'.[6] But their analysis neglected some crucial factors. Coal production in the Valley had once again begun to increase. By 1970 more tons of coal were being mined than ever before—but with only one-third of the miners that had been employed to produce a similar tonnage in 1950. More wealth was being produced per head from within the Valley than in all the non-coal sectors of the economy in the rest of the county—but it scarcely benefited the Valley. While in the rest of the county many of the small businesses and 89 per cent of the land were locally owned and widely distributed, in the Valley roughly 85 per cent of the land and most of the coal wealth continued to be owned by the single absentee owner.

Moreover, in an important sense, the coal valley of today is not isolated. It is an important part of the national and international economy. The owner of the land and the coal, the American Association, Ltd., of London, is connected to one of Britain's largest and most complex multinational financial empires. Most of the coal is produced from mines run by the Consolidation Coal Company, the wholly-owned subsidiary of Continental Oil Company, one of the world's largest energy conglomerates. Three or four times a week, in train loads of over 100 cars each, the coal is transported from the Valley on the lines of the Southern Railway Company, owners of one of the largest transportation networks of the region, to be burned in the furnaces of the Georgia Power Company, a wholly-controlled subsidiary of the Southern Railway Company, owner of utilities in Florida,

[6] *Claiborne County Census Summary,* (East Tennessee Development District, Knoxville, Tennessee, 1973), p. II, p. 6.

Mississippi, and Alabama as well. The electricity that is produced is used primarily by the industries and consumers of the urban, industrial centres of the South, from which the communities of the Valley are said to be apart.

So the Appalachian coal valley of today is not poor; yet its people remain so. They are not 'on the outside looking in', but very much on the inside, at the bottom, looking up at the nation's inequalities.

Contemporary Culture. Though economically linked to the mainstream, the communities of the Central Appalachian region maintain the distinctive culture of miner-mountaineers. In its traditional aspects, this culture places a value upon rural lifestyle, relative isolation, and a harmony with nature not found in urban areas.[7] There is a strong importance attached to personal relations and personal interaction, and to the social organizations of kin, neighbour and church.

Yet, intermingled with the traditional rural values are others common to industrial labour forces, that grow out of the work experience of the mines and the community organization of the densely-populated coal camps.[8] The collective identity of 'mountain people' or (more derogatorily) 'hillbillies' is flavoured with that of 'little people' or 'working folks' who must 'stick together' against the 'bosses' and the 'rich folks'. A common language and pride in work are important. The single industry of mining has added an integrative bond to the existing bonds of the traditional culture. One sees within the community, both within individuals and within groups, differing combinations of these values lying along the scale from the individual mountaineer to the solidarity-inclined miner.

At the same time the subculture of the miner-mountaineer

[7] For studies which emphasize the traditional 'folk' aspects of the Appalachian culture, see particularly Weller, *Yesterday's People,* op. cit.; John Fetterman, *Stinking Creek* (E.P. Dutton and Co., New York, 1967) and Ford, 'The Passing of Provincialism', op. cit., pp. 9–34.

[8] For description of the impact of the mining industry upon mountaineers' culture, see for instance, Caudill, *Night Comes to the Cumberlands,* op. cit.; Helen M. Lewis and Edward E. Knipe, 'The Impact of Coal Mining on the Traditional Mountain Sub-Culture: A Case of Peasantry Gained and Peasantry Lost', in Kenneth Morland, ed., *The Not So Solid South* (University of Georgia Press, Athens, 1971).

is being affected by the impact of the more dominant culture of American society. In this sense, mountain communities are often seen as communities in transition between folk society and 'mainstream' or 'mass' society.[9] Although the literature on the subject differs over its causes and virtues, assimilation is occurring,[10] giving rise to further differentiations within the community according to the place of individuals or groups along an exogenous-endogenous value scale.

This scale is linked to the economic stratification of the community. At the top of the ladder are the external élites of the Valley—the owners and managers of the absentee institutions that impact upon it. They are the most likely to be part of the metropolis and to adhere to its values. Within the region, often in the trading centres close to the Valley, occasionally within the Valley itself, is another élite—the owners of the small mines, the businessmen, and the professional people. Though they may appear an upper class within the local situation, they are viewed more appropriately in relationship to the external élite to whose interests theirs are tied and to whose values and lifestyles they are likely to hold some allegiance. In certain circumstances the local élite may emphasize their identity with the local culture; at other times, they are likely to express contempt for those beneath them who retain more traditional ways.

Beneath the local élite are the active miners, the manufacturing workers, and the small farmers of the Valley. Within the local situation, when their income is compared with that of the local élite and the 'underclass' beneath, they appear a middle class; yet, in the broader social spectrum, they are members of a working class. They retain a spoken pride about the culture of the miner-mountaineer; yet they have also adopted some of the values of the outside world, such as the importance of education for their children or an appreciation of consumer goods.

[9] For instance, Berton H. Kaplan, *Blue Ridge: An Appalachian Community in Transition* (West Virginia University Bulletin, Morgantown, 1971); and John B. Stephenson, *Shiloh: Case Study of a Mountain Community* (University Press of Kentucky, Lexington, 1968).

[10] That is, some studies see it as a relatively conflict-free process of integration of the subculture into the mass culture; others, as penetration by the dominant culture of the traditional society.

Beneath this stratum is perhaps the largest group in the Valley. They represent America's 'underclass' of poor, under-employed or unemployed. They or their families are likely to have been part of the culture of the miner-mountaineers for decades. They are likely to live the furthest off the main road in the Valley, 'up the hollers', along the creeks.[11] They probably have been to the cities at some point, to work or to visit members of the family who work there. Yet they return again and again to the same area. They adhere most strongly to the traditional culture, but at the same time, they are the most likely to accept the degradation or inadequacy ascribed to that culture by mass society or the local élite.

Thus the cultural identity of the people of Clear Fork is a mixed one, understood as a combination of the values of rural mountaineers and industrial miners, or in relationship to the more dominant culture which surrounds and affects it. At different times, among differing groups or within the same group, various combinations of the values may appear.

There is a tendency in Appalachian studies to consider either the culture or the political economy of the region, placing the reasons for the perpetuations of poverty within one explanatory framework or the other.[12] Yet, the stratification patterns suggest that the economic and cultural variables may be interrelated empirically. To the extent that they are, the cultural values may contribute to the field of power resources which serve to maintain the inequalities. In general, the means by which certain values can be evoked over others at certain times for the protection of certain interests, and, in particular, the extent to which the values of the dominant interests impact upon the political actions and conceptions of the non-élites will continue to be a focus of this study.

Everyday Inequalities. In the life of a community whose culture is tied to the land and work upon or within the land,

[11] Fetterman, op. cit., for instance, points out that status can often be judged by the geographical relationship of a family to the creek. Those along the main branch (where the land was flatter and more farmable) were often the better-off; those along the side branches were of lower status.

[12] Lewis and Knipe, for instance, describe the 'culture of poverty' and the 'exploitation' schools of thought on Appalachian under-development. See 'The Colonialism Model: the Appalachian Case', op. cit.

the ownership or use of that land might be expected to be
the most contentious of inequalities. During the coal camp
era, the company that owned most of the land in the Valley,
the American Association, Ltd., had remained in the background of conflict. Other companies who leased the coal,
ran the mines, and built the communities had been more
visible antagonists. With the closing of the mines in the
1950s, the situation altered. The American Association
took possession of the homes. Other companies still operated
the mines, but they were smaller and less powerful. The
American Association, Ltd. emerged even more clearly as the
coal and land lord of the Valley.

Although the community remained poor, the profits of the
Company, derived primarily from rents and royalties, steadily
increased. Most of the profits went to the shareholders, the
majority of whom were in Britain. The primary shareholder
and Chairman of the Board of the Company was Sir Denys
Colquhoun Flowerdew Lowson, a former Lord Mayor of
London, who also presided over some ninety other companies
around the world. The value of the Company, including the
65,000 acres of land and coal, represented to Lowson in
1972 an estimated one-half of one per cent of the total
value of his £200 million empire. The profits that did not go
to the shareholders were invested, not within the Valley, but
across the mountain, for the development of a Holiday Inn
for tourists at the Cumberland Gap, and a marina and golf
course 'to attract the wealthier citizens of Pineville and
Middlesboro'.[13]

It need not be expected that these inequalities—the extraction of wealth, and the re-allocation of it for the pleasures
of the upper and middle classes in the area—would bring
protest in the contemporary valley. The pattern is but a
continuation of that developed in the 1890s and maintained
since. If any inequalities have come to be routinely accepted
they are these. But with the mechanization of the mines and
the development of strip mining, the coal communities
themselves were under threat: 'the people would be better
off, we would be better off, if they would be off our land',
the local Middlesboro manager, Mr. Alvaredo E. Funk,

[13] American Association *Annual Report,* 1970, p. 8.

went on record as saying.[14]

The policy of depopulation was most visibly symbolized as the coal camp houses were torn down and not replaced. More than two-thirds of the company houses were torn down between 1962 and 1972, and the Company has made it clear that more will go. The houses that remain are in extremely poor condition. Leases, if granted at all, are for thirty-day periods. Rent is often collected by an agent with an armed guard. If the people don't like it, they can leave. A memorandum posted on the doors of the stores or the post office, or at the mines, reads, 'No specified reason is needed if the owner desires to have the house vacant . . . No one is obligated to remain in a house. If he is unhappy about his surroundings he is free to move immediately.'[15]

Those who stay, either upon company property or upon other land around it, have to contend not only with dilapidated housing but with another consequence of the change in company policy—strip mining. Strip mining in the area literally means blasting away the sides of a mountain, bulldozing the debris over the edge, and shovelling out the coal. The process is fast, profitable to the operators, and highly destructive. Over 600,000 acres have already been despoiled in this fashion in Central Appalachia.[16]

In Tennessee, the Company has had on its land more strip-mining operations than any other landowner in the State. In 1972, over 187·9 linear miles of open cuts had been made in layers along the steep mountainsides of the Valley.[17] Piles of refuse hover above clusters of homes in several of the hollows. They threaten to break loose, reminding people of the slag heap that collapsed in 1955, destroying overnight with a flood of water an entire coal camp, killing two children. In other places, mixture of rocks and mud covers the roads after rain, making them temporily impassable. The hillsides are defoliated, but of more consequence to the people is the

---

[14] *Nashville Tennessean,* 18 September 1971.

[15] Memorandum 'To All Concerned' from A. E. Funk, General Manager of American Association, 10 April 1970.

[16] Of several powerful descriptions of the effects of these unchecked mining practices see, in particular, Harry Caudill, *My Land is Dying* (E. P. Dutton and Co., New York, 1971).

[17] Figures from Tennessee Department of Geology, 1972.

erosion that has filled the creeks below with silt, mineral particles, and acid. Once deep and clear, the Clear Fork Creek 'can no longer be used for those purposes for which it was once used, such as drinking water, swimming, fishing, baptizing, washing clothes, and other purposes for which mountain people use creeks . . .'.[18] The flooding which now occurs four or five times a year deposits upon the land a thick muck-like substance, killing the garden crops of sweet potatoes, cucumbers, corn, and beans.

Strip mining in the Central Appalachian Valley is more than an act of environmental demise. The loss of jobs and the destruction of the land mean the demise of a culture, a way of life. 'Everytime they stick a dozer blade into the mountain its kind of like stickin' a knife into a mountain person's heart', describes one woman, '25 or 30 years more, no end to it that I can see', says Funk. 'I'm quite certain that whole mountains will be moved . . . will simply be taken into the Valley and the coal stripped and it'll end up a level piece of land.'[19]

Perhaps the people could move elsewhere, as the Company suggests; but in the Valley, as throughout the rural areas of Central Appalachia, there are few 'elsewheres' that are suitable. As in the 1930s, corporate ownership of massive blocks of land—more valuable to its owners for the coal beneath than for other uses—still prevents the development of alternative housing or jobs. Even here, the Company has refused to free any of its land for factories, housing, or even a health clinic. Meanwhile government programmes continue to avoid the controversial question of land ownership.

If outmigration in the 1960s was the result, it was more a matter of 'push' than 'pull' to the benefits of the 'urban industrial society'. A government survey in the area in and around the Valley in 1969 found that: 'the local conditions of rural areas, with all their "undesirable characteristics" are not forces powerful enough by themselves to cause people in

[18] *Lewis Lowe, et. al.* v. *American Association, et. al.,* complaint filed in Chancery Court for Claiborne County, Tennessee, 1973.

[19] Transcript of interview with Granada TV for 'World in Action', *The Stripping of Appalachia* (programme transmitted 6 November 1972).

rural, isolated places to leave their communities'.[20] Migration to an urban centre may mean a slightly higher income, if a job can be found, but it by no means guarantees an escape from relative deprivation—as the 'Appalachian ghettos' of places like Cincinnatti, Chicago and Detroit indicate.[21] And, other studies show, a slightly higher income is not the first preference of these miner-mountaineers.[22] In the contemporary coal valley, as in the 1930s, the people would rather stay where they are.

In staying, they may expect little relief from the Company, which continues from London to mine and mind the land and the coal. In 1974 manager Funk told a BBC reporter:

BBC: Don't you have sort of a moral responsibility to maintain the people who wish to stay in that area, and who have been working their fingers off to keep them in a reasonable condition of living?

Funk: No, sir, these people don't work for us and never have worked for us—they're just people.

BBC: But they're living on your land aren't they?

Funk: We don't have any responsibility for them . . .

BBC: You mean they get in the way of strip-mining operations?

Funk: Well, I don't say they get in the way, but they just don't add anything to the assets of the company.[23]

In the contemporary coal valley there is a conflict between the interests of the community and those of the Company. In a larger sense, the conflict represents the tension between the economic and energy demands of the industrial society and the development needs of the rural hinterland within it. What is the response of the people of Clear Fork to the inequalities they now experience? Does a mobilization of bias still serve to legitimate and protect certain interests? If

[20] Samir N. Maamary, 'Attitudes Toward Migration Among Rural Heads of Household in Campbell County Tennessee', Appendix B, report of Campbell County Demonstration Project, East Tennessee Development District (September 1969), p. 8.

[21] A summary of the literature may be found in Gary L. Fowler, 'Up Here and Down Home: Appalachians in Cities', Working Paper No. 1 of Urban Appalachian Council (mimeo, September 1974). For a specific case study, see Todd Gitlin and Nanci Hollander, *Uptown: Poor Whites in Chicago* (Harper and Row, Evanston, 1970).

[22] See Larry C. Morgan and Brady J. Deaton, 'Psychic Costs and Factor Price Equalization' (mimeo of paper presented to Southern Agricultural Economic Association, 1974).

[23] Transcript of interview with BBC's 'News Extra', transmitted 14 May 1974.

so, how has it been re-shaped or strengthened over time? How in the modern situation do power and powerlessness affect the actions and conceptions of the people in the Valley?

In considering these questions, it should not be necessary to show how basic patterns of quiescence or rebellion are created, for that has been demonstrated in previous chapters. Rather, the focus must be upon how the historically-shaped patterns are altered or maintained. The following chapters will examine several potential modes of action upon inequalities in the community. As it happens empirically, the first two chapters, dealing with local government and union participation, involve the study of power as it serves to maintain quiescence. Then Chapters 8 and 9—involving the community organization, the media, and the protest group—provide a study of how challenge to the Company began to emerge, and against what obstacles.

6

VOTING AND VULNERABILITY: ISSUES AND NON-ISSUES IN LOCAL POLITICS

A pluralist or one-dimensional approach to community power might suggest a focal point of analysis to be the formal arenas of local government. In a federalist democracy, it is there that citizens should go to air their grievances on local matters; and it is there that power and powerlessness can be discovered through an examination of 'who participates, who gains and who loses, and who prevails in decision-making' about key issues.[1]

But in the rural county seat of Claiborne County, across the mountain from the Clear Fork Valley, none of the matters of potential community conflict identified in the previous chapter appear to have been considered as issues in the affairs of local government. Study of the minutes of the various governing bodies, interviews with local officials, and observation of government meetings show the key issues of the county to be such things as a low tax rate, distribution of beer licences, and the renovation of the courthouse, not the poverty, inequality, or demise of the Clear Fork Valley. The chief executive officer of the county, the county judge, insists that there are no particular problems 'out in the county', and that what problems there are receive adequate attention.[2]

The researcher could have either of two responses to the discovery of the 'non-issueness' of the Valley's problems in the county courthouse. The one that would be most likely with the decision-making methodology would be to conclude that if the problems have not appeared for observation in the deliberations of government then perhaps they are, in fact, non-problems or at least problems whose significance

[1] Polsby, *Community Power and Political Theory,* op. cit., pp. 4-5, (refer also to prior discussion, Chapter 1).
[2] Review of local government documents, 1960–70; interviews with local county officials.

cannot be assessed in a study of power.[3] The other approach would step outside formal decision-making arenas to ask whether an intervention of power, in its second and third dimensions, might lie, between the potential issues and governmental consideration of them. Using the latter approach, if no power barriers are identified then the conclusions of the former would have to be accepted. On the other hand, if intervening power processes are identified, then a more complete understanding of community conflict will have been acquired than could have been gained with the former methodology.

In this chapter, I will take the latter approach, beginning first with a further look at one example of an important non-issue: taxation of corporate coal wealth. I will then ask, what keeps this issue from arising in the arenas of local politics?

6.1 A NON-ISSUE AT THE COURTHOUSE: NON-TAXATION OF CORPORATE COAL WEALTH

For local governments the taxation of property is the primary means of financing such things as schools, roads, and local services. In rural counties like Claiborne County, Tennessee, establishing the rate for property taxation and budgeting the revenues generated are the primary responsibilities of the major decision-making body of the local government, the 'county court'.

But Claiborne County, like other poor counties of Central Appalachia, does not have much tax revenue to allocate for its pressing needs. The per capita local government expenditure of $155 is less than one-half the average amount spent per capita by other local governments in the nation. Approximately one-third of Claiborne's revenue is generated from local sources, while the average county can generate two-thirds of its budget from local sources. And, while 43 per cent of the budget of the average county in America is generated from the property tax, Claiborne County raises only 26 per cent by this means. For most of the rest of even

---

[3] See, for instance, Polsby, op. cit., p. 96; Wolfinger, 'Nondecisions and the Study of Local Politics', op. cit., pp. 1063-80.

its limited funds, it must depend upon state and federal aid.[4]

The irony of the apparent poverty of the Claiborne County local government is that the major property resource of the county—coal—goes relatively untaxed. And the major owner of the coal, the Company, whose 44,000 acres of coal-rich land represent some 90 per cent of the county's coal resources and 17 per cent of the county's property surface, provided in 1970 only 2·38 per cent of the county's property taxes. From one of its mines, the one leased to Continental Oil's subsidiary, the Company averaged in 1971 $4,500 a week in royalties; yet the land upon which this and other mines are located was appraised for taxation at only $25-30 an acre, a fraction of the $130-275 per acre value applied to the tillable land belonging to local farmers.[5] According to a 1971 study, this pattern in Claiborne County of non-taxation of corporate coal wealth was found in other counties in Tennessee as well. The value of coal was simply not considered in the local property tax base, despite state laws to the contrary.[6]

In spite of the apparent inequalities and the legal authority potentially available for their remedy, the non-taxation of Claiborne County's mineral wealth in 1971 had not been an issue in the Claiborne County courthouse. Not since 1940 had the question been considered by the county court. For most of the period since 1940, the tax assessor had been re-elected every four years, had carried out his tasks routinely, and had seen no problem in the situation. The county judge saw no reason for concern, though he added, 'I just can't explain to you how Al Funk and his boys—and tell Al I'm a good friend of his when you see him, won't you—get away with paying so little if that's what they do.'[7] The representative

[4] Census of Governments, 1967, as published in Appalachian Data Book (Appalachian Regional Commission, Washington, 1970); Claiborne County Data from county financial statements, 1970.

[5] Based on study of property tax records in Claiborne County for 1971. See John Gaventa, Ellen Ormond, Bob Thompson, 'Coal, Taxation and Tennessee Royalists' (xerox for Vanderbilt University Student Health Coalition, August 1971).

[6] ibid., and Tennessee Code Annotated 67: 605-7.

[7] Quoted by Simon Winchester, 'The Stripping of Clear Fork', *The Guardian* (London), 6 May 1974, p. 11.

from the Clear Fork Valley to the county court also sat on the Tax Equalization Board—the tax appeals body which holds yearly hearings—but he had done little to raise the issue. His major action had been to lower, for no apparent reason, the assessment on his own property from $25,990 to $17,960. In fact, the only appeal before the Board in 1971 relevant to the major tax inequality had been an appeal by the Company, arguing that its taxes were *too high,* and claiming that its 44,000 acres of coal land were worth only $320,000, or five dollars an acre of coal-rich land.

It is immediately tempting to view the 'non-issueness' of this potential issue as an isolated phenomenon—perhaps to be explained individualistically in terms of corruption of the local officials involved. Yet to do so would be too simple. This non-issue is but an example of many other potentially important issues which remain latent within Claiborne County, and, in turn, the pattern of the county is but an example of the pattern found throughout the Central Appalachian Region. Broader questions must be asked. Why the apparent quiescence? Is there a form of power that intervenes between the community and the courthouse in action upon this and other latent issues?

Across the mountain from the courthouse, in the communities along the Clear Fork Creek, partial answers quickly emerge. In the Valley, generally, there is an awareness of the pattern of undertaxation of certain interests—but there has been such awareness for years. Recognition of the inequality alone does not make it an issue. Rather, about this and other identifiable potential issues, there is a sense of inevitability, a prevailing belief that nothing can be done. 'To get anything done you have to go over there,' says one woman, 'but then you don't get it done when you go over there,' she quickly adds. 'The county government is just poor grade, that's all I can say . . . it's just poor grade,' says another miner. 'Now all the years I've lived in the holler, you've got a very little bit of county help.' Among some, generalized cynicism gives way, as the matter is discussed, to angry identification of particular power interests—the Company, coal operators, a few families. Among others, particularly as questions are raised about action, there is a rapid withdrawal, often accompanied by expressions of fear, not of defeat, but of reprisal. Residents cited possible loss of welfare benefits, housing, jobs or businesses if they signed a complaint challenging the under-taxation of company coal land.

In a historical context it is possible to understand the genesis of this prevailing 'law of anticipated reactions'. Yet, for a contemporary study of power, further questions must be asked about whether and by what means the law is still being enforced.

6.2 VOTING: A POWER-POWERLESSNESS MODEL

In theory, in a democracy, voting in elections is a principal means by which a deprived public may act upon its concerns. Candidates are chosen as representatives and mandated by the electorate to act upon their interests. Why have the potential issues in the Valley not become manifest in the local decision-making arenas via this electoral process?

A host of studies in political science argue that the poor may not participate, or may not participate effectively, because of low income, poor education, lack of information, and other factors of a socio-economic-status (SES) scale.[8] Often other more cultural reasons such as traditionalism are given for the political behaviour in rural under-developed regions.[9] A recent study of political participation among blacks, Indians and Appalachians looked at Claiborne County, Tennessee for its Appalachian case. Based on random interviews with residents about personal backgrounds and feelings of voting efficacy, the study concluded that patterns of participation for those groups were related to their 'cultural diversity' from the American mainstream.[10] Like so many others, the study failed to take a view 'from the bottom up' to ask whether the apparent apathy or traditionalism might be related to the power processes of local politics.

Elections in the Valley. Election day in the Clear Fork Valley

[8] See discussion, Chapter 1, pp. 0-0. For summaries of these studies see also Lipset, *Political Man*, op. cit., pp. 179-263; Verba and Nie, *Participation in America*, op. cit.

[9] ibid., Lipset, pp. 258-9.

[10] John Paul Ryan, 'Cultural Diversity and the American Experience: Political Participation Among Blacks, Appalachians, and Indians' (Sage Publications, Beverly Hills, 1975).

is considered a special day, and, like other special days, it has its ritualistic elements. People dress in their best clothes and make their way to the schoolhouse to vote. Many of the men slip their pistols into their pockets, as they do for all important gatherings. At the polls the voters take their time, for the event gives a chance to visit—the men meeting out by the cars, the women in the halls or empty class-rooms of the dilapidated building. Leaflets are distributed, a few campaign remarks are made, but very quickly amongst most of the people the conversation moves to other matters—the crops, the family, deaths that have occurred since the last common event. Election days, in an important sense, are integrative occasions, a coming together of the community, like the church 'home-comings' or 'house-raisin's' of days past.

In Presidential elections, unlike the rural Republican farming communities of surrounding parts of eastern Tennessee, this coal community votes Democratic, as it has since the days of the New Deal and the union. But the striking factor about Presidential politics is their remoteness in the local situation. During the 1972 contest between Nixon and McGovern, for instance, despite the headlines in the city's television and newspapers, very few of the Valley's residents talked of the election or its issues. There were no campaign rallies held; no literature was distributed. In national politics, this community neither gives nor receives much attention.

Local contests, on the other hand, are more intense, though party identification is rarely mentioned. Long-standing factions, primarily headed by competing élites or families of élites, appear to be the basis of the cleavages. All the candidates for the Valley's representatives to the county courthouse since 1960 have been the representatives of one of three factions—one based around the largest strip mine owner, and the other two based around the largest local landowners in the Valley. Political identification is usually that of being 'for the——bunch' or 'against the——bunch', with the name of the 'bunch' being the family head of that particular group.

In recent years the dominant faction has been that of one of the local landowners, to be called the 'Family'. One of the brothers of the Family served as the magistrate on the county court from 1966 to 1972, when he was replaced by the principal brother, the 'Godfather'. The son of the Godfather heads the school-board, and used to run the poverty programme. Though the primary linkage between the Valley and local government in the last decade has been through this group, few people other than its members seem to respect the Family. Rather, their 'influence' seems to rest on the fact that the Godfather is viewed as the broker of benefits or reprisals of the two major institutions that immediately affect the welfare of the Valley's residents—the Company and the courthouse.

There is a historical basis to both relationships. The dominance of the Family in the Valley developed out of their position as large landowners and coal owners in the area; their 550 acres were second only to the Company's 45,000. During the earlier coal camp days the Family served as the supervisors, landlords, and merchants within the coal camps on their land. As their mines began to close down, they appeared to form an unofficial alliance with the larger absentee landlords. The Family became viewed as mediators between the Company and the community, gaining further power as brokers of favours concerning jobs or home tenure.

From their economic base the Family play a political role. During the days of the Depression, oral history suggests, the good grace of the Grandfather was necessary to get employment on the public works programmes. Even now, people say, those who live in company housing or work in mines on company land are expected to vote in the Family's favour. Those on welfare, which comes from the courthouse, associate the Family with control of their food stamps, while those who work the relatively lucrative county jobs, such as schoolteachers, feel similarly vulnerable. As in the coal camp days, the powerlessness is maximized by the numerous points of vulnerability—for instance, welfare recipients,often those who live in the poorest housing, the company housing, fear not spending their food stamps at the Godfather's store, lest they lose their welfare, or face eviction—or both. As one miner described the rule-of-thumb of local politics, 'If you don't vote for me, I won't 'commodate you. Otherwise, if you stamp on my toes too hard I can make it hard on you.'

In recent years, other factions, based around other élites have begun to emerge. But they, too, possess, or are considered by the non-élite to possess, similar coercive capabilities. Because of the 'brokerage' capacity of local élites, the analysis of local politics in the Valley must take place in two areas: that which gets into the electoral arena, and that which is kept out.

Though intensely fought, the conflict which emerges into the local political arena is rarely substantive compared with what could emerge. The candidates do not raise questions potentially challenging to either Company or courthouse—such as why the locally derived wealth is not redistributed through local taxation. Rather, the campaigns are flavoured by charges and counter-charges amongst the factions—of corruption, of broken promises, of 'dirty tricks'. Stories abound of ballot boxes being stolen, of campaign literature disappearing from the mails, of excessive patronage; yet, the schools and roads for which promises of improvement are made continue to worsen for lack of funds. Local politics in the Valley take on the air of a ritual battle whose well-defined rules, though unwritten, are widely understood.

Public challenges by the non-élite, as candidates or as critics, are deterred by feelings of inadequacy, fear of reprisal, or simply the sense that the outcome of challenge is a foregone conclusion. When challenges do occur, the ritual can be re-enforced by the threat of a more coercive power. Élites may convey instructions for the 'appropriate' behaviour of the non-élite at places of vulnerability. For example, the Godfather may keep the 'recommended' slate at the cash register in the store or the company agent may call the men out from the mines at the lunch hour and 'suggest' how they vote. Private challenges, i.e. in the ballot box, are pre-empted by the fear that the deviant might be discovered, a fear unmitigated by a thought about whether any of the candidates offer substantive enough reason to take the risk. How the challenges would be discovered in a secret ballot is a question asked by the outsider but rarely brought up by the local poor. There is merely the sense that somehow those who run the machines would know, for the machines represent 'them'. And, for the illiterate, there is the dependency upon an 'interpreter' of the ballot or the machine, strengthened by the self-recognition of that dependency. Every so often, those thought by the élite to have been rebels find themselves conspicuously evicted from their homes or blacklisted from their next jobs—offering symbolic re-enforcement to the fear of detection. More generally, it is not the actual exercise of coercion but the constant possibility that it might be exercised that supports the routines of non-challenge.

While the benefits of the status quo are high for the powerful, the costs of challenge are potentially higher for the powerless. Over time, that which is kept out of local politics seems to become as clearly understood as that which is allowed in. From this perspective, low income, status, or education are themselves insufficient explanations of voting patterns but may be indicators of potential vulnerability. And resignation is not an indigenous product of culture, but of the power situation in which the non-élite find themselves.

The Voting Data. If the model generated from observation is valid, then it should be reflected in voting returns. Testing for subjective factors such as fear with quantitative data is difficult. However, using voting returns Salamon and Van Evera have been able to establish the role of fear amongst blacks in elections in rural Mississippi.[11] Does 'vulnerability' also effect the voting patterns of whiles in Appalachia?

To explore the question, data have been collected for local and national elections for four different precincts in Claiborne County. The communities are similar in that their residents rank low on indices of income, education or status (see Table 6.1). They vary, however, according to the level of corporate dependency, i.e. vulnerability of the voters to loss of jobs or housing owing to the uniform control of a corporate élite (see Table 6.2). The precincts may be seen more particularly as follows:

Company Town. One of the first of the coal camps developed near Middlesboro, this community has declined

[11] Salamon and Van Evera, 'Fear, Apathy and Discrimination', op. cit., pp. 1288-1306; also, Sam Kernell, 'Comment: A Re-Evaluation of Black Voting in Mississippi', *American Political Science Review*, 67, (1973) 1317-18; and Salamon and Van Evera, 'Fear Revisited: Rejoinder to Comment by Sam Kernell', *ASPR* 67, (1973) 1319-26.

Voting and Vulnerability:

TABLE 6.1

COMMUNITY BY INCOME, EDUCATION, AND OCCUPATION[a]

	% below poverty level	% 8th grade education or below	% emp. in mining	% emp. in agricult.	% emp. in constr. or mnftg.	% trade, service, finance	% other
Company Town	HIGH	HIGH	HIGH	LOW	LOW	LOW	HIGH
Coal Community	52	45	47	4	0	20	29
County Seat	37	44	1	9	36	37	17
Rural Community	41	41	3	17	34	26	20

[a] Data are from the *1970 Census,* provided by the East Tennessee Development District. Because the census divisions do not correspond precisely to political divisions in the county, the data represent only approximations of the characteristics of the voters. In the company town, totally incompatible boundaries make approximations impossible; personal observations, interview and courthouse data provide the basis for the estimations.

since the closure of the mines in the 1950s. All of its remaining forty-eight dwellings are company houses. All but four of the dwellings—which consist of a few rooms with timbered walls, no running water or electric heating—were built by the Company before 1935, most in the 1920s. Their residents represent the underclass of Appalachia: the unemployed or intermittently employed, disabled or retired. The 'good graces' of the Company or its agents are probably important for their housing tenure, jobs or welfare benefits.

Coal Community. On the other side of the company property, in the centre of the Valley, is the coal community. This area was once a cluster of the traditional company towns. Now, the decline of the mines has left a mixture of tenants amongst independent home-owners, of active miners amongst retired or unemployed workers. Some 50 per cent of the families live in rented housing, though not all of the homes are owned by the Company; 84 per cent of the workers are employed by private companies or local government; 75 per cent in non-supervisory or non-ownership

TABLE 6.2

COMMUNITY BY DWELLING AND JOB 'VULNERABILITY'[a] [b]

	% in rented homes	% employed by private corp. or local gov.	% self-employed or State/ Fed.	% male clerical, operative, labourer except farm	% male professionals, manag., foremen, farm owners, Craftsmen
Company Town	100	HIGH	LOW	HIGH	LOW
Coal Community	50	84	16	75	25
County Seat	22	75	25	56	34
Rural Community	13	55	45	36	64

a Data are from the *1970 Census* (see above).

b Vulnerability is seen as a function of home tenure and nature of employment, similar to the measure proposed by Salamon and Van Evera (see n. 11, p. 00). Those employed by a private corporation or local government are assumed to be more vulnerable to pressure of local élites than those self-employed or employed by state or federal government. Those working in clerical, operative or labouring positions are assumed to be more vulnerable within the workplace than the professionals, managers, foremen, farm owners, or craftsmen. In the last two columns, data were available only for males. Data do not include farm labourers owing to their insignificance in this context.

capacities, though not all work for the same employer. Thus, vulnerability in the coal community is relatively high, though not as great as in the company town, and the susceptibility is to a less singular powerholder.

County Seat. Across the mountain from the coal community is the political, financial and trading centre of the county, the county seat. It is the least poor of the communities. Though in a non-coal area of the county and containing few miners, its business élites probably benefit from the coal industry in the county. Approximately 73 per cent of its employed work force are in construction, manufacturing, trade, service, or finance. Some 75 per cent of its work force are employed in private corporations or local government, though only 56 per cent are in the more vulnerable positions, and only 22 per cent rent their homes.

Rural Community. While each of the communities are rural, this one, separated from the coal communities by the giant Cumberland Mountain, is rural in the agricultural sense. Once almost entirely a farming area, 17 per cent of its work force are still employed in agriculture, while others now commute to small industrial, construction, or trading jobs nearby. Only 13 per cent live in rented homes; 45 per cent are self-employed in the 'safer' government jobs, and some 64 per cent are in relatively non-vulnerable jobs at the workplace. While the least vulnerable, its poverty, traditional air, and relative isolation otherwise make it very much like the rural subculture of the other areas.

In general, it should be expected that if the 'vulnerability model' is a valid one, then the company town should show extremely high support of 'company candidates'. Though vulnerability will affect some of the residents of the coal community, the aggregate results may give the appearance of competition, owing to the developing factions of élites. The county seat and rural community should give less support and should, as relatively independent communities, provide some test of the extent to which vulnerability may help to explain the voting behaviour in the dependent communities. However, the county seat, as a financial and trading centre, may tend more than the rural area to vote similarly to ways 'encouraged' by the corporate élites.

On the basis of elections in which one of the candidates is known from other data to be protective of the Company's interests, the power pattern appears to hold.

The chief executive officer of the county, the county judge, a Democrat on record as thinking of himself as a 'good friend' of the company manager, received in the 1970 election 100 per cent of the vote in the company town, 79 per cent in the coal community, and only 42 per cent and 65 per cent in the third and fourth communities respectively. The same person in his race for county sheriff in 1968, received 97 per cent of the vote in the company town, 61 per cent in the coal community, 51 per cent in the county seat and only 39 per cent in the rural community.

While one might argue that this cleavage represented party cleavages in progressively less Democratic communities, the

TABLE 6.3

VOTING FOR 'COMPANY' CANDIDATES BY COMMUNITY[a]

	Company Town	Coal Community	County Seat	Rural Community
		[(% for 'company candidate')]		
County Judge (1970)	100	79	42	65
School-board (1970)	94	31	63	28
Sheriff (1968)	97	61	51	39
School-board (1966)	88	40	57	40
Tax Assessor (1940)	89	73	54	52
Sheriff (1940)	94	70	46	46

[a] All voting data in this chapter are from original Claiborne County Tally Sheets, as filed with the Tennessee Secretary of State and recorded in the State Archives, Nashville, Tennessee.

same pattern held true for another 'company candidate', a Republican and son of the Godfather, in his race for school-board member, a powerful position by virtue of its control over government jobs in the county. In the company town the son received 94 per cent of the vote, in the nearby coal community only 31 per cent and in the third and fourth communities 63 per cent and 28 per cent respectively. Roughly the same pattern was found in an election in 1966 when against the same competitor he received 88 per cent in the company town, 40 per cent in his home coal valley, 57 per cent in the county seat and 40 per cent in the rural community. In that same year, in a three faction race, the 'company' ticket, including the brother of the Godfather, received 96 per cent of the vote in the company town, while the coal community was split amongst the factions—26 per cent for the 'company' group, 35 per cent for the strip mine operators' group, and 38 per cent for the third group. The fact that the 'company' candidates received highest votes in the company town, while receiving low support in their own, less dependent, coal communities nearby, suggests some factor at work in the company community not at work in the other similar area. And the fact that the Family, who are large merchants in the Valley, also received high votes in the county seat may reflect their common interests with the financial and trading élites of the county's centre.

Vulnerability as an underpinning of voting behaviour may

have been more to be expected in the earlier coal camp era. In fact, in his first election for tax assessor in 1940, the tax assessor who had underassessed the company mineral wealth in 1970 received 89 per cent of the vote in the company town, 73 per cent in the coal community, and only 54 per cent and 52 per cent in the other two communities. That same year, Frank Riley, the county sheriff, known for his 'union busting' attitudes in the miners' rebellion of 1931, received 94 per cent of the vote in the company town, 70 per cent in the coal community, and only 46 per cent in each of the other two communities. The support of the sheriff for the company interests was seen six months later when, with the company manager at his side, he attempted to shoot his way through a 'Jones boys' picket line at the mines in the company town.

In each of the above cases, then, the choice expressed in the vote by the people of the company town appears different both from what may have been expected on the basis of the interests reflected in the candidates' positions on issues or potential issues, and from the voting pattern of other similar poor communities. Rather, the voting patterns appear to reflect other interests of the voters, not visible in the public arena—e.g. the maintenance of 'good relations' with the Company or its élites. Are these examples indicative of a general pattern? How can one tell on the basis of aggregate data, where the positions of each of the candidates are not known? It may be possible to develop yet more general patterns of the 'power model' by looking at variations amongst community and election types by measures of homogeneity or fragmentation, participation and divergence. The measures are explained more fully below.

Homogeneity and Fragmentation. Single industry communities are, by their very nature, relatively homogeneous. Related concepts of the 'occupational community' and of the 'isolated mass' are often used to explain the political and industrial behaviour of mining areas. The absence of cross-pressures and the interrelationships between workplace and community life are thought to lead to a degree of solidarity and radicalism not found elsewhere.[12] Thus, the argument could be made

that the highly concentrated voting returns in the company
town and in the coal community merely reflect the natural
homogeneity of those communities. However, these concepts, which place explanations in factors endogenous to the
single industry working community itself, are insufficient. A
focus upon common occupation or isolation, like the focus
upon socio-economic status, does not explain variations in
voting behaviour amongst similar communities or variations
in the same community amongst differing election types.

A more developed explanatory model might be this:
political behaviour may be understood in terms of the interaction of the isolated occupational community with other
external factors, such as the power field around it. In certain
situations, the homogeneity of the mining community may
lead to workers' solidarity and radicalism, but in other
situations, homogeneity may equally mean uniform vulnerability.

The two approaches may be tested by looking at a measure
of how homogeneity or fragmentation appears in the voting
patterns of varying communities in varying election types.
In general, if the 'occupational community' approach is
itself sufficient explanation for voting behaviour, then the
level of homogeneity in voting in a single community should
remain roughly the same amongst election types and the
difference in levels of homogeneity (range) amongst the
communities should remain roughly consistent. If, however,
vulnerability to power exercises is an intervening factor, then
voting homogeneity should increase in the dependent communities for elections in which power processes are likely
to be at work, while it should remain the same in the more
independent communities. Power exercises may be expected
to occur where results immediately beneficial to the powerholders' interests are most likely to be obtained. Thus, in

---

[12] For a discussion of the occupational community concept as it affects voting,
see Lipset, op. cit., especially pp. 193–4. Further development regarding miners in
Chile is found in James Petras and Maurice Zeitlin, 'Miners and Agarian Radicalism', *American Sociological Review*, 32, (1967), 578–86. The concept of the
isolated mass is developed by Kerr and Siegel, 'The Interindustry Propensity to
Strike', op. cit. Both concepts are usefully developed in relationship to mining
communities by Bulmer, 'Sociological Models of the Mining Community,' op. cit.,
pp. 61–92.

this particular case of testing for power of the corporate élite within Claiborne County, the exercise of power should be expected to produce variations in level of voting homogeneity or fragmentation more in local elections than in national elections, more so in the dependent communities than in the independent communities, owing to the potential capacity of the local élite significantly to affect outcomes.[13]

Participation. If power is being exercised towards certain outcomes in certain elections then it might also be expected that the more vulnerable the community, the more likely will be unusually high turnout for those elections. In their studies of black voting in Mississippi, Salamon and Van Evera found low participation in elections to be related to fear amongst the blacks that the exercise of the vote might bring economic or other reprisals.[14] However, in differing circumstances, especially for local elections in small communities where who votes can easily be observed, abstention may bear its costs, and vulnerability may be related to high participation. Unfortunately, data on number of registered voters were not available in Claiborne County.[15] Level of participation will

[13] The degree of homogeneity or fragmentation in voting behaviour amongst non-uniform election types has been measured by several methods in other studies, one in relation to French elections by Mark Kesselman, 'French Local Politics: A Statistical Examination of Grass Roots Consensus', *American Political Science Review*, 60, (1966), 963–73, another in Douglas W. Rae and Michael Taylor, *The Analysis of Political Cleavages* (Yale University Press, New Haven, 1970). Further discussion about these two measures and others is presented in Rae, 'A Note on the Fractionalization of Some European Party Systems', *Comparative Political Studies*, 3 (1968), 413–18. Both the Kesselman and Rae measures were computed, with no substantive difference in patterns found between the two. The Kesselman index was used because of its constant lower limit of 1 and easily definable upper limit as being equal to the number of candidates, making significance more readily interpretable. As Kesselman observes (pp. 968-9) 'The index measures the degree to which votes in a commune are distributed among competing candidates or lists. It increases as the number of candidates or lists competing increases, and as the proportion of the total vote received by candidates of lists converge.' The index is:

$$I = \text{antilog}_e - \sum_i^k p_i \log_e p_i$$

where k = number of candidates; p_i - proportion of vote for its candidates; p_i = 1.

[14] Salamon and Van Evera, op. cit.

[15] Of all the records in the local courthouse those on voters registered are the most tightly controlled. Initial visits to the Elections Commissioner evoked the response that the information was not available. Telephone calls brought no answer. Data finally acquired through the county judge were for the most recent elections only, making them unusable over time. Such records are not kept on the state level.

be measured as a ratio of persons voting in a given election to the number voting in the congressional elections in that given community for that given year.

Divergence. If power is found to affect the level of homogeneity and the level of participation in local elections, then it may also affect the results within those elections. It may still be difficult, however, to assess significance of results where other data on the candidates are not known and where party labels are not important—or, indeed, not available. What may be of interest (and also measurable) is the extent to which the direction of voting varies amongst communities and election types. Thus, one community, the county seat, has been taken as a standard, and the direction and extent of divergence of the results of the other communities has been measured against it. Divergence is the difference (positive or negative) between the percentage of the votes received by the leading candidate in the standard community and the percentage received by that candidate in each of the other communities.

For national elections, where the local corporate power is not expected to be exercised, the level and direction of divergence amongst communities should be relatively stable, reflecting, perhaps, the difference in occupational types of the communities. For local elections, where power processes are expected to be at work, the level and direction of divergence may be quite different, reflecting more the relative vulnerability of the non-élite within the communities.

The data are presented for six types of elections from eight election years during the period 1956–70,[16] a period corresponding to the decline of the mines during which the fear of loss of job or home was probably high. Consideration of the results in the four communities, excluding missing data, provides ninety-four election results for analysis.

Vulnerability and Homogeneity. For each of the election types, the company town had the lowest level of fragmentation

---

[16] On the national level, election types analysed were Presidential and Congressional races; on the local level, they were county judge, tax assessor, sheriff, and school board. Owing to the abolition of the 'company town' as a separate precinct, this analysis could not go beyond 1970.

Voting and Vulnerability

in voting, i.e. the highest level of homogeneity (see Table 6.4). Except for the Congressional elections, the coal community, too, appeared to have less division than did the occupationally more diverse county seat and rural community; though the differences were not nearly so strong as in the case of the company town. While these results have been predicted on the basis of the 'occupational' approach, what would not have been predicted are the variations in the levels of homogeneity in voting amongst the communities in differing election types. Except for the tax assessor's race, the variation or range increased remarkably for the local contests.

TABLE 6.4

HOMOGENEITY IN VOTING
BY ELECTION AND COMMUNITY[a]

	Company Town	Coal Community	County Seat	Rural Community	Range	Mean No. Candidates	Adjusted Range[b]
President	1·85	1·89	2·23	2·09	0·38	2·27	16·7%
Congress	1·62	1·93	1·84	1·80	0·31	2·14	14·4%
County Judge	1·34	2·28	3·06	3·05	1·72	3·44	49·9%
Tax Assessor	1·66	1·83	1·89	1·86	0·23	2·00	11·5%
Sheriff	1·61	2·22	2·37	2·18	0·76	2·86	26·5%
School-board	1·34	1·92	1·92	1·89	0·58	2·00	29·0%
Federal	1·71	1·91	1·96	1·90	0·25	2·18	11·0%
Local	1·55	2·12	2·31	2·20	0·76	2·66	28·0%

[a]Computations employ the Kesselman Index, see n. 13.
Lowest possible fragmentation, i.e. a unanimous result, equals one.
Highest equals the number of candidates for that election.

[b]Because the fragmentation level varies according to mean number of candidates, an adjustment has to be made to allow comparisons amongst elections. A crude adjustment was made by the formula

$$\text{range} \times \frac{1}{\text{mean number of candidates}} \times 100\% = \text{adjusted range}$$

standardizing to a % variation on a common scale of one.

Within the company town may be seen the reasons for the variations in fragmentation. While for the more independent communities the amount of fragmentation in local elections is roughly equal to or greater than that for the national elections, for the company town fragmentation in voting decreases. The county judge races, for instance, attract the most number of candidates and might be expected on the basis of probability to show the highest level of fragmentation in the voting returns. While the expectation holds true for the independent communities, the opposite is the case for the company town: despite the increased choice available and the increased competition in the other communities, the level of fragmentation in this, the most vulnerable community, is the lowest of all the election types (except that of the school-board, to which it is equal).

When the level of homogeneity in voting is graphed over time, other very important patterns emerge. In general for the national elections the range between levels of homogeneity in the various communities appears stable, indicating a consistency in political differences (Graph 6.5A). For local elections, on the other hand, the difference in level of voting fragmentation amongst the communities varies enormously (Graph 6.5B). In certain years (in particular 1962, 1966, 1968), a high 'consensus' in the company town abruptly emerges, while in other years the pattern is similar to that of the more independent communities. Moreover (as can be seen especially by the graph of a single illustrative election type, Graph 6.5C), the consensus in the dependent community tends to occur when dissent is highest in the other communities. If corporate power is the variable which explains these differences, it would appear that the power is more likely to be exercised in the dependent communities the more tightly contested and unpredictable are the outcomes in the more independent communities.[17]

Vulnerability and Participation. In general, observation of elections in the Clear Fork Valley suggests that interest is likely to be higher in local elections than in federal elections, because of the perceived remoteness among the residents of all but the local contests. If the conclusions based on the homogeneity measures are correct, then local participation

[17] The low range of fragmentation levels for the tax assessor's race is explainable by the fact that the tax assessor has been relatively uncontested making the need to exercise power to ensure certain outcomes relatively low. In his first race in 1940, however, fragmentation K was 1·4 in the company town, compared with 2·46 in the independent rural community, a range more consistent with the pattern. Presumably in other years, as an incumbent able to distribute favours and build influence in all the communities, he was able to win on his own.

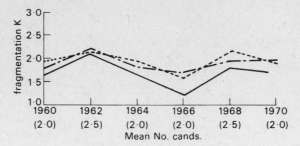

A National Elections 1960–70

	1960	1962	1964	1966	1968	1970
Mean No. cands.	(2·0)	(2·5)	(2·0)	(2·0)	(2·5)	(2·0)

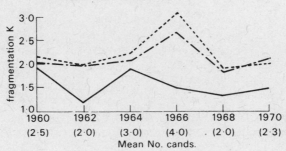

B Local Elections 1960–70

	1960	1962	1964	1966	1968	1970
Mean No. cands.	(2·5)	(2·0)	(3·0)	(4·0)	(2·0)	(2·3)

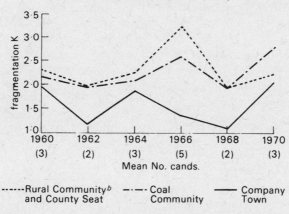

C Local Elections: County Sheriff Only 1960–70

	1960	1962	1964	1966	1968	1970
Mean No. cands.	(3)	(2)	(3)	(5)	(2)	(3)

······ Rural Community[b]   —·—· Coal   —— Company
and County Seat   Community   Town

6.5 Relative Homogeneity and Fragmentation Amongst Communities Over Time [a]

[a] Lowest possible fragmentation, i.e. a unanimous result, equals one. Highest, i.e. maximum division within the community, equals mean number of candidates.

[b] The differences in levels of fragmentation for the rural community and county seat were marginal. To facilitate clarity, the two have been combined.

should be inordinately higher in the most dependent community in elections where power is probably being exercised to swing uncertain outcomes in the powerholders' favour.

TABLE 6.6

RELATIVE PARTICIPATION BY ELECTION AND COMMUNITY[a]

	Company Town[b]	Coal Community	County Seat	Rural Community
	%	%	%	%
President	242	211	144	154
Congress	100	100	100	100
County Judge	510	300	234	266
Tax Assessor	308	135	152	136
Sheriff	332	245	156	168
School-board	510	219	105	112
Summary:				
Federal	157	211	144	154
Local	358	231	158	167

[a]Data on number of registered voters were not available. Level of participation is measured as a ratio of persons voting in a given election to the number voting in the Congressional elections in that community for that given year.

[b]Very low turnouts in certain years for the Congressional races help to account for the high index in the company town. For instance, in 1968, according to records, only two persons in the company town precinct voted for Congressman, while thirty voted for President. To account for a possible error in the data, the figure for that year has been altered, making it more in line with the patterns of previous years. The adjustment provides weaker evidence for the argument regarding inordinately high participation in the company town for local elections. However, even with the conservative figures (given above) the pattern remains the same.

In general (as Table 6.6 shows), participation was higher in local elections than in national elections in each of the communities. For instance, in each of the communities the county judge's race had a higher rate of participation than did the Presidential elections.

Amongst the local elections, however, further differences emerged. While in the relatively independent communities the rate of participation dropped in the elections other than those for judge, in the company town it remained relatively high. In the independent communities, while turnout for the tax assessor's election was only slightly higher than turnout for the Congressional races, in the company town—whose residents had the least property to be assessed—it was three times higher. Similarly, the school-board race (which has always involved a member of the Family) received high turnout in the company town, lower turnout in the coal community and very low turnout in the two independent communities. The data suggest, then, that vulnerability may also be a factor in predicting who turns up at the polls to be counted—though by the boss rather than by the ballot.

The pattern of pressure to vote in the company town is further supported when correlations are made between the rate of participation and the levels of fragmentation. It might be expected, for instance, that the higher the competitiveness in the local elections, the higher will be the turnout. In the independent communities, a positive relationship appears to hold true. (Correlation R is 0·839 in the rural community, 0·767 in the county seat and 0·464 in the coal community.) However, in the company town, there is a negative relationship. (R equals −0·505.) There a high degree of 'consensus' and high rates of turnout in local elections appear to go together.

Vulnerability and Divergence. In aggregate terms the elections since 1954 show that the highest variations in outcome amongst the communities are found in the Presidential, county judge and school-board races, respectively. (Table 6.7.) In each case, one extreme of the range is found in the outcome of the company town, but the significance of the fact for the various election types is quite different. For Presidential elections, the company town votes least like the county seat and rural community and most like the other coal community, perhaps reflecting the similarity of the single occupational type, the miners. In local elections for the judge and the school-board representative, however, the company town votes the least like the coal town and most like the county seat, the economic and political centre of the county, to whose financial and political élite the community's poor may be most vulnerable.

Vulnerability and Economic Climate. Intuitively, one might expect vulnerability to have been more of a factor affecting voting behaviour in the earlier coal camp days than in contemporary America. However, further considerations

TABLE 6.7

DIVERGENCE BY ELECTION AND COMMUNITY
(difference between winner in county seat and same
candidate in other communities)

	Company Town %	Coal Community %	County Seat %	Rural Community %	Range %
President	−30	−16	0	8·7	38·7
Congress	5·8	−2·1	0	4·2	7·9
County Judge	4·2	−29·4	0	−13·6	33·6
Tax Assessor	2·7	6·0	0	0·6	6·6
Sheriff	8·2	0·2	0	−7·4	15·6
School-board	13·9	−14·3	0	42·9	56·8
Summary:					
Federal	−7·7	−6·3	0	4·0	11·7
Local	9·7	−6·3	0	−9·5	18·2

in this Central Appalachian valley might argue for a reverse expectation. Following the closing of the mines, the miners' labour became less of a bargaining resource; countervailing union strength declined; jobs and homes in the area became scarce; the coal communities became smaller and more marginal—all of which may have increased the part played by vulnerability in the political process. In order to compare the voting patterns since the decline of the mines with the patterns of earlier periods, seventy-six more voting results from the four communities have been analysed for the years 1930-52.[18]

In doing so, results in Table 6.8A suggest that the coal communities were more homogeneous than were the county seat and the rural community for all election types, as they are today. However, with the exception of the county judge's race, the range of difference in the level of homogeneity amongst the communities did not increase in the local contests, as it has in the contemporary era. Table 6.8B indicates that in general the level of participation in local elections was not markedly higher than participation in national elections in any of the communities, and, more particularly, that the pattern in the most dependent coal community did not differ significantly from the pattern in the others. Finally, Table

[18] The years were chosen which compared most closely with other time periods considered in this study, so the 1940s were excluded.

TABLE 6.8

VOTING PATTERNS PRIOR TO 1954

6.8A Fragmentation by Election Type and Community

	Comp. Town	Coal Comm.	County Seat	Rural Comm.	Range	Mean No. Candidates	Adjusted Range %
President	1·60	1·89	1·93	1·95	0·35	2·00	17·5
Congress	1·52	1·82	2·37	2·26	0·85	3·00	28·6
County Judge	1·28	2·40	2·77	2·43	1·49	3·00	49·3
Tax Assessor	1·68	1·83	1·89	2·07	0·39	2·25	17·3
Sheriff	1·74	2·19	2·46	2·47	0·72	3·20	22·5
Summary:							
Federal	1·55	1·85	2·20	2·14	0·65	2·61	24·0
Local	1·67	2·07	2·27	2·30	0·63	2·80	22·0

8B Participation by Election and Community (pre-1954)

	Company Town %	Coal Community %	County Seat %	Rural Community %
President	152	202	120	137
Congress	100	100	100	100
County Judge	195	161	138	189
Tax Assessor	147	158	133	124
Sheriff	174	185	140	159
School-board	na	na	na	na
Summary:				
Federal	152	202	120	137
Local	168	172	137	149

8C Divergence by Election and Community (pre-1954)

	Company Town	Coal Community	County Seat	Rural Community	Range
President	17·9	−4·9	0	−8·6	25·5
Congress	−18·8	−12·5	0	−17·4	18·8
County Judge	42·4	13·3	0	10·8	42·4
Tax Assessor	−5·0	−21·4	0	17·4	21·4
Sheriff	16·1	−11·6	0	−3·8	19·9
School-board	na	na	na	na	na
Summary:					
Federal	−5·0	−9·6	0	−13·9	13·9
Local	10·3	−13·1	0	−4·0	14·0

6.8C shows that the company town voted unlike the independent rural community in both national and local elections, as
is the case today, yet there was little discernible pattern in
the directions of the differences amongst the various election
types for the various communities.

In general, then, the aggregate data for the earlier coal
camp period do not show as clearly the pattern found in the
contemporary mining era. While it is difficult to make
further conclusions without more information one point is
clear: we cannot make the intuitive assumption that the
contemporary era has ushered into the Appalachian coal
hollows new levels of political freedom.

6.3 CONCLUSIONS: POVERTY POLITICS AND SOCIAL REFORM

Though the single case study alone does not support a general
theory, the data argue for a further development of a power-
powerlessness model of voting behaviour for deprived groups,
along the lines begun by Salamon and Van Evera for Mississippi
blacks. Factors such as low income, low education and low
status may, in fact, be reflections of a common index of
'vulnerability' or social and economic dependency of a non-
élite upon an élite. Through processes of coercive power,
those most likely to challenge inequalities may be prevented
from challenge, while those least likely to challenge maintain
the political game as a ritual whose rules are clearly understood by all parties. Over time, there may develop a routine
of non-conflict within and about local politics—a routine
which may, to the observer, appear a fatalism found in
'backwardness'. As regards voting, this section has suggested,
the phenomenon would be better understood as a product
of power relations, such that actions of challenge—and even,
over time, conceptions of such actions—by the powerless
against the powerful become organized out of the political
milieu.

While one might have expected these power relationships
to have existed historically, they persist in the contemporary
Appalachian Valley. Their persistence is despite major
programmes for social reform that have emerged in the 1960s
and 1970s and is of vital consequence to the impact these
programmes have had upon the region, as is seen in the

politics of the War on Poverty and development planning.

'Today for the first time in our history, we have the power to strike away the barriers to full participation in our society', President Johnson proclaimed in presenting War on Poverty legislation to Congress on 4 March 1964.[19] Aspects of the Economic Opportunity Act did somewhat alter obstacles to participation faced by the poor in the Clear Fork Valley, as in other parts of the country. Legally, local Community Action Programs (CAPs) were established with the mandate of 'maximum feasible participation' of the groups served. Symbolically, the new legislation, as the National Industrial Recovery Act of 1933 had for labour, added a subjective resource: the poor could now claim the *right* to participate in the courthouse domain.

If our theory of power is correct, this shift in the power field might be expected to lead to new patterns of participation among the Clear Fork residents. In fact, elections to community action boards were held: and none of those elected were among the traditional political élites or appeared to be aligned with them. A community centre opened, and was described by residents 'as the first time poor people felt like something was theirs'. Initially unthreatening activities of the poor led to more challenging ones. Recipients of food stamps at the community centre began to stop shopping at the Godfather's store. One day when the food stamps did not appear from the welfare office, forty of the Clear Fork residents hired a bus, went to the courthouse, sat in until they got their stamps—and sent the bill for the trip to the welfare offices. Not only did participation occur, but the definition by the poor of 'maximum feasible' was well outside the traditional rules of the political game.

The theory of power also suggests that the emergence of these new forms of activity among a previously quiescent group would invoke a response from the powerholders, who would seek to re-establish their control. Indeed, pressure (combined with ill health) brought the resignation of the programme director, who was replaced by the wife of the bank president, a prominent Republican from the county seat and a close ally of the Family in the Valley. A political manoeuvre by the

[19] Quoted in Hanna H. Meissner, ed., *Poverty in the Affluent Society* (Harper and Row, New York, 1966), p. 209.

county court displaced the outspoken valley representative to the CAP board and replaced her with a 'safer' representative of the poor. Invocation of certain symbols—such as the label 'communist'—forced the resignation of the former Catholic nun who served as staff organizer. She was replaced initially by a sister in the Family, followed shortly by the Godfather's son. People withdrew from participation in the centre, which was soon closed down except for occasional use. By the middle of 1968, though the poverty war was still being fought, the flurry in this Appalachian valley was essentially over. There was little question but that the poor had lost.[20]

The national response to the failure of these reform attempts has been a shift in concern from poverty, remedied through full participation of the poor, to development, achieved through planning by a professional élite. For Appalachia, the Appalachian Regional Commission (ARC), with a staff of over 100 headquartered in Washington, was created to direct 'a combined federal and state effort to solve the region's problems'. Locally, seventy development districts—multicounty planning units—were set up to chart the growth of 397 Appalachian counties.

Both the ARC and development districts alike have been criticized for taking the politics of poverty further away from the region's poor. Issues like those in the Clear Fork Valley have failed to appear on the agendas of these extra-local governmental institutions, just as they did at the county courthouse. As the *Courier Journal*, Kentucky's largest paper, has written, the ARC has evaded 'the whole question of economic colonialism—perhaps most serious since absentee ownership and control of Central Appalachia's one-industry coal economy is the tap root of the area's problems'. It has 'failed in Central Appalachia where success was desperately needed'.[21]

Theoretically, the new professionals of the Appalachian Regional Commission are accountable to the governors of the Appalachian States, and the staffs of the development

[20] A more complete account of a similar pattern in another Appalachian community may be found in Perry, *They'll Cut Off Your Project*, op. cit.
[21] *Courier Journal* (11 April 1973).

districts to the elected officials in their areas. But where pluralism at the local level, as in the Clear Fork Valley, fails to exist, the elected boards serve as legitimators of the planners' actions. For instance, when confronted as to why the development district for sixteen east Tennessee counties had not dealt with problems caused by the corporate coal owners, its director replied, 'The local election is coming up. That's where you ought to be working to get your concerns represented.' He added about the Clear Fork Valley:

I've been kind of appalled up there. . . . They tell me horror stories about local government, about how local government is unresponsive to their needs, and I say 'O.K. run for county court, damn it, throw the bastards out'—And nothing happens.[22]

The reasons, he argued, for the inaction were the 'greater apathy' of rural areas, perhaps due 'to the origins of the people of the area' or the 'we–they attitudes' emerging from union struggles. His attitude, as the very structure for his accountability, failed to recognize that electoral non-challenge may be a function of the power situation in which the relatively powerless find themselves.

In the later 1970s, this method of attempting to solve local problems through multicounty or regional planning efforts has been exported to parts of the country other than Appalachia. Health Systems Agencies have been set up. A bill proposing development districts across the nation has been introduced in the Senate. Regional energy authorities have been discussed. By policy makers and political scientists alike, the trend is applauded for offering new opportunities for creative federalism and rational planning. But if the politics of Claiborne County are any indication, these programmes take place in fields of power controlled by local élites, who have the ability to exclude certain issues and participants from the local political process. If the building blocks for the new governmental forms are themselves faulty, then the new forms need not imply greater responsiveness to the needs of local communities. In fact, they probably place decision-making further away from the local non-élites, while adding to the mobilization of bias new forms of maintaining and legitimating important non-issues.

[22] Meeting in Knoxville, 22 October 1974 and interview 8 January 1975.

7

POWER WITHIN THE ORGANIZATION: REFORMISM AND ANTI-REFORMISM IN THE UNITED MINE WORKERS OF AMERICA

On 31 December 1969 a reform candidate for the presidency of the United Mine Workers of America (UMWA), Joseph (Jock) Yablonski, his wife and daughter were murdered in their home near Clarksville, Pennsylvania. The murder came only three weeks after Yablonski had been defeated in his bid to oust the incumbent president of the union, W.A. (Tony) Boyle. It was the culmination, courts later found, of a conspiracy by Boyle, other union officials and union members to destroy their opposition. And it was the beginning of a long series of further efforts by the insurgents, the Miners for Democracy, for reform within the UMWA.

The struggle for power within the organization raises important questions for the study of rebellion and quiescence. During the 1950s and 1960s the union leadership had become increasingly dictatorial and corrupt in caring for the interests of the membership. Yablonski, and, following his murder, the Miners for Democracy, sought to bring rank and file control to the union, to clean up its corruption, and to begin more militant action on issues of health, safety and wages of the men. Rather than supporting the insurgents, however, the miners in an around the Clear Fork Valley—the area known as District 19—remained loyal supporters of Boyle and actively worked to oppose the reform movement. In the 1969 election, though Yablonski managed to get 36 per cent of the votes throughout the nation, he received only 2 per cent in this district, the lowest of any district in the country. In a new election in 1972, following intervention by the Department of Labor as well as widespread publicity of corruption amongst the union leadership, Arnold Miller, the new reform candidate, received 55 per cent of the miners' votes overall, but only 19 per cent from the coal regions of north-eastern Tennessee and south-eastern Kentucky. Moreover, District 19 was the area to which Boyle turned to develop his conspiracy to murder Yablonski: the three top district officials and a local union president were convicted for their part in the plot, while dozens of other men were questioned as knowledgeable witnesses in the ensuing trials.

The cursory picture that emerges is not only one of rank and file support of an undemocratic and corrupt regime, but also one of active opposition by the membership to a movement for greater participation, equality and militance within their organization. Why?

As in broader questions of social or political power, an answer is dependent upon the level of analysis of power relationships, each of which is 'ineradicably evaluative.'[1] A first-dimensional approach might conclude that the voiced support to the Boyle regime, as reflected in the voting patterns, meant consensus of the men to the *status quo* within the union. The second-dimensional approach to power might discover that there were grievances which were blocked from expression in the voting arena—as indeed there were. Yet, as will be seen, even when a more open process was maintained by Department of Labor supervision, 81 per cent of District 19 miners apparently still voted against more opportunity for voice in the governance of their own affairs. Rather than accept these conclusions, the third-dimensional approach would ask whether the power of the regime might have been used to shape the apparent consensus to it of the non-élite. If such a situation were found to be the case, then the view might be put forward that the apparent consensus against democracy might, in fact, represent proof of the need for greater democracy within the organization—i.e. a democracy that would limit the power of the élite to preclude opposition and to shape beliefs in its own legitimacy at the expense of the interests of the membership.

This chapter will analyse power within the organization by using each approach—that of the first, second and third dimensions. The conclusion will be presented that the first two approaches prove insufficient, while the third approach provides a more complete methodology for interpreting the

---

[1] See Lukes, *Power,* op. cit., p. 1; and earlier discussion, Chapter 1.

working-class anti-reformism that was seen within the union.[2]

7.1 A THEORETICAL NOTE: MICHELS RECONSIDERED

Before turning to the empirical work, a brief comment should be made about an early and important contribution to the theory of power within the organization. Robert Michels's *Political Parties*. The work is significant to this study not only for what it says but also because of a contradiction within it, the resolution of which may contribute understanding to the third dimension of power.

Michels is known, of course, for his development of the Iron Law of Oligarchy in reference to voluntary organizations, most significantly reform or revolutionary associations seeking to alter 'aristocratic power'.[3] The initial need for strong leadership within the organization leads to the adoption of 'militaristic ideas and methods'.[4] In attempting to build power to combat the external situation, the reform organization develops oligarchic tendencies, such as monopolization by leaders over finances, communications, and the bureaucratic apparatus itself, limiting the participation of the membership.[5] The oligarchic power in turn has effects upon the consciousness of the powerholders, leading to a belief in their own superiority: 'The consciousness of power always produces vanity or undue belief in personal goodness.'[6] Not only does oligarchy derive from the 'tactical and technical necessities' of political aggregates but the 'explanation of the oligarchial phenomenon which results is partly *psychological*: oligarchy derives that is to say from the psychical transformations which the leading personalities in the parties

---

[2] For background material on the national leadership and the reform movement, I have benefited from Brit Hume, *Death and the Mines* (Grossman Publishers, New York, 1971); Joseph Finley, *The Corrupt Kingdom* (Simon and Schuster, New York, 1972), and McAteer, *Coal Mine Health and Safety*, op. cit., especially pp. 37–103. The material on District 19 is drawn mostly from primary sources including interviews with miners; previously closed United Mine Workers archives (cited as UMWA Files), including correspondence and documents; and extensive transcripts and documents relating to the Yablonski murder trials, especially as found in *Commonwealth of Pennsylvania* v. *W. A. Tony Boyle* (1974) and *Commonwealth of Pennsylvania* v. *Wm. J. Prater* (1972), to be cited, unless otherwise indicated, as *Trial Files*.

[3] Robert Michels, *Political Parties* (Jarrold and Sons, London, 1915), pp. 3–14.
[4] ibid., pp. 46–9.
[5] ibid., 99–144.   [6] ibid., p. 219.

undergo in the course of their lives'.[7] In an interesting way, then, Michels presents a three-dimensional approach to understanding the impact that power within the organization may have upon the organization's powerholders. Once having prevailed in the decision-making of the organization (first dimension), the leaders develop barriers for the exclusion of certain participants and issues (second dimension), having a further effect upon their consciousness of their own power (third dimension). (Refer back to Figure 1.1.)

What is often overlooked in Michels though, is his notion of the contribution made by the psychology of the masses to the 'Iron Law'. Oligarchy develops not only because of the tendencies of leadership but also because of the innate acquiescence of the non-élite themselves. There is a political indifference of the masses, an 'immense need for direction and guidance', and an 'incapacity for acting'.[8] Moreover, the 'gratitude felt by the crowd for those who speak on their behalf'[9] and their 'profound need to prostrate themselves . . . to pay adoring worship' to 'temporal divinities', are 'the more blind in proportion as their lives are rude'.[10] There develops among the masses a 'cult of veneration'[11] of the led for their leaders, a 'messianism' which regards 'leaders as heroes'.[12] Indeed, the 'incompetence of the masses is almost universal throughout the domain of political life and this constitutes the most solid foundations of the power of the leaders'.[13]

What Michels fails to do is to show why the psychology of the masses is 'inherent' while the psychology of the leaders develops from their own power situation. That is to say, while Michels examines the effects of power upon the wants and values of the powerful, he does not allow for similar effects upon the powerless. The failure leads to a contradiction within Michels's work, for the political indifference of the masses cannot be 'universal'[14] if also the 'desire to dominate, for good as for evil, is universal'.[15] What might be used from Michels to explain the indifference among some but not among others is this insight: 'He who has

---

[7] ibid., p. 248.   [8] ibid., p.59.   [9] ibid., p. 66.
[10] ibid., p. 73.   [11] ibid., p. 69–70.   [12] ibid., p. 58.
[13] ibid., p. 92.   [14] ibid.   [15] ibid., p. 219.

acquired power will almost endeavour to consolidate it and extend it, to multiply the ramparts which defend his position and to withdraw himself from the control of the masses.'[16] Not only might such ramparts include barriers, serving to exclude the voice of the membership, but they may also include a constructed sense of powerlessness, allowing direct and indirect forms of the shaping of perceptions. Indeed, if the fact of power amongst the leaders produces 'consciousness of power' that is re-enforcing to the drive to control in the leaders, then the fact of powerlessness of the non-élite may also produce a 'consciousness of powerlessness', that is re-enforcing to the acquiescence of the led.

The growth of autocracy within the UMWA under John L. Lewis and his immediate successors provides a classic example, to which allusions are often made, of Michels's theory of the development of organizational oligarchy.[17] What, though, has been the impact of oligarchy upon the mass within the organization, and how is that impact analysed in the three approaches to the study of power?

7.2 THE ONE-DIMENSIONAL APPROACH

The pluralist methodology assumes a consistency between the benefits reflected in the decisions of the organization and the recognition of those benefits by the potential actors whose interests are affected. If outcomes are favourable to a potential actor's conception of his interests, then he is expected to respond either by quiescence or by expression of consent; if unfavourable, he is expected to voice opposition, as well as to be able to make his grievances heard. With reference to the miners of District 19 and the performance of their leaders in the UMWA, several conclusions might be drawn from this methodology on the basis of voting and decision-making data:

a) The lack of conflict within the key decision-making arena, the International Executive Board, and the lack of expressions of grievance by the representatives on the Board from District

[16] ibid.
[17] See for instance, in S. M. Lipset, 'The Political Process in Trade Unions', in Galenson and Lipset, eds., *Labor and Trade Unionism* (John Wiley and Sons, New York, 1960), pp. 216–42.

19 reflected a harmony between the benefits of the Boyle regime and the interests of the members in the District.[18]

b) The overwhelming support of the Boyle regime, as expressed in a 98 per cent vote by the miners in 1969 and an 81 per cent vote in 1972 indicates, too, a rank and file consensus to the actions of the Boyle regime, as being consistent with the membership's conceptions of their interests.

c) The fact that the support was significantly greater in this district than in any other suggests that the benefits allocated by the union leadership were more favourable to this population than to any other population of miners in the union.

One can assess the plausibility of these conclusions by comparing the miners' conceptions of their interests to the benefits reflected in the decisions of the organization. If the two are relatively synonymous, then, in fact, the pluralist methodology in the situation may be appropriate. If, however, there is a significant gap between perceived interests and objectively measured outcomes, one may suspect the expressed 'consensus' of the miners to the regime to involve other dimensions of power.[19]

Interviews with miners and participation in various union affairs in the Clear Fork Valley and other parts of District 19 reflect a relative unanimity amongst the rank and file about the criteria for assessing the union's performance in representing the miners' interests. Generally, they have to do with 1) job security over time; 2) overall union strength; 3) health and pension benefits; 4) safety and workplace conditions and 5) wage and fringe benefits. Feelings about this form of unionism are intensely held, and there are few other conceptions of the role to be played by the union, such as there might be with syndicalism or revolutionary unionism. In a summary fashion, a measurement may be made of the extent to which the United Mine Workers' leadership from the middle 1950s to the election of 1969 'delivered' upon these interests.

[18] Based on Review of 'Minutes of the International Executive Board', 1955-72, United Mine Workers of America.

[19] By taking the approach of measuring outcomes in relation to expressed interests, rather than objective interests to perceived outcomes, I am still within the broadly pluralist arena. 'Who prevails' or 'who benefits' can be measured; the problem of imputing interests is avoided.

1) *Job Security over time.* In 1947 the number of jobs in unionized mines in District 19 had reached a high of 20,000. After the war, the number decreased rapidly, so that in 1964 there were only 4,589 miners' jobs in the district. This loss of jobs in the Southern Appalachias was to a degree due to structural factors such as mechanization and post-war decline in demand for coal. However, a series of complicated court cases have held that responsibility rested at least in part in the policies of John L. Lewis and the leadership of the UMWA—policies of conspiring to aid the development of mechanized larger companies at the expense of driving the smaller owners of the Southern Appalachian region out of business.[20]

At the end of the war, Lewis and the larger coal operators reached the conclusion that there were too many men employed in the coal industry to obtain optimum efficiency and benefits for those that were needed. Their response was to negotiate contracts and private deals whereby favourable conditions were obtained for fewer men in the larger companies, while unfavourable demands were made upon the small companies, thus making them non-competitive. For instance, the UMWA allowed some companies 'sweetheart contracts' while pressing claims for payment of royalties upon others; it provided loans to certain companies from the union-owned National Bank of Washington; and it even went so far as to buy controlling interests in one coal company which then negotiated sub-market prices with the Tennessee Valley Authority, leading to lower prices being paid to the smaller suppliers in the area.

Though Lewis's position may have benefited miners in other areas, the effect upon the job situation of the miners of Southern and Central Appalachia was clearly disastrous. In a few short years an era of underground mining was laid waste, and the consequent effects of unemployment, out-migration, and transformation of workplace structure are

[20] The three key cases were *Ramsey* v. *UMWA, Lewis* v. *Pennington,* and *Southeast Coal Co.* v. *UMWA.* Summaries of these and their significance are found in T. N. Bethell, 'Conspiracy in Coal', in *Washington Monthly* (Mar. 1969) reprinted by Appalachian Movement Press (Huntington, West Virginia); Finley, *op. cit.,* pp. 159–77; Hume, *op. cit.,* pp. 22–7; and McAteer, *op. cit.,* pp. 92–7.

still being felt throughout the region, as they are in the Clear Fork Valley.

2) *General Union Strength.* Particularly amongst the older miners who fought the organizing battles of the 1930s, a general notion of maintenance of the organizational strength of the union is an important policy to be pursued by union leadership. However, the effects of the 1950s policies created a situation ripe for non-unionism and even 'company' unionism. Relatively few employees per mine and high unemployment made the miners more susceptible to company threats against union membership. Large numbers of mines dispersed any union organizing drives, while strict Taft-Hartley laws made any activities that might resemble secondary boycotts illegal and expensive. The requirements of the Protective Wage Agreement Clause in 1958 and suits by the union to collect royalty payments from small operators caused more of the UMWA contracts in the region to be broken. A major and often violent organizing drive in 1959 had little effect in countering non-unionism. In fact, there developed at the same time the Scott County Miners Union, later known as the Southern Labor Union (SLU), a company-dominated workers' association which provided workers with few benefits but gave to operators legal protection from UMWA organizing attempts. A special committee of the International Executive Board of the UMWA found in 1961 that there were only 3,305 dues-paying UMWA members in the District while there were 2,606 non-union miners. Where District 19 had been almost completely unionized at the end of the Second World War, by 1964, of 254 mines in the district only fifty had contracts with the UMWA. Despite a few letters to local officers from national officers expressing 'astonishment' at the extent of the SLU's control in the area, little was done about the growth of non-unionism at either district or national level. The hegemony of the UMWA in this region—for which the miners had so vigorously fought —was broken.

3) *Pension and Welfare Benefits.* One of the greatest contributions of 'John L.' in the eyes of the Appalachian miners was the establishment of the Welfare and Retirement

Fund, a trusteeship providing pension and health benefits to retired and working miners.[21] With the ageing work force and declining employment in the southern coalfields, the pensions were vital to the well-being and even survival of many miners. Moreover, in this region where health conditions are among the worst in the country, a health card giving free medical treatment for all UMWA miners and their families, plus a chain of Appalachian Miners' Hospitals, provided some of the most valued benefits of union membership.

However, under the Boyle regime the policies of the Welfare and Retirement Fund seemed to begin to discriminate against the Southern Appalachian miner. By 1969, the Fund's management was riddled with squander and mismanagement. The major aspects of the Fund's failure to provide its potential benefits to the miner may be summarized as follows:

a) A series of decisions by the trustees of the fund gradually limited the health care benefits that John L. Lewis had provided. The result of the decisions was that men who had been forced out of jobs in the 1950s and who had then fought to prevent the development of company unionism found that their 'reward' was the loss of their union benefits. Moreover, in 1962, the Miners' Hospitals were suddenly sold, after being in operation for only six years.

b) Another series of decisions affected pension benefits for older miners. In 1961, the pension was cut from $100 per month to $75, because of deficits in the Fund's operations. In 1965 it was raised to $85, but the requirements were modified to state that a miner must have worked twenty years with the *last year in a union mine*. Men who had worked for union mines most of their lives until forced to take non-union work because of growing non-unionism in the district, found themselves ineligible to draw pensions, regardless of past service to their union.

c) The above cuts in benefits occurred while the Fund was being mismanaged. A lawsuit filed in August 1969 by seventy union members and their families brought some of the failures

[21] Established in 1950, the Fund receives royalty payments on each ton of coal mined by UMWA signatory companies. Responsibility for the funds is vested in a three-person trusteeship consisting of a union representative, an industry representative, and a 'neutral' trustee.

to public attention. The decision handed down by Judge Gesell of the District of Columbia Federal District Court found that for a twenty-year period the Fund had kept non-interest-bearing cash deposits in amounts ranging from $14,000,000 to $70,000,000 in the National Bank of Washington (in which the union owned 74 per cent of the voting stock). As a result, the complainants charged, the Fund had lost a minimum of between $2,000,000 and $5,000,000 a year. Moreover, the money of the Welfare Fund that had been invested had been so mismanaged as to lose nearly $10,000,000 on a $44,000,000 portfolio. A close, interlocking relationship between the officers of the Bank, the Fund and the union had allowed the union's officers to use the Fund for their own purposes. As a result, the court determined, the Fund had been used 'in disregard of the best interests of the beneficiaries'.[22]

d) The losses to the pensioners resulting from the misuse and mismanagement of the Fund were offset somewhat by a single gain. On 24 June 1969, only a few weeks before the election and only one day after he had replaced Lewis as union trustee of the Fund, Boyle declared a $35 a month increase in the monthly pension. The move was challenged by the reform forces as an irresponsible political manoeuvre to gain votes. The court later found it had been taken in 'unnecessary haste', without adequate consultation amongst the trustees and without 'adequate regard for the trustees' fiduciary obligations'.[23]

4) *Miners' Conditions and Compensations.* The mining industry of the United States has more fatalities, more disabling accidents, and a higher incidence of pneumoconiosis ('black lung') than that of any other Western industrialized coal-mining nation.[24] Despite that fact, the Boyle regime during the 1960s was doing little to protect the safety of the men or to gain compensation for their disabilities.

The attitude of the union leadership was revealed following

[22] *Blankenship* v. *Boyle*, 329 F. Supp. 1089 (1971), p. 1104.
[23] ibid., p. 1108.
[24] J. Davitt McAteer, 'Safety in the Mines: A Look at the World's Most Hazardous Occupation; A Comparative Study of Coal Mine Health and Safety in Europe and the United States', Center for Study of Responsive Law (Washington, 1971).

the death of seventy-nine miners in Farmington, West Virginia when President Boyle told newsmen and families of the dead, 'As long as we mine coal, there is this inherent danger'; and he added that the Consolidation Coal Company, operators of the mine, was 'one of the best companies to work with as far as cooperation and safety are concerned'. Strikingly different from the belligerent attitude taken by Lewis in earlier years, this stance was indicative of other union inactions upon health and safety.

For instance, though there had been no major safety legislation in the United States since 1952, the Boyle regime did little or nothing to promote further legislation. In fact, the passage of the relatively progressive Coal Mine Health and Safety Act of 1969 was in spite of the union leadership. Senator Harrison Williams, chairman of the Senate Labor and Welfare Committee which considered the bill, remarked, 'the rank and file men wanted the strongest law but the union did not. The union was not as demanding as we (the committee) were. Boyle really waltzed that one; we had to fight him at every turn. What he did was unconscionable in terms of a labor organization.'[25] The union at the time was spending its funds and energies on the Hill as a part of the National Coal Policy Conference, an industry lobbying arm.

Though pneumoconiosis (black lung) had been recognized and compensated as an industrial disease in Great Britain since 1941 and though it similarly affected the work force in the United States, it received little attention there, by the UMWA or anybody else, until 1968. At that time, it was the anger of 43,000 miners in West Virginia that brought the problem to public attention. They went on strike for eighteen days to demand state black lung compensation benefits—but were opposed by union leadership. The Black Lung Assocations that sprang up as pressure groups amongst the rank and file in this campaign later served as key elements in the Miners for Democracy movement.

5) *Wages and Fringe Benefits*. The final criterion left which might offset the above failures of the leadership in

[25] Quoted in McAteer (1973) op. cit., p. 57. The movement for safety legislation was led in Washington by Ralph Nader and Congressman Ken Hechler, of West Virginia.

representing the interests of the miners, as defined by the
miners themselves, is that of wages and fringe benefits. While
there were more advances in this area than in the others, they
were still not very impressive. Between 1958 and 1963 no
new contract was negotiated for the miners. A lawyer for
the UMWA pointed out about Boyle's first negotiated contract in 1964, that though it 'produced the same two dollars
a day wage increase that Lewis had obtained during his last
three sessions, it still had no paid holidays, a benefit enjoyed
under almost every other union contract in the country in
the U.S.'.[26] In 1968, following the first authorized strike
over a contract in seventeen years, and in a time of relative
profits for the industry, the miners received an 'immediate
three dollar raise to $30·25 a day' and 'two subsequent
raises to $34·25 a day by 1970'.[27] There were more fringe
benefits, though the royalty rate to the Fund remained the
forty cents per ton negotiated by Lewis in the 1950s.

Thus, while the miners were receiving a small increase in
wages, other interests were being neglected in the areas of
job security, general union strength, welfare and retirement
benefits, and safety conditions—especially for the miners in
the Southern Appalachian region. Meanwhile, though, the
interests of others were gaining—namely those of the UMWA
leadership and the coal industry itself.

For instance, President Boyle and the union's treasurer
Owens made comfortable salaries of $50,000 and $40,000 a
year respectively. In addition, they had handsome expense
accounts and extended their benefits through patronage:
Boyle's daughter made $43,288 a year as the union attorney
in Boyle's home state of Montana, one of the smallest mining
districts of the country. A brother of Boyle and two sons of
Owens were generously worked into the payroll. Eleven days
before the union election, a Labor Department audit of the
UMWA's financial affairs revealed that the top officials had
authorized expenditures in violation of the union constitution,
that an unnamed official had been charging his vacation to

---

[26] Finley, op. cit., p. 253.
[27] Hume, op. cit., pp. 71–2.

the UMWA for years, and that there was improper reporting on loans of union funds totalling $1·4 million dollars.

The policies of the UMWA during the late 1950s and 1960s reflected a general tendency towards a business unionism, often of more benefit to the industry than to the membership. The coal industry was a sick industry when Lewis made his decision to support the larger mechanized mines. By 1967 the industry had recovered—but the union had not. As the McAteer study shows, the union's policies were 'many times more oriented toward the production of coal than improvements of conditions of the miners'.[28]

How, then, at this one-dimensional level of power analysis, can one interpret the apparent quiescence of the miners to their condition? The acquiescence was by no means universal, as indicated by the miners' rebellion to the contract in 1964, the West Virginia Black Lung Movement in 1969, and the emergence of the Yablonski candidacy itself. But the miners of District 19, whose interests were perhaps most negatively affected by union policies, expressed the greatest support to the regime. Why?

One response that the pluralist approach might take would be to suggest that since the leadership did manage to increase wages (even though incrementally) the consensus indicated satisfaction of the miners with the gains in standard of living found in business unionism. The relative poverty of the Southern Appalachian area made miners there all the more happy with the increasing wages. But this explanation will not do. Whereas 87 per cent of the pensioners nationally voted for Boyle in 1969, only a bare majority of the workers —whose wages had been increased—gave him their support. And in District 19, the only votes opposing Boyle came from the working locals. Thus, Boyle received the least support from the working populations who benefited from the wage increases, and the most from the retired miners who did not.

For the retired miners, one could argue similarly: that the 30 per cent pensions increase made by Boyle shortly before the election gained their support. Yet, as was found by the courts, the move was actually unsound, and affected at best

[28] McAteer, (1973) op. cit., p. 101.

only the miners' short-term interests. Moreover, it was a group of seventy West Virginia miners and their families who made the point that, 'It is all too obvious that *increased benefits to various classes of disabled and retired mine workers could have been granted in the past.*'[29] Past losses, one could equally argue, should have been thought to offset the single gain.

If no basis can be found for the apparent consensus with the strict use of this approach, another alternative for the pluralists (one we have often seen used) would be to explain the apparent inconsistencies between what the leaders did and how the miners responded, in terms of the apathy, ignorance, isolation, etc. of the miners. Apart from the fact that this would be an unproven assumption, it would also be taking the élitist stance the pluralists sought to avoid, by suggesting that while the miners must recognize their own interests, they cannot recognize when these are being acted upon. In such a situation, in which the objective measurement of benefits contradicts the subjective definition of their own interests by those affected, it is incorrect either to accept the apparent consensus or to explain it away by blaming it upon the victims. Rather, it is precisely in such a case that the analyst must move away from the measurement of conflict in the committee room and the ballot box to an investigation of the possibilities that the second and third dimensions of power may be 'lurking behind' the apparent acquiescence of the led to their leaders.

7.3 THE TWO-DIMENSIONAL APPROACH

Any approach that had sought the opinions of the rank and file miners themselves would have known, of course, that the imputing of their consensus to the situation would have been invalid. The miners recognized their grievances—that their jobs were being lost, that the union was declining, that their pension and health benefits were being taken away, and that their conditions were not safe—after all, they were the ones who daily suffered the consequences of the corruption and defaults of the national leadership.

[29] From complaint filed in *Blankenship* v. *Boyle* Civil No. 2186 (D.D.C. August 6, 1969). Also quoted in McAteer, (1973), op. cit. p. 90.

In the 1960s, letters to the UMWA office in Washington, often hand-scrawled, pleading, sometimes angry, show in a poignant fashion the extent of the growing dissatisfaction with the state of the union in the south-eastern Kentucky and north-eastern Tennessee coalfields. These letters received little response.

It was grievances such as these that Jock Yablonski, a disillusioned member of the International Executive Board, set out to remedy in announcing his candidacy on 29 May 1969. Speaking in a guarded press conference in Washington's Mayflower Hotel, he said his challenge was out of a 'deep awareness of the insufferable gap between the union's leadership and the working miners that has bred neglect of miners' needs and aspirations . . . In recent years, the present leadership has not responded to its men, has not fought over their health and safety, has not improved grievance procedures, has not rooted itself in the felt needs of its membership, and has rejected democratic procedures, freedom of dissent and the right of rank and file participation in the small and large issues that affect the union.'[30]

Why did the grievances of the miners not translate themselves into support for the Yablonski challenge? Why did the growing unrest remain latent? The second-dimensional approach looks at the blockages that prevent grievances from emerging into overt conflict within the organization.

Of course, the previous approach, with its assumptions of an open decision-making arena was something of a 'straw man' exercise. The UMWA was not a democratic organization, even in principle, and in practice it had developed an apparatus of oligarchy that serves to organize into consideration matters of consensus, and to organize out matters of complaint. Elements of the apparatus may be seen in the representative, the consultative, and the electoral relationship of the leaders to their constituents.

The Representative Relationship. The 1933 rebellion of miners in District 19 for more rank and file control in their union was examined in Chapter 4. In the late 1960s, this district, like twenty-one others in the union, still continued

[30] Quoted in Hume, op. cit., p. 173.

as a 'provisional district', without rights of autonomy. Though
the members were represented on the union's governing
body, the International Executive Board, by the president,
secretary-treasurer and another delegate from the district,
these representatives were appointed by the union president,
not elected by the membership.

This top-down representative relationship gave the hierarchy the capacity to repel grievances by more means than
might be seen in the line relationships of authority in the
organization. At district level, the union officers played the
role of brokers of a variety of benefits and reprisals much as
that played by the local corporate élites in the political
process. (See previous chapter.) They served as mediators
between bureaucracy and rank and file, companies and
work force. There developed a relationship of fear—one that
served to preclude complaints—between the men and their
district officers, who could be ruthlessly arbitrary in the
dispensation of positive or negative sanctions involving
hospital cards, pensions, union positions, even jobs. At the
same time, there continued among the rank and file a loyalty
to the national leaders, with whom there was little daily
contact. Letters to the national officers during the 1960s—
many of which were anonymous or contained the request
that the identity of the writer not be revealed to the district
officers—voiced the fear of the lower level of the hierarchy,
and its faith in the upper level to provide assistance in sorting
out the district's affairs. Most of the letters received the reply
that grievance procedures started at district level. They were
usually referred back to the very person they had sought to
avoid, Albert Pass, the secretary-treasurer, whose reputation
amongst the local miners was of a man 'you had better not
get in the way of'.

When dissent did develop—as it did with the emergence of
the Yablonski candidacy—the combination of non-account-
ability and fear in the representative relationship could be
used to mobilize support for the oligarchy from the more
dependent elements of the organization. In the Yablonski
murder and the ensuing attempts at cover-up, the linkages
between the levels of the hierarchy and the consequent
accumulative nature of power are dramatically seen.

On 23 June 1969, just under a month after Yablonski had announced his candidacy, Tony Boyle stepped out of a meeting of the International Executive Board in which a fiery confrontation had taken place between the two candidates. According to later court testimony, he said to Albert Pass, 'We are in a fight. We have to kill Yablonski or take care of him.' Pass, a Lewis-appointee, was himself intent, according to some, on becoming UMWA president. He had plenty of reason to court Boyle's favour, and responded, 'If no one else will kill him, District 19 will.'[31]

Though not so much of a moving force, in normal times or in the murder plot, Turnblazer, the District 19 president, went along with the plan. Both he and his father had the union hierarchy to thank for their positions. Later, when in Kentucky to make a speech, Boyle called at Turnblazer's home and commented, 'you've got a fairly nice home; don't let Yablonski take it away from you'—a comment construed by Turnblazer as a threat that the actions against Yablonski should be carried out, if he did not want to lose his livelihood.[32]

Neither Pass nor Turnblazer would carry out the plan themselves, but they could mobilize the resources of the organization to compel others to do so. Pass turned to a field worker in the north-eastern Tennessee area, fifty-four-year-old Bill Prater. The son and grandson of miners, a long-time organizer who had led the organizing drives against the Southern Labor Union in the early 1960s, Prater was highly regarded by the men as one of the fairest and hardest-working officials they had. His involvement would later surprise many of them. But Prater himself described, 'Albert knew of my intense loyalty to the UMW of A, and also I had done things previously that he requested me to do . . .'[33] He added, as Turnblazer had, a suggestion of threat. 'During this period of time, the atmosphere in District 19 was one of fear; fear that jobs would be lost due to the lack of successful organizing activities . . . Threats to that effect had been made by Albert Pass.'[34]

Prater, in turn, moved down the hierarchy and approached Silous Huddleston, a sixty-three-year-old retired miner, a

[31] Turnblazer in *Boyle Trial,* vol. 11, p. 176.
[32] Turnblazer in *Boyle Trial,* vol. 11, p. 178.
[33] Prater in *Boyle Trial,* vol. 9, p. 161.   [34] ibid., p. 164.

trusted friend, and president of local union 3228, a twenty-three-member pensioners' local, in Lafollette, Tennessee. Huddleston, too, was loyal to the union, and his loyalty had been encouraged in the past by the granting of some lucrative committee posts at International conventions. It was not difficult for the hierarchy to convince Huddleston that the new man, Yablonski, 'was going to destroy the United Mine Workers and the things I had fought for all my life, the things all the old men had fought for . . .'.[35]

Huddleston, in turn, contacted his daughter and son-in-law, Annette and Paul Gilly, Appalachian migrants to Cleveland, to carry out the actual job. The Gillys recruited two other unemployed urban Appalachians to assist them. With the use of 'loans' from the International, a secret fund of $19,920 designated as 'organizing expenses' was set up in District 19 to reward the assassins. In addition, Paul Gilly was told by Prater that he would see that his father, a disabled coal miner, received his union pension which had previously been denied.

For the 'loans' from the International to be transformed into cash to pay the assassins, an elaborate 'kick back' scheme was developed. It involved other field organizers and twenty-two pensioners, not initially aware of the actual use of the money. Pass called the field officers into his office and said that the names of the most trusted men in the area were needed for a Research and Information Committee. The purpose of the committee, the organizers were told, was to gather information on non-union operations, to help locate black lung victims, and, according to Pass, to 'preach the gospel of the union'.[36] The pensioners of this important—but mythical—committee were then approached by the organizers and taken to banks to cash cheques for their 'services' on the committee. The money was returned, through the organizers, to Pass and Prater to pay the gunmen. The pensioners were told that the money was being 'kicked back' to be used to defeat William Bell, an organizer of the company-oriented Southern Labor Union, who was running for judge in Bell county. Their obedience in carrying out

[35] Huddleston in *Prater Trial,* vol. 2, pp. 733–4.
[36] Pass in *Prater Trial,* vol. 4, p. 517.

instructions from officers was only the repetition of a long-instilled pattern of loyalty and duty without asking questions. As one of the pensioners testified, 'This here judge was in opposition, the fellow that was running for judge was in opposition to our union. I thought I was helping my union by doing this, helping our organization.'[37]

In actuality, of course, the money was being used to finance a sordid plot to murder Yablonski. After the murder, when law enforcement agents surged into the district, the organizers and pensioners were again reminded by a representative of the union hierarchy of the story they were to tell. Gradually, as the men realized that the money may not have been used for what they had been told, a choice developed between protection of the union hierarchy or co-operation with the law. Again, the power that linked together the levels of the organization showed its strength. The men unanimously lied, to the FBI and to the Grand Jury, about how they had 'spent' the money they had never really received.

At later trials, at various levels in the chain of command, testimony revealed the reasons for perjury. Turnblazer, the president of the district, said, 'The only reason that I can give for agreeing to this false testimony was self-protection and fear of Tony Boyle's wrath.'[38] Prater, in turn, said of Pass, 'his powers of persuasion are great'.[39] While other district organizers elaborated:

District Organizer 1: . . . I would say that Mr. Pass ruled with an iron hand. I knew that if I disobeyed his orders that I would have no job. That was in my mind . . .[40]

District Organizer 2: I knew that if I told the truth that I would in all probability lose my job.[41]

The pensioners, who at that point had nothing to hide from the law, testified as to why they had complied with the union:

Pensioner 1: A. Well, I thought I had to you see.
　　　　　　 Q. Why did you think you had to?
　　　　　　 A. Well, I was, I've got a hospital card.
　　　　　　 Q. I can't hear you.
　　　　　　 A. I've got a hospital card and draw benefits from the union and I was afraid on that account . . .[42]

[37] President of Local 6927, Clairfield, Tenn., in *Prater Trial*, vol. 2, p. 835.
[38] Turnblazer confession, *Trial Files*, p. 30.
[39] Prater confession, *Trial Files*.　　　[40] *Boyle Trial*, vol. 10, p. 206.
[41] *Boyle Trial*, vol. 11, p. 67.　　　[42] *Prater Trial*, vol. 2, p. 826.

Pensioner 2: Q. Why did you listen to Prater?
A. Well, I was under a fear.
Q. A fear of what?
A. Well, I was expecting my benefits to be cut down.
Q. Your benefits, what?
A. Welfare, hospital . . .[43]

Pensioner 3: A. For the biggest reason, I was afeared I would lose my pension check and my hospitalization . . .
Q. You were trying to protect yourself, is that right?
A. My income. [44]

At the time of these statements, the pensioners had maintained their stories in the face of constant questioning by the FBI for some three years. As witnesses in various inquiries, they had sat sequestered, away from their families for days at a time in strange cities. Wearing their home dress of overalls, keeping to themselves in a group, they had maintained a loyal solidarity, re-enforced by common fear. Yet, during the Prater trial in 1973, they gradually had the feeling that they and their union had been betrayed. In a meeting amongst themselves, one of the pensioners, a Holiness preacher, was particularly adamant that the time had come to tell the truth. In an emotionally charged gathering in their hotel, the men told Prater that they could no longer go along with the story. In his and subsequent trials, in response to questions by lawyers as to why they had now decided to tell the truth when before they had lied under oath, their answers revealed a shift in allegiance to a power greater than that of the union organization:

Pensioner 1: Q. Why have you decided to tell the truth?
A. Because there's a higher power that would hurt me inside I couldn't risk. And I just had to come out and tell the truth.[45]

Pensioner 2: A. . . . It just got to workin' my heart, I couldn't go no further with it.[46]

Pensioner 3: A. . . . God got hold of me and I just couldn't live with it.
Q. Who got hold of you?
A. God.[47]

Pensioner 4: A. Well, I was condemned over what I had done and I had to do something or I couldn't go on. I had to right my wrongs if I could.[48]

[43] *Prater Trial*, vol. 2, p. 845.   [44] *Boyle Trial*, vol. 10, p. 153.
[45] *Prater Trial*, vol. 2, p. 826.   [46] *Boyle Trial*, vol. 10, p. 153.
[47] *Boyle Trial*, vol. 10, p. 121.   [48] *Boyle Trial*, vol. 10, p. 143.

'Lawfully', Michels wrote in beginning his work on the Iron Law, 'the monarchy can be abolished by God alone, and God's will is inscrutable.'[49]

The Consultative Relationship. In addition to the representative relationship between the International Union and the locals, the constitution of the United Mine Workers also provides for an international convention to be held every four years for officers' reports and resolutions from the membership—in theory a forum for the expression of consensus or grievances. In practice, however, the 1964 convention, which convened with Boyle as president, provides a classic study of agenda control.

First, there was control over participants: the miners' convention was held far from the coalfields in the grand meeting centre of Bal Harbour, Florida, making dissidence expensive. Potentially friendly delegates were financially assisted by the International to make the trip, particularly those from some 400 pensioner locals which contained no active members but whose representatives would be well aware of who controlled the Welfare and Retirement Fund. Secondly, there was control over the issue-formulation process: when a local union could not afford to send its representatives to the convention's committees, the administration itself appointed the replacement. Committee members were paid $60 a day for their services and more for expenses. For instance, fifty-two members of the Appeals and Grievance Committee received $1,457 each for their expenses at the ten-day convention, and no appeals or grievances were voted out of committee. A similar process of non-conflict occurred in the fifty-five-man Scale and Policies Committee, the forty-eight-man Order of Business Committee, and a sixty-seven-man Officers' Reports Committee.

Third in the agenda control process was the invocation of supporting norms and rituals. As the miners (and their wives) assembled in the ballroom of the Miami Hotel, they heard two prayers, a speech by the mayor, and a speech by the manager of the hotel—all extolling the virtues of the miner and

[49] Michels, op. cit., p. 3.

his role in the labour movement. An introduction reminded
the convention that Boyle was from a mining background,
had been recruited personally by John L. Lewis into a position
of leadership, and was a humble hard-worker: 'The man
never said "no"; he didn't know how to say "no". You could
pass the building any time of the night, say until midnight
and sometimes later, and you could see the lights lit and his
whole staff working, if it was necessary, to try to keep the
work off the officers in our union and do it himself to
protect this great institution of ours.'[50] After this introduction, a 'spontaneous' demonstration of support for Boyle
lasted forty-seven minutes—to the music of five bands im-
ported especially by Boyle for the occasion, and to the tune
of $390,000 from the union treasury. A flag was presented
to Boyle from his home state of Montana. A large delegation
of miners from eastern Kentucky and Tennessee, each wearing
a white hard hat bearing the insignias of 'Tony Boyle' and
'District 19', presented Boyle with a similar miner's hat.
Boyle rose to speak, asking first for a moment of silence for
Thomas Kennedy, his deceased predecessor, and then saying:

The accomplishments of this administration, as in past administrations,
have been the result of the determined membership of this union which
cooperated with its National officers, ignoring of course, the critics
inside and outside our Union who would weaken or destroy this organization.

I am reminded at this time of some irresponsible people who have
been making irresponsible statements to the press . . . I have read that
there are some people who would return this Union to its membership.
Well, I have only been your president for a little over a year and nine
months and I did not know that I had taken it away from you . . . Take
it away from you? What would I do with it? So, you see, this fellow is
in line with the enemies of organized labor in this country . . .

Boyle concluded his speech by saying, 'we are looking forward
to a harmonious constructive convention', and by expressing
thanks for the previous 'great demonstration of cooperation
and loyalty to this union'.[51]

The tone was thus properly set. The new president himself
could now legitimately preside over the silencing of the

[50] UMWA, *Proceedings of the Forty-Fourth Consecutive Constitutional Convention,* vol. 1, p. 11.
[51] *Proceedings,* pp. 15–16, 19–20.

'enemies of organized labor' who sought to question him. So the fourth technique of agenda control was to ignore objections of parliamentary procedure, such as the fact that the wives were voting by voice with the members: to which Boyle could say, 'I don't think we have to worry too much . . . from the demonstration you saw here this morning, as to the closeness of the votes that might occur . . .'[52]

Finally, force was reserved as the mechanism for dealing with dissent that might manage to break through the other barriers—and it could be authoritatively invoked. District 19 'whitehats' were stationed at the microphones, and the first day of the convention saw the dissidents' volume turned off as these 'ushers' physically beat up critical speakers and 'escorted' them, bleeding, from the convention floor.[53] After this show of force on the first day, the convention proceeded without expression of grievance. The non-critical committee reports were introduced and carried without opposition. The authority of the union élite was re-enforced until the process repeated itself at the next convention in Colorado in 1968.

The Electoral Relationship. With the demonstrative processes of power seen in the union in the past, it is perhaps not surprising that a campaign by an opposition candidate was no easy task. While the prior exercises of power had not been aimed particularly at this candidate, they did have the perhaps unintended consequence of thwarting the support he might have otherwise received. A similar effect would have been to keep Yablonski from entering this Tennessee and Kentucky region, for fear of use of force against his life, similar to that seen in the 1964 convention against other dissidents.

As the electoral challenge to Boyle developed, the first serious challenge to the president of the union in decades, other forms of power within the organization served to ensure that the pattern of non-challenge would not easily be broken. These grew from the mobilization of bias, or control over the resources of the organization by the oligarchy. Their

[52] *Proceedings,* p. 23.
[53] Hume, op. cit., p. 48. No mention in official *Proceedings.*

effectiveness rested in the fact that the insurgents lacked mobilization of counter-resources, and were thus relatively powerless in getting an equal hearing for their viewpoint. Three examples of these overt mechanisms for thwarting electoral opposition within the organization may be demonstrated, while a fourth factor, a set of 'non-decisions', later proved to be the key to the maintenance of Boyle's power.

The first mechanism was Boyle's control over the bureaucracy and its officers. A week after Yablonski announced his candidacy, he was dismissed by Boyle from his post as Acting Director of Labor's Non-partisan League—for not spending enough time on the job. This move also made Yablonski seem an outsider acting with a personal vendetta in his candidacy. However, other personnel of the bureaucracy were mobilized to spend their time working for Boyle's re-election. Inactive pensioner locals were also activated in support of the regime, particularly to get the necessary number of nominations for the candidacy, while Yablonski struggled to recruit personnel and even to find locals willing or able to put his name into the ring.

The second asset of the mobilization of bias was the control by the regime of funding within the organization. Lewis had started the practice of 'loans' to the districts; it had continued under Boyle as a primary means of cultivating support. For instance, in the half-year prior to the 1964 convention in which the District 19 'whitehats' had so visibly demonstrated their loyalty to Boyle, the district had received $661,000 from the International, 'five times as much as any other district and one third of all the money paid to all the districts'.[54] In 1967–8, District 19 received $724,290 in loans, while in 1969, 'loans were increased with particular emphasis on those areas where there was enemy strength'. Yablonski's home district in Pennsylvania, for instance, whose offices were controlled by Boyle men, 'had its quota of money doubled'.[55] Meanwhile, Yablonski and his supporters paid for most of their expenses and small staff out of their own pockets.

Third, and perhaps most important, was monopoly over the means of communication with the members. In the highly dispersed 150,000-member organization, the union's bi-weekly *Journal* was a key to dissemination of information, for it was read religiously in the coalfields. Boyle had always made good use of the instrument as a bit or propaganda—it normally carried extensive coverage of the union hierarchy, with no coverage of dissenting voices, and seemed bound only to the editorial policy of escalating its adulation of the leadership as dissent appeared to be emerging. At the time of some opposition to the 1964 contract, for instance, the 15 May issue had twenty-eight pictures of Boyle in twenty-four pages. A similar pattern held true in this election: five editions of the *Journal* following Yablonski's announcement carried 166 references to and sixteen pictures of Boyle, with no references to or pictures of Yablonski. Similarly, Boyle refused to allow the union to mail any Yablonski literature to the membership, though such was required by the union constitution.

While the incumbents could thus mobilize resources within the organization, the insurgents could only attempt to appeal to a counter-mobilization of bias outside the union. They did so primarily by effective publicity and by the strategic use of legal challenges to eliminate obstacles to participation, calling particularly upon federal laws aimed at guaranteeing internal union democracy. They were successful in getting the courts to re-instate Yablonski in his position, in obtaining coverage in the mineworkers' *Journal,* in getting the union to send a mailing of Yablonski campaign literature to the union members, and, *post facto,* in proving the misuse of union funds for campaign purposes by officials. Yet, Kalis points out, 'A few lawsuits . . . brought by Yablonski were largely unsuccessful in combating the oligarchy at work in the UMW during the 1969 campaign.'[56]

If the power of the oligarchy to contain issues within the organization was thus the key to the outcome of the conflict, equally important were a set of 'non-decisions' founded simply in the inertia of the courts and governmental bureaucracies to which Yablonski appealed. In a sense, the conflict itself

[54] ibid., p. 46.   [55] Finley, op. cit., pp. 245–6.

[56] Peter Kalis, 'Private Litigation and the UMW', *Yale Review of Law and Social Action,* 3 (1972). The summary of the above legal actions is from the Kalis article.

had grown out of a need to counter what had *not* been done by the federal agencies: A Department of Labor suit to get the UMWA to comply with the law by eliminating the 'trusteeship' status of districts had lain dormant for six years. The Department of Labor similarly had not enforced finance reporting clauses of the Labor Management Representatives and Disclosure Act of 1959 (LMRDA), thus allowing corruption to develop and go unnoticed. Yet, when the challenges by Yablonski did come about, and extensive briefs were filed by Attorney Rauh for intervention to guarantee a fair election, the courts denied the requests, declaring that the Secretary of Labor could act only *ex post facto,* not in anticipation of possible miscarriages of justice in the future.[57] And when Yablonski decided to pursue further his challenge for another, fairer election after the first defeat, the failure of the Pennsylvania police to check into Yablonski's reports of a strange car with Tennessee licence plates watching his home, and the general failure to provide him with protection despite requests, contributed to his murder, the final quelling of the dissent. The point is not to suggest collusion between the Boyle regime and the government bodies. It is to argue that non-decisions—what is not done because of institutional neglect or inertia—must be considered as a form of power.

A second-dimensional power analysis suggests, then, that the apparent consensus of the members of District 19 to the incumbents may have been due to the barriers put before the insurgents and their supporters which made the floating of issues, the development of a candidacy and a campaign, and the holding of fair elections difficult or impossible. Indeed, it might be argued that the case is remarkably clear-cut: if Yablonski was unable even to gain access to the potential voters, then it is no wonder that he failed to gain their support. However, this approach, while necessary for the analysis, is not sufficient, for it does not explain two very significant facts in the conflict.

In this case the observer was provided with an unusual control to the power plays found in the first election. Another campaign and election were held in December 1972, after the government had determined the irregularities of the first to

[57] Hume, op. cit., p. 225 and *Yablonski* v. *UMW* 72 L.R.R.M. (D.D.C. 1969).

have been in violation of certain laws. Allegations were made and substantiated by the Department of Labor that 'the union had failed to provide adequate safeguards for a fair election; Yablonski observers were denied entrance to some polling places; the union violated provisions of its constitution; secret balloting was not provided for in all polling places; some members were denied opportunity to vote; money from dues was used to promote Boyle's candidacy; and the union failed to keep public financial records'.[58] The insurgents charged in addition that there had been violence used against Yablonski during the campaign; that Boyle had raised pensions to support his re-election bid; that some 600 local unions were 'bogus' locals composed only of pensioners, contrary to the UMWA Constitution; and that paid employees were campaigning for Boyle.

The second campaign sought to provide guarantees of an open system. Not only was the election supervised by the Department of Labor but the internal conduct and financing of the union was also monitored. Moreover, despite the tragic murder of Yablonski, the insurgents had overcome certain barriers in their own organization. They had formed the Miners for Democracy with a new slate of candidates, headed by Arnold Miller, a retired miner from West Virginia. The Yablonski murder had attracted more publicity and support to the effort; and campaigning was carried out (under armed protection) in District 19 where Yablonski had previously refused to go. The incumbents' oligarchy seemed to be starting to crumble. Among the factors that might have increased the erosion of support for the regime between the first and second elections were the indictment of the officers of District 19 for conspiracy to murder Yablonski, one having already been convicted; abundant, though not yet proven speculation of Boyle's role in the conspiracy; and Boyle himself facing a jail sentence of up to five years for thirteen counts of conspiracy to embezzle funds, and violations of campaign contribution laws. In addition, the Federal District Court had found the UMWA, the Welfare and Retirement Fund, and the union's bank guilty of a breach of trust— and Boyle had been ordered to resign as a trustee of the Fund;

[58] Kalis, op. cit.

and well-publicized Congressional hearings had revealed further corruption within the union regime.

Given the government controls, the development of the organization of the insurgents, and the further revelations of the decay of the regime, Miller's victory by 70,373 votes to Boyle's 56,334 in the second election is not surprising. What does need explanation is that Boyle still received 81 per cent of the votes in District 19—despite all his 'sins' against the union. For the sake of the strict empiricist, one might say that the second dimension of power, as tested in the repeat election, accounted for only a 17 per cent drop in the 98 per cent level of consensus seen in the first contest.

The second factor unexplained by the two-dimensional approach is this: as the opposition to Boyle by Yablonski and then Miller increased, the number of grievances against the regime expressed by the rank and file in District 19 decreased. Unlike the earlier part of the decade when grievances were expressed though ignored, such indicators as correspondence from the rank and file of the area tended in 1969–72 to express hearty support and loyalty to the leadership. This change in attitude plus the 81 per cent support for Boyle at the ballot box despite his proven corruption, suggests the possibility of yet another dimension of power serving to affect the conceptions of the miners of District 19 about the conflict.

7.4   THE THREE-DIMENSIONAL APPROACH

The three-dimensional approach must examine the perceptions of the miners about the conflict and link those perceptions to power processes. On the basis of the model put forward in Chapter 1, two sorts of process may be suspected: a) 'consensus' as an indirect consequence of the miners' power position, that is from a sense of powerlessness; and b) 'consensus' as a more direct consequence of the shaping of cognitions by the powerholders, made more possible by the sense of susceptibility of the relatively powerless.

The indirect forms of consensus shaping grew out of the history of non-participation within the union. As has been seen, for decades democracy within the union had been suppressed. Any participation by membership other than loyalty and obedience had been viewed as a threat, facing numerous barriers, including force. Enforced quiescence over a period of time tended to develop internalized accept-ance of the appropriate relationship of the led to their leaders, expressed in such similes as 'this man Tony Boyle is like Moses leading the children of God from bondage'.[59] Over time, the understanding of the relationship could become so internalized that power could be exercised with-out any specific act on the part of the powerholders. For instance, though the pensioners helped in the cover-up of the Yablonski murder because they feared a loss of benefits if they did not, no overt threat against them to that effect had actually been made. A pensioner testified:

Pensioner 3: Q. Now, did Mr. Prater say that you would lose your pension and your hospitalization if you didn't sign?
A. No, sir.
Q. Did Mr. Prater threaten you at all in any respect if you didn't do what he wanted you to do?
A. No, sir.
Q. But he was a good friend of yours is that right?
A. He was supposed to have been, yes sir.[60]

One is reminded of the description of the ritualized power roles of Ancient China described by Pocock: 'If a man finds himself playing his appointed part . . . it no more occurs to him to play a part other than that appointed to him than it occurs to a dancer to move to a different rhythm that that played by the orchestra.'[61]

But the internalized understanding by the membership of the appropriate relationship to their leaders carried with it a trained scepticism about conflict amongst men at the top. Like Boyle, Yablonski was seen as one of the élite, so that little real distinction was thought to exist between the two candidates. Both had access to power, position and money. Nothing in the historical experience of the powerless made credible the claims that the new leader would be any more accountable or allow any more participation than the old. With no perception of cogent reasons to support one member

[59] *UMWA Files,* letter to Boyle from local union officer, April 1970.
[60] *Boyle Trial,* vol. 10, p. 153.
[61] Pocock, 'Ritual, Language and Power', op. cit., pp. 45–6.

of the union élite over another, but with plenty of knowledge of the possible costs of defying the established regime, it was simply safer for the miners of District 19 to go along with the incumbents. In such a situation votes for Boyle reflected neither consensus nor coercion, but a socially constructed assessment of the costs and benefits in taking sides in what was perceived by the powerless to be inconsequential conflict amongst the powerful.

The choice of 'safety' based on powerlessness within the organization was supplemented by another factor. Despite its internal repressiveness, the union offered a sense of security for the miners and their families within the broader field of power relations—i.e. within the even more hostile and exploitative political economy of the region. Powerlessness within the organization still represented power relative to what might have been the case without it. That dependency allowed, as it had since the initial organization under 'John L.', the hand-in-glove process of shaping into the organization uncritical loyalty while shaping out of it the voicing of challenge. Over time, just as non-participation led to acceptance of the role of non-participant, so, too, would cultivated loyalty lead to its internalization. In the poverty of the Southern Appalachias, for instance, relief could be a chief means of buying allegiance. Even after the benefits had ended, the loyalty it invoked could continue. The pattern may be seen in a 1959 resolution from a destitute coal camp of the Clear Fork Valley:

We the members of the Local Union—, District 19 . . . wish to thank the officers of the National United Mine Workers for the grocery orders we have been receiving through our Local Union and District 19 office.

   Although the grocery orders have been stopped and we still have forty five members not working because some ramps and tipples where the truck mines sold their coal have never signed the present contract with our union, we will still remain loyal to our great union . . . we want to thank you for everything you have done . . .[62]

Where leadership was not to be questioned and exit was not a choice, then loyalty was the only response possible for the powerless.

[62] Letter from local union to Thomas Kennedy, vice president UMWA, 24 October 1959, *UMWA Files.*

Given the normally hostile political environment, government intervention in the second election to protect the miners' rights of expression could also play a role supportive to the regime. From below and afar, it was viewed by the workers as an attack upon their affairs, as harassment by a government in which the miners felt no part and among whose agencies and actors they drew few distinctions. Intervention from outside was considered a threat, as it had been in the past; it demanded—and received—a response of unity amongst the rank and file, and support for the union leaders.

These indirect means by which the powerholders gained support were supplemented by more overt means of shaping perceptions of the emerging conflict. Various myths amongst the miners about Yablonski and the Miners for Democracy developed into beliefs. That they developed and took the particular form they did was no accident. The myths were evoked by the élite and interjected into the situation through their communication with the membership—speeches, the *Journal*, letters, and their agents in District 19. The barriers to other communication from within the organization—i.e. from Yablonski—meant that the regime enjoyed a relative monopoly of the dissemination of information about the conflict. Loyalty within the organization combined with distrust of the media of communication from the broader social environment to cause the myths to be believed. The relationship of the leaders to the led often gave the myths a directive character. Historical experiences and social circumstance added to the symbols in the myths certain emotive meanings. The resulting shaping of cognitions must be considered the product of power. The primary myths at work can be summarized as follows.

1) *Yablonski was financed by coal operators and rich people.* In the first instance, opposition to Yablonski was considered an act of militancy against corporatism and the power of the wealthy. Local miners were told that the reform effort was really a front for coal operators to destroy the union from within. Secretary-treasurer Owens, for instance, argued that the challenge was the result of an 'organized, deliberate policy conceived by anti-union groups and international

corporations that control—three hundred and sixty-five of
them—that control all the corporations in the world, [to]
destroy the United Mine Workers of America . . . the citadel
of the labor movement'.[63] George Titler, vice-president of
the UMWA, specified, writing, 'Yablonski was working for
the biggest coal operator in the world, the Rockefellers. He
travelled in the airplanes of the steel companies. Oil company
lawyers were showering the UMWA with lawsuits.'[64] Silous
Huddleston, a local union president in District 19 convicted
for his part in the conspiracy to murder Yablonski, testified
that he was told 'by the leaders' of the insurgents:

A. (Huddleston) . . . Continental Oil, big oil and gas powers were
    behind them and they intended to bust the union, get rid of it,
    control it . . .
Q. (Lawyer): Does Continental Oil operate out of Kentucky and
    Tennessee?
A. They own coal lands all over the nation or practically all over,
    what don't belong to the steel companies . . .[65]

Another miner wrote to Boyle, 'This old bunch of War
mongers is trying every way they can to destroy us miners
and our union. So, I say, Mr. Boyle—back you and our union
at any cost . . . show these old slavedrivers and murderers
what we want and where we stand.'[66]

2) *The 'instant expert' as 'fink'.* If 'corporations' and
'rich people' are terms of abuse in Appalachia, so too are
middle class, social reformers' ('instant experts') and company
informers ('finks'). Early in 1969, Ralph Nader, the consumer
advocate and Congressman Ken Hechler, a former college
professor, were given the two latter labels when they began
to attack the UMWA leadership for its failures in the areas
of health and safety. The *Journal* ran a special 'Message to
Miners' on its front page which read, in part:

The French have a name for such persons. They are called *agents provocateurs.* Agents provocateurs are secret agents hired to incite others

    [63] Minutes of the IEB, 22 January 1970, p. 302.
    [64] George Titler, *Hell in Harlan* (BJW Printers, Beckley, West Virginia, 1973),
p. 216.
    [65] Huddleston in *Prater Trial,* vol. 11, p. 761. At the time Consolidation had
two large mines in his area of Tennessee. Consolidation Coal is a subsidiary of
Continental Oil, which in turn is partially controlled by Rockefeller investments.
    [66] *UMWA Files,* letter from miner in Baxter, Kentucky, to Boyle, 15 June 1971.

to actions that will make them liable to punishment.

The American Labor movement has a shorter and more concise term for such troublemakers. We call them finks. A fink is a spy, a strikebreaker, an informer and a stool pigeon, among other things.

In our book persons who accuse the United Mine Workers of America and its dedicated International President W.A. Boyle of not doing their jobs in behalf of the health and safety of coal miners are finks. . . .

Don't allow cheap politicians and other 'instant' experts to try to split you away from the leadership of the United Mine Workers of America. The coal operators have tried in the past to their regret.[67]

This message brought response. Numerous letters and petitions of support came back to the International from men in District 19 expressing resentment to the 'false and untrue statements that are being circulated by the Nader click';[68] and saying, 'As for Mr. Nader, we don't like the news he puts out about our leaders and union for he don't know what he is talking about, for you have to be a coal miner to know most of the bad faults of coal mining and conditions of a miner for it is not always peaches and cream as some people think it is.'[69] This line of attack was transferred to the Yablonski candidacy, which received the support of Nader, Hechler, and other liberal outsiders.

3) *Yablonski would take away miners' pensions.* Not all the myths acquired their meaning from the social environment outside the organization. The prior experiences of these miners in the politics of relief in the union made them believe the false claim by the union leadership that Yablonski would take away the miners' pensions. The claim was evidently drawn from Yablonski's plan to integrate pensioner locals with working locals, as was required under the constitution of the UMWA, but it was interpreted by the mediators of that information as something far more threatening. Huddleston's confession of his participation in the murder reflected a belief about Yablonski widely held amongst the pensioners more generally:

Yablonski tried to get all the pensioners out of the union, if the pensioners were out of the union they would not be entitled to their pensions. The pensioners fought to get the benefits the miners now

[67] *UMWA Journal* (1 Feb. 1969).
[68] Resolution from a local union, 12 May 1969. *UMWA Files.*
[69] Letter from miner in Whitwell, Tenn., 10 May 1969. *UMWA Files.*

have, and without their pensions, they might as well be dead. I participated in the plan to murder Yablonski to keep him from destroying the union.[70]

4) *'Outsiders' and 'radicals' seeking to 'destroy our union'.* A final group of abusive terms sought to mobilize the miners on the basis of a general appeal against those who would 'destroy' or 'control' the union. For instance, the 1 October 1972 *Journal* was headlined 'The Radical Left Supports MFD', referring to the favourable stance of the *Daily World, Militant,* and *The Guardian* towards the Miners for Democracy. The editorial continued in language hearkening back to that used by the local élite to interpret the 1930s conflict:

Why are these radicals part of the MFD campaign team? We don't profess to know for sure, but the people who back these papers either want to nationalize (socialize or communize) American coal mines or they want to destroy the UMWA and thus knock down what they call the Establishment: What they really want is to destroy the American form of government. Radicals still believe that the only way this can be started is through control of the labor movement, or second best, by neutralizing it. Coal miners! The Three Stooges are being backed by these people. Why? What have they offered the militant, radical, non-miner left-wingers? These outsiders are bad news for you diggers. Just like the clique of Washington lawyers and foundations, they want to destroy your union.[71]

In another performance, a speech by Boyle and Owen to the International Executive Board, the opposition were attacked at different points as being 'outside people—doctors, lawyers, politicians', 'totalitarian liberals', 'right and left wingers', 'great bleeding hearts', 'traitors to their families' and 'to their country', and 'do-gooders'—all trying to destroy the union.[72] While the outside viewer may find it difficult to take these myths seriously, they were intensely believed—and with good reason—by many of the miners, especially in District 19. Their common factor is the extent to which they were grounded in the powerlessness of the miners, within both their social situation and their organization. The myths had special meaning gained from past experiences of exploitation. They were believed because of the relationship implanted between

[70] Huddleston confession, *Trial Files,* p. 21.

[71] *UMWA Journal* (1 Oct. 1972), used by Ridgeway in 'Politics Mine-Workers Style', *New Republic* (4 Nov. 1972).

[72] Minutes of IEB, 22 January 1970, *UMWA Files.*

the leaders and the led in the process of combating that exploitation. The relationship was well expressed by Silous Huddleston when he was asked why he believed the information:

A. I never heard anybody dispute it.
Q. But you didn't check it out?
A. No, I didn't check it out. I don't have that kind of money. No, member does. That's what they have representatives for . . .
Q. After Mr. Pass told you . . . did you go to Mr. Turnblazer and ask Mr. Turnblazer whether he knew?
A. No, I didn't ask Mr. Turnblazer because you can't expect and see every representative, every secretary-treasurer and on up to the president and everybody.
   If you're not going to believe your leaders you're in pretty bad shape.
Q. You're the kind of fellow that believes your leaders, is that right?
A. Yes, sir, if you don't follow your leaders what use have you got for people? . . . You gotta accept somebody's word. If you don't accept your leaders word, who you going to accept? [73]

Power is accumulative by nature; each dimension serves to re-enforce the others. The patterned dependency of the non-élite plus the effective wielding by the leadership of information about the emerging conflict allowed the élite to shape their own legitimacy, to breed their own consensus.

7.5 CONCLUSIONS

I can now return to the original question of 'Why did the miners of District 19 oppose the potentially favourable reforms and reformers within the organization?'. In the first-dimensional approach, examination has shown that it could not have been simply because they were receiving favourable benefits from the regime. By the miners' own conceptions of their interests, the organization was 'delivering' to other interests, often contradictory or detrimental to their own.

Going outside the formal decision-making arenas, the second approach revealed that the miners did, in fact, have grievances about the organization and its leaders very similar to those being expressed by the reformers. But the grievances were translated neither into issues in the representative and consultative relationships, nor into support for the insurgents.

[73] Huddleston in *Prater Trial*, vol. 11, pp. 759, 762, 764.

In the electoral challenge, bureaucratic blockages, invocation of a supporting mobilization of bias, and non-decisions were all found partially to explain the gap between grievances and apparent action upon them. However, the 81 per cent continued support for the hierarchy, seen in the controlled situation of the second election, still remains unexplained by this approach.

From the third-dimensional perspective, then, opposition to Yablonski and support for Boyle from the miners of District 19 grew from more than non-decisions and blockages to recognized grievances. Rather, it grew from an instilled conception of the appropriate relationship between the leaders and the led. The position of dependency within the union relative to the powerlessness outside it, allowed and encouraged the response of loyalty to the regime when challenge to it occurred. The loyalty was both strengthened by and made the men more susceptible to, belief in information handed to them from the union hierarchy—information consisting of key symbols from past struggles developed into myths for interpreting the internal conflict. Because of the power relationships, expressed grievances against the hierarchy declined as the reformist opposition to the hierarchy increased, even though the reformist platform may have expressed the miners' own wishes.

The consequences of this position are, of course, numerous. If the 'consensus' of the led to their leaders can be a product of power, then non-conflict in the organization need not be evidence of acceptance of the *status quo* by the membership. At least, where its costs are the murder of opposition and the internal exploitation of the rank and file to the extent seen in this chapter, then 'consensus' itself may be evidence of the need for change, i.e. for the institutionalization of democracy within the organization to allow latent conflict more freely and openly to emerge.

By most interpretations of the law, as in behavioural social science, such phenomena as corruption and murder are understood primarily in terms of individuals' actions. Where several people are involved, such as in the Yablonski murder, responsibility may be placed in a conspiracy, consisting of the sum of the actions of the individuals involved. But the power we have observed that allowed the hierarchy to carry on its corruption at the expense of its membership and even to murder its opposition, was more than the sum of the power exercised in the observable actions of individual participants. Rather, it grew from patterns of behaviour and belief shaped out of past processes of power and exercised by individuals or groups not involved in this particular conflict. It involved prior non-decisions, or neglect, of government institutions. And it involved a position of social powerlessness of the participants that encouraged susceptibility to the manipulation of their actions and thoughts within the organization. Without general factors of power such as these, the actions of individuals, or a conspiracy of individuals, might neither have occurred nor have been successful.

It is perhaps this understanding that helps to explain the particular role played by the miners of District 19 in support of the regime. In the Central Appalachian environment of unitary economic and political power, the powerlessness of the miners and their families allowed and encouraged a dependency upon the union organization to a degree greater than in other districts. That dependency, manifesting itself in uncritical loyalty, in turn allowed and encouraged manipulation of the organization by the leaders to their own ends. From this perspective, only as the broader relationships of economic and political inequality that dominate the region are altered may the power relationships within the organization themselves be fully changed.

PART IV

THE CHALLENGING OF POWER RELATIONSHIPS

8

COMMUNITY DEVELOPMENT AND COMMUNITY MEDIA: PRE-PROTEST ARENAS OF COMMUNITY CONFLICT

It is fitting that the emergence of contemporary conflict in the Clear Fork Valley involves challenges about the ownership and use of the land. From the days of the first settlers, the life and work of the Appalachian has been upon and within the land. But since the colonization of these rural valleys by industrial capital in the late 1800s, the ownership of the land has been separated from the people who live and depend upon it. With the development of a modern technology that carves and moves the land, the people of Appalachia have become increasingly severed from it. And it is the control of the land by others who neither live, work, nor depend upon it that the power to maintain these essential inequalities in the mining Valley is drawn.

However, as one first enters the Valley and listens for challenge about the ownership and use of the land, there is a peculiar silence. One listens further; the political quietness has certain forms.

Among some, especially those who benefit from it, there is satisfaction with the pattern of the land's ownership and use, expressed in unsubtle terms: 'Strip mining is good for the mountains', says one strip mine owner leasing land from the Company. 'To me, black is beautiful, I mean coal. I mean its our livelihood, and black coal to us means money, which is beautiful.'[1] Among others, anger is poignantly expressed about the loss of homeplace, the contamination of streams, the drain of wealth, or the destruction from the strip mining all around. But the anger is individually expressed and shows little apparent translation into organized protest or collective action. Among the middle-income working people the demise may be recognized, though accepted as legitimate: 'They're just businessmen out to make a buck: I'd do the same if I

[1] Quoted from transcript of *The Stripping of Appalachia*, Granada TV, op. cit.

could', is a statement often heard. Among the lower classes a certain fatalism initially seems to preclude action: 'It'll hurt you a "trying" ', says one unemployed miner sitting on his front porch. 'You can't do anything about it and the end is near at hand anyway', says a woman once she is convinced that the questioning outsider is neither lawyer, insurance agent nor tax collector.[2]

Among the non-élite, one listens more closely: beneath the expressed sense of legitimacy or fatalism is fear. The post-mistress says quietly, 'Everybody's afraid of them, they've always had a lot of money, and people in the Valley here doesn't have money or have backing from any other source, political or religious or otherwise.' She continues, 'Everybody understood that, and nobody would dare say anything to them because if they did they would be reprimanded, they'd have to move out of their houses or they'd lose their job or they'd be persecuted in some form.'[3] A shopkeeper adds from the back room of the store, 'The American Association is really a dirty word around here; its more like sayin' Hitler, I guess.'

One listens further: within the Valley are roughly nine small communities or clusters of homes each of which is upon or adjacent to the property of the Company, and each of which is directly affected by this property's use. Within each of the communities, individuals articulate grievances about the Company, but rarely do they indicate awareness of other individuals in other communities having similar grievances against the same Company. This non-communication does not appear to be merely a product of isolation. About certain matters—illness, deaths, local politics—word travels quickly, carried through interaction at work, at the store, with the postman, or on the telephone. But about the matters of the land and the Company, common information amongst the communities remains unshared.

One listens even more closely: despite the non-communication there is a widely shared sense of the Company's existence and its pervasive influence. To the people it is simply the 'land company' or the 'sociation. There is a vague

---

[2] Interviews by author.
[3] Transcript of *The Stripping of Appalachia,* op. cit.

knowledge that its real headquarters lie elsewhere, and among some a particular knowledge that the 'elsewhere' is England. Beyond that the identity need not be specified, for the Company's presence appears unchanging. Its fluctuations of policy are understood primarily in terms of the personalities of the local agents through which the policies are communicated. Even the speech patterns of the non-élite reflect the perceptions of immutability. As one listens a distinction is heard in the language between 'private property' (small, individually-owned plots) and 'company property' (the large, corporately-owned plot). The two are discussed as separate categories, unrelated to the same criterion of inequality or use. Conflict may emerge amongst the owners of the 'private property'—perhaps over the equalization of taxes or the sorting of livestock—but conflict over the allocation of the Company property appears neither to be discussed nor to occur.

This silence about the land is not uncharacteristic of the broader political culture of which it is a part. For almost a century, the ownership and use of land throughout Central Appalachia has been controlled by a handful of absentee corporations, whose interest has been speculation and profit-making resource development, not the needs of local communities. Corporate control of land for agriculture, timber, energy or recreation is growing throughout other parts of rural America as well. Yet, unlike many parts of the world, land reform has not emerged in the United States as a widespread demand amongst those most affected by the land inequalities.

It is in valleys like the Clear Fork, where the contrast is so sharp between those who live and work the land and those who glean and own it, that the silence about land reform might be expected to weaken. But given the power relationships that have been found, how does protest emerge? In an atmosphere of fear, fragmentation and non-communication, how do issues become formulated and actions upon them begin? What happens when a small rural community begins, or potentially begins, to raise its grievances against the multinational corporate coal and land lords of its valley?

Part IV of this book examines the emergence of challenge

in the Clear Fork Valley, setting it against the historical development of power relationships seen in Part II, and the contemporary workings of power, seen in Part III. This chapter looks at the formulation of issues and strategies in what might be called pre-protest arenas of community conflict; in particular, it examines the role of the community development organization and the media in shaping consciousness and action upon grievances. Chapter 9 examines what happens as the Clear Fork citizens attempt to take their grievances beyond the Valley, to corporate and governmental powerholders.[4]

8.1 THE COMMUNITY ORGANIZATION IN THE EMERGENCE OF PROTEST: FROM GARBAGE COLLECTION TO LAND REFORM

The quietness within the Valley is much like the 'culture of silence' described in Paulo Freire in oppressed communities, especially those of the *latifundisia* in Latin America. Freire is one of the few theorists to consider how from within such closed societies the challenges of a subordinate group develop against their subordinators.[5] The process, in Freire's terms, is one of 'conscientization'. It begins with self-determination by oppressed groups of 'limit acts': 'The starting point for organizing the program or content of education or political action must be the present, existential, concrete situation, reflecting the aspirations of the people.'[6] The aspirations define certain 'limit situations' upon which action is thought possible. The 'limit situations' may not be, at first, the major issues of oppression but they provide initial grievances

---

[4] In terms of the model put forward in Chapter 1 for the emergence of protest, this chapter examines the formulation of issues and strategies (i.e. the movement from a three- to a two-dimensional power situation) and Chapter 9 looks at attempts to act upon clearly recognized articulated grievances (i.e. the move from a two- to a one-dimensional power situation).

[5] See especially Paulo Freire, *Education for Critical Consciousness* (Seabury Press, New York, 1973) pp. 21–31, for discussion of the 'silence' in reference to large landholders.

[6] Paulo Freire, *Pedagogy of the Oppressed,* op. cit., p. 68; I know of no word in the English language which captures the ideas of 'conscientization'. Both politicization and mobilization are implied in the term, but 'conscientization' need not be implied in either of them. Consciousness development or consciousness raising will not do for they imply an outside agent; 'conscientization' has a more reflexive implication. Freire calls it 'the deepening of the attitude of awareness characteristic of all emergence'. ibid., p. 81.

around which self-determined action may occur. 'As critical perception is embodied in action, a climate of hope and confidence develops which leads men to overcome limit situations . . . As reality is transformed and the limit acts are superseded, new ones will appear, which in turn will invoke new limit acts'.[7] With this dialectic process of articulation and action, along with the reflection about what is occurring, consciousness and confidence necessary for more widespread challenge begin to grow.

If correct, Freire's notions provide useful insights into the relationships of power and participation, powerlessness and non-participation examined in this study.[8] In situations of oppression the powerful try to prevent any real participation of the powerless, for non-participation serves to preclude 'conscientization'. If opportunities for participation not subject to the dominance of the powerful do emerge, and if they allow self-definition by the dominated of their concerns, then the involvement of the latter will probably occur. Combined with opportunities for reflection, the new participation of the previously quiescent should carry with it the development of political consciousness, leading to action upon more far-reaching demands. The simple breaking of patterns of non-participation will be a threat to the powerful, even though, at that point, their interests are not being challenged directly. They will try to re-instil the quiescence of the powerless. Their actions will either be successful or will serve to escalate the conflict. Because they have the potential to serve as a catalyst in this dynamic process, many community action or community education programmes may be more significant for social change than they at first appear.

These ideas may be examined more concretely by looking at one form of community action in the Clear Fork Valley, the community development corporations (CDCs). In the aftermath of the War on Poverty, community development corporations sprang up in many rural and urban, poor and minority neighbourhoods across America. They are usually non-profit grassroots organizations which try to increase community self-sufficiency and self-determination through

[7] ibid., p. 72.
[8] Refer back to Figure 1.1.

locally-controlled political and economic institutions. Hopes
have been expressed that the CDCs would serve not only as
a means of local economic and political development but also
as vehicles of broader social change.[9]

Within the Valley has developed one of the most extended
examples of this form of community action amongst rural
whites in the United States. Initially it sprang up not as a
movement for general social change but as a pragmatic
response to local conditions. Following the takeover of the
War on Poverty programmes in the Valley, several local
citizens and community workers met with state officials
to see what other government programmes might be attracted.
They were told that there was little assistance available for
rural areas, and most of the funds were going to the ghettos
through the Model Cities programmes. Consequently, the
citizens started their own programmes with funds from
foundations, churches and individuals. They dubbed their
efforts 'Model Valley'.[10]

There is no doubt that these relatively independent efforts
for change in 'Model Valley' brought patterns of participation
different from those seen in government or union affairs.
With the help of a community organizer, a twenty-five-
member board was formed composed of miners, other
workers, unemployed and retired poor people, a shopkeeper, and an office worker. With the assistance of church
or foundation funds, a community-owned, -operated and
-managed pallet factory was opened, providing badly-needed
jobs. In an area of immense health needs, there developed
four community-owned clinics, each governed by a local
board of directors. In one of the communities, board members are elected in specially held community-wide elections.
The four clinics in turn elect representatives to the twenty-
four-member United Health Services of Kentucky and
Tennessee, Inc. which co-ordinates funding and personnel.

[9] See for instance Brady Deaton, 'CDC's: A Development Alternative for
Rural America', *Growth and Change* 6 (Jan. 1975), 31–7, or Gar Alperowitz,
'Notes Towards a Pluralist Commonwealth', in Lynd and Alperowitz, *Strategy
and Program: Two Essays Toward a New American Socialism* (Beacon Press,
Boston, 1973).

[10] I am grateful to members of Model Valley Development Corporation for
interviews and use of portions of their files.

In such a fashion, a population of approximately 7,000 residents, most of whom are poor or working people, own and run their professional health care system. Other community developments have included a crafts co-operative, a child development centre, and a housing project.

To say that participation occurred is not to say that it did so universally or without problems. Amongst many, the developments were viewed with cautious scepticism, arising from past experiences with other collective organizations. For those who did participate, local control meant endless meetings, negotiations, and effort to resolve differences and keep the organization going.

Nevertheless, evidence on behalf of one expectation remains: a previously dependent and acquiescent population of lower- and working-class people participated differently in circumstances of relative independence. The single case helps to substantiate the position that poverty, poor education, low status, and rural nature of the population are themselves insufficient explanations of apathy or non-challenge in this segment of America's poor.

What was the impact of these developments on the consciousness of the participants? Their conceptions of themselves and their situation seemed to change with increased participation. The first collective action defined by the group to be in their interests was a garbage clean-up; the next was a health clinic; then came the crafts co-operative. Only as such actions successfully occurred did conceptions of interests upon which to act move to notions of independent housing, jobs and economic development. At that point there was a major external blockage: the lack of suitable land. After being rejected several times over requests for land from the Company, the group located another thirty-acre spot upon which the factory and a community centre were built. That success, in turn, led to broader ideas for action. A participant described:

One of my impressions was in the first couple of years, everytime we would raise a question about anything like this, the response was 'we can't get any land . . .'

And, you know, it wasn't until . . . we got this land made available to us that we began to think with a new vision . . .

The 'new vision' included the idea of a model Appalachian town in which housing and community industry could be developed—provided that land could be obtained from the Company. Perceived interests began to include recovering some control of the land itself. In the space of about five years, through a process of deciding upon and carrying out actions, definitions of interests shifted from those involving little conflict against the existing order (garbage collection) to the development of alternatives to that order (a factory, clinics) to the notion of challenging the order itself (land demands).

Intertwined in these changing ideas about action was a change in conception of where the responsibility rested for conditions of poverty experienced in the Valley. In the first instance, that of garbage collection, the responsibility was felt to lie in the inadequacy of the community. A participant explained, 'At that time, our mentality was lets try to get some industry into the area, but we should clean it up first.' A successful clean-up—but the failure of industry to follow—led the group to consider that other forces were responsible for obstacles to a better life in the area. The view then became one of a community which had been 'left out' of the benefits of society because of government inaction or corporate neglect. But as actions were taken by the community itself to solve its problems, it faced further obstacles from government and corporate interests. The notion of contradictory interests began to emerge, and external forces were seen as being responsible for internal conditions. The statement of a miner about the desire for a new community shows the shift:

We want to make that town into a model Appalachian town. We want to show people that it is not because of *us* that things have been like they have in this part of the country—it's because we have been under the thumb of companies like American Association. Now, the planners, they tell us it can't be done. But we showed them with the factory and we'll show 'em with this—that, given half a chance, folks can have a decent life in the mountains.

Through local actions, the sense of powerlessness began to fade. From instilled quiescence a feeling of possibility began to emerge:

In the last two years you can tell the difference in the 'holler', in the attitude of the people. They've begun to get a little self-respect, or, I don't know, whatever you call it. It used to be ten years ago they didn't seem to care one way or another.'

A visiting reporter from the *Washington Post* wrote of the community:

In pride and amazement they refer to the new factory in town. It is the first industry ever for Clairfield (after coal) and the people got it with no R and D grants from the government, no cash from the highway-happy Appalachian Regional Commission and no lobbying from trade associations in Washington. The story of the new Clairfield pallet factory may be seen as the last gasp of a dying town or as the first breath of one pulsing again to life. The second is the view here . . .[11]

Participation in the present was inspired by new, less fatalistic attitudes towards the future:

Well, as a part-time mother, I look in the future when my son will be going to school, or be looking for a job . . . They'll never be enough students here for a high school, but there is a possibility that we can get a road; there is a possibility that we can get better housing; there is a possibility that we can get better communications with county seat or get our own communications; but it's not going to be done if people don't get out and try it. And that's why I'm here.

As actions upon perceived limit situations were successful, more participation occurred, leading to further action. In a concrete situation an interrelationship begins to be seen between participation and consciousness, so that one becomes necessary for the development of the other in the process of community change.

As was to be expected, growing consciousness and participation brought a response from the powerholders. Freire writes that the emergence of action amongst a non-élite is also a 'moment in the developing consciousness of the power élite . . . Just as there is a moment of surprise among the masses when they begin to see what they did not see before, there is a corresponding surprise among the elite in power when they find themselves unmasked by the masses.'[12] Local participants described what happened more simply but with equal insight:

[11] Colman McCarthy, 'In Appalachia: Putting a Big Stake on a Small Business', *Washington Post,* 19 March 1972.

[12] Freire, *Cultural Action for Freedom,* op. cit., p. 65.

Nothing happened over here unless they pushed the button to do it . . . Like when they lost control and didn't understand what was going on . . . some people over there (the courthouse) got nervous.

Well, the way this 'holler' is right now . . . a few control it with what money they've got. Why, they've got the land, what private property there is they've got. —— (the largest strip mine operator in the Valley) has got $100,000 a year payroll . . . Suppose you got other money comin' in—why that's gonna threaten their control a little.

In the first instance, the strongest hostilities came from those immediately threatened by a loss of control—the élite in the Valley. The opposition came early in the development process and took its usual initial form—the invocation of symbols and violence against the outsiders involved, even though they were involved at the request of and with the support of the local non-élite. In this case a primary organizer, a former nun and middle-aged community worker, was labelled an 'outsider', a 'communist', and a 'Catholic', the last causing most suspicion in the fundamentalist, Protestant area. One woman described the fear:

We thought Catholics were mean and cruel. We never knew no better. There weren't any around. That's what we were told to think. We didn't have any other ideas. We were told they were organized, would band together, unified, and do what they were told to do. They'd try to take over and wouldn't listen to any of us . . . I was afraid of them.

Where myths and symbols failed to prevent effective development of the community organizations, more violent intimidation was attempted: twenty-two bullets were put through the community worker's home, the office of the health and development group was burned down, and an alternative school destroyed by fire. But the developments continued.

Meanwhile, the response of the political élite at the county courthouse was initially one of neglect, combined at times with the voicing of similar evocative symbols against 'troublemakers' or 'communists'. Then, as the citizens began to take their concerns directly to the courthouse, the tacit neglect became more overt. For instance, one county court session was immediately adjourned when citizens came to inquire why their road had not been paved and where the county funds allocated for it had been spent. When the issue of Company taxes was raised an official of the State Department of Property Appraisal was sent to the county to investigate the charges that several million dollars' worth of coal property was going untaxed. After interviewing the county and Company officials, he ended up across the mountain from the courthouse, in the Valley, threatening to increase the taxes on the $30,000 worth of property at the community-owned factory—while ignoring the 45,000 acres of undertaxed Company property which he had originally been sent to investigate.

While the response to local community development activities was thus open hostility on the part of the political élite, that of the absentee economic élite—the Company and its officers—was initially one of uncooperative aloofness. As they owned some 85 per cent of the land in the Valley, with the local élite owning most of the rest, their stance of containment could be witnessed in their policy towards the land. Though much of it was unused, they refused to part with it for local industry. Though they were tearing down company houses, they refused to free land for alternative housing development by community groups. Though a school in one of the coal camps fell vacant, they refused to release it for a child development programme. A request by a doctor for a quarter of an acre of land on which to build a clinic was denied. The doctor later described the attitudes expressed to him by the company manager, Mr. Alvaredo E. Funk:

When I went to talk to him about it I was treated I suppose about the rudest I've ever been treated in all my life . . . I was told that they would not give land to anybody else for anything over here, and I said 'Why not? ' and he said 'Well, a bunch of communists and do-gooders over there; all they're interested in is destroying us.'[13]

The Company's attitude expressed through the land policy towards the lower-class valley residents was in sharp contrast to its policies expressed across the mountain in the more middle-class suburbs. There upon the edge of seventy acres of land it had donated for a reservoir, the Company proposed to build a golf course, marina, and condominium to 'attract the wealthier citizens of both Middlesborough and Pineville'. It also donated a site to a humane society for building a dog-pound.

[13] Transcript of *Our American Association*, produced by Thames TV and transmitted 25 July 1974.

The obstacles to community development here, as elsewhere, do not reside simply in the opposition of local powerholders. One study in Appalachia has found, for instance,
that 'the major reasons why community economic development groups experience difficulties stem from factors which
are external to them and therefore out of their control . . .
For community economic development in Appalachia to
succeed, the major policy and strategy changes must be in
the helping institutions, the economic and legal system and
the Appalachian Region itself . . .' Necessary experts are
often ideologically unsympathetic or insensitive to the needs
of community groups. Assistance in funding is difficult to
obtain, undependable, or bound to rigid bureaucratic guidelines. Existing laws, especially security laws, make the development of community-controlled enterprises even more difficult.
'What all these points illustrate', the study concludes, 'is the
helping system is not operating as it is supposed to operate
. . . Things are not working as they are said to work.'[14] Or, in
the terms of this study, the community development organization is faced with a mobilization of bias, that serves to
handicap its potential for change within either the community,
or more broadly.

What effects did these encounters with power have upon
the actions and conceptions of the emerging activists? Theoretically one might suspect either that the prior patterns of
quiescence would be re-instilled; that the activities would be
neutralized into a relatively unthreatening form; or that
further actions and more militant consciousness would
develop. While these are analytically distinct possibilities, the
case study suggests that in practice each may occur, in varying
degrees, simultaneously. The emergence of challenge involves
constantly mediating and resolving the various responses.

Thus, on one level, the activities continued to increase in
scope, as has been seen. Yet, the victories themselves began
to provide leverage by which the powerholders could effectively neutralize the community actions. The successful

[14] Neil Tudiver, 'When Aid Doesn't Help: Obstacles to Community Economic
Development in Appalachia', (mimeo by Commission on Religion in Appalachia,
Knoxville, 1972). See also, Geoffrey Faux, 'Politics and Bureaucracy in Community Controlled Economic Developments', *Law and Contemporary Problems,*
36 (1971).

development of alternative organization meant that the group had more to lose in direct conflict.

Although the group made statements like the 'members have grown in understanding the economic and political forms that come to play in rural coal mining communities', that very understanding led to a choice of avoiding confrontation for fear of losing materials and markets for the community factory, a loan from a bank, a grant from a foundation, community legitimacy, buildings (through fire or sabotage), certification from authorities to deliver health care or carry on legal aid, and so on.

On the other hand, in the Clear Fork Valley the community development activities did help to create a climate for the emergence of protest.[15] In time, a more direct confrontation about the ownership and use of the land would occur. The unfolding process through which it developed will be seen when the role of the media in community conflict is examined.

8.2 THE MEDIA IN COMMUNITY CHANGE: "CAUSE THEY'VE NEVER BEEN NOTIFIED ABOUT IT . . .'

An extensive literature in the social sciences suggests that the media may exercise power by 'setting the agenda' of political conflict.[16] In relationship to a relatively powerless group, the process may occur in two ways. In the first instance, power may be exercised by controlling the distribution

[15] Co-operatives and community organizations have been found in other countries to be an important first step to more general demands for land reform. See, for instance, G. Hizer, 'Community Development, Land Reform and Political Participation', in Theodore Shanin, *Peasants and Peasant Societies* (Penguin Books, Harmondsworth, Middx., 1971), pp. 389–411; or William Hinton, *Fanschen* (Alfred A. Knopf, New York, 1966), especially pp. 200–12.

[16] Anthony Smith, *The Shadow and Cave* (University of Illinois Press, Urbana, 1973). Smith points out that since the Second World War there have been over 10,000 studies on the media and its effects. Much of the vast literature goes unconsulted in political science. I have resorted to several edited collections. See, especially, F. Gerald Kline and Phillip J. Tichenor, *Current Perspectives in Mass Communications Research* (Sage Publications, London, 1972); Denis McQuail, *Sociology of Mass Communications* (Penguin Books, Harmondsworth, Middx., 1972); and Jeremy Tunstall, *Media Sociology* (Constable and Co., London, 1970). For a summary of the discussion on 'agenda setting' see Maxwell E. McCombs, 'Mass Communication in Political Campaigns', in Kline and Tichenor, op. cit., pp. 169–94.

of the message, thus limiting the extent to which potential
support for challenges may be mobilized. Often referred to
by the useful term 'gatekeeping', this process was seen at
work in the coverage and non-coverage by the press of the
miners' rebellion of 1931.[17] Secondly, though, what is
distributed by the media is thought to have an effect upon
the conceptions and actions of an audience, and may also be
a form of power. An example of this has been seen in the
means by which the information disseminated by union
leaders helped to shape the opposition of the miners of
District 19 to the Miners for Democracy. While social science
literature disagrees about the precise effects of the media
upon an audience, one element of its impact for agenda-
setting is clear: 'It [the press] may not be successful much of
the time in telling people *what* to think, but it is stunningly
successful in telling the readers what to think *about.* '[18]

In the Clear Fork Valley, the media does little to encourage
people to think about the important issues they face, nor
about themselves as actors upon them. The issues of potential
significance to the life of the community simply do not
appear upon its pages or its screens. The power of the media
rests just as much in what is unwritten and unsaid as in what is.

For instance, residents of the Clear Fork Valley may have
received any of five local papers from the three counties of
which the Valley is a part. But numbers should not imply
diversity of style. All the papers (four weekly, one daily) are
published from the county seats or townships. All depend
upon local advertising, primarily from local businessmen
within the county seats. Most of the news in all of the papers
focuses upon the events that happen within the county seat
or town, most of which would appear from the coverage to
be uncontroversial—e.g. deaths, church services, weddings and
relatively uneventful county court meetings. Rarely on the

---

[17] See discussion by Donahue, Tichenor and Olien, 'Gatekeeping: Mass Media
Systems and Information Control', in Kline and Tichenor, op. cit., pp. 41-70. See
also Michael Lipsky, *Protest in City Politics* (Rand McNally, Chicago, 1970).
Lipsky writes: 'To the extent that successful protest activity depends on appealing
to, and/or threatening, other groups in the community, the communications
media set the limits of protest activity.' (p. 169).

[18] McCombs, op. cit., p. 182 quoting B. C. Cohen, *The Press, the Public and
Foreign Policy* (Princeton University Press, Princeton, 1963).

pages of the press do either the events or the potentially critical issues of the outlying areas appear, especially any which might involve the power élite of the county, most of whom live in the county seat. A result, as one of the community workers described, is that 'the unethical politicians, professional or business persons never get exposed. The public is led to believe that the only bad guys are those that get drunk, hold up the bank, or get caught with moonshine.' At least one reason for the non-exposure is not hard to determine. The editor of the comparitively large and liberal *Middlesboro Daily News* says about the American Association, its subsidiary Cumberland Gap Corporation, and its manager Funk, 'In this town, they are like the Trinity—the Father, the Son, and the Holy Ghost.' Needless to say, neither he nor the other editors are likely to take the names in vain.

This neglect by the urban media of the potential issues of the coal valley is just as pervasive as that of the local media, though perhaps for different reasons. Papers may be delivered to the Valley from the city of Knoxville, seventy miles away, but their major clientele is the urban, middle class; there is normally little coverage of the rural, poverty situation, although the urban papers may be approached successfully for publicity as conflict emerges, i.e. in the mobilization process. In general terms, however, the further the papers are from the local power situation the more likely they are to cover local challenges. For instance, while the controversy about the American Association, Ltd. has appeared in the *Nashville Tennessean,* the *Louisville Courier Journal,* the *Washington Post,* the *New York Times,* several London newspapers and even the *Hong Kong Standard,* it has yet to be reported in the *Claiborne County Progress* or the *Middlesboro Daily News.* Thus, it is also ironically the case that those papers most likely to cover controversial issues in the Valley are least likely to be read by the local non-élite, who are most likely to act upon them; and the image portrayed at home emphasizes the stability of what elsewhere would be portrayed as a situation of conflict.

Though the outside newspapers, and to some extent the local press, are rarely read by the residents of the Clear Fork Valley, more families in the Valley have a television set than a car, a member of the household with a job, or a flush toilet. While the Clear Fork area is the least prosperous sector of Claiborne County, more of its families have televisions (93·5 per cent) than in any other area, except the most prosperous, those in the county seat (94·2 per cent). The televisions are watched often, and for long periods of time. Yet what is watched, like the print media, generally appears alien to the local situation. Progammes which present people like those of the Clear Fork Valley do so usually as stereotypes of passive, quaint or backward characters. Where mountaineers do appear as major actors, it is in a conflict-free, system-supportive fashion. For instance, the 'Beverly Hillbillies', a popular comedy about illiterate mountaineers who move to a Southern California estate after striking oil, portrays the myths that the people own their resources, that the system is open for quick financial gain to those who are lucky, and that wealth will be used to buy passage into a filmstar dreamland. 'Hee Haw' portrays the culture in its most nonsensical fashion for the pleasure of urban audiences, while 'Gomer Pyle' would seem to suggest that even 'country bumkins' have a place in the armed forces—albeit the place of the jester. One Appalachian writer has written, 'If similar programs even approaching the maliciousness of these were broadcast today on Blacks, Indians or Chicanos, there would be immediate public outcry from every liberal organization and politician in the country . . . But with this, as with all things Appalachian, *silence.* America is allowed to continue laughing at this minority group because on this America agrees: "hillbilly ain't beautiful".'[19]

What are the effects of non-coverage or degrading coverage by the media upon people like those of the Clear Fork Valley? What impact does it have upon their political actions and their conceptions of themselves as local activists? Social scientists really do not know. Studies of the media have focused little attention upon the effects of the media on relatively powerless groups in our society.

Speculations can be made, though, based upon what is known about the media generally. If the mass media normally help to legitimate the dominant values and concerns of a

[19] James Branscome, 'Annihilating the Hillbilly', op. cit., p. 1.

society, then the neglect of other values and concerns may ascribe to them a subordinate or unimportant status.[20] What a society sees of itself on television may provide its mainstream with a kind of collective self-image, by which individuals and sub-groups evaluate themselves and others. Where a positive self-image is not portrayed for a particular group, that group may develop a sense of inadequacy about itself, re-enforced by how other groups project their media stereotypes upon them. Moreover, the lack of coverage of a subordinate group keeps the members of the group isolated from one another, unaware that others similarly situated share common concerns or are pursuing challenges upon common issues. Much as communities in the past have been disenfranchised of their right to vote or dispossessed of their land, so rural communities like those of the Clear Fork Valley are 'disconnected' from one another in the communications process.

While it is normally difficult to test such assertions in the life of a small community, it may be possible to begin to do so by observing the impact of alternative media upon a relatively powerless group. Two such opportunities have been provided in the Clear Fork Valley, one to do with community videotaping, the other with the making of a film about the Company by Britain's Granada Television.

Videotape technology provides a medium that can be used as a tool for alternative communication amongst 'disconnected' communities. The equipment is easy to use, portable and relatively inexpensive. It has the advantage of instant playback through anyone's television set, thereby giving a certain legitimacy to its form while allowing a different content to what ordinarily might be watched on the screen. Experiments with this alternative medium in the Clear Fork Valley and elsewhere in the Appalachian region have demonstrated several important effects. Where a rapport has been established, the presence of a camera can lend a sense of

[20] 'The cultivation of dominant image patterns is the major function of the dominant communications agencies of any society', writes George Gerbner, 'Mass Media and Human Communication Theory', in McQuail, op. cit., p. 50. See, too, Raymond Williams, *Communications* (Penguin Books, Harmondsworth, Middx., 1962).

importance to what is said—an importance often denied the statements of powerless people. Grievances and ideas for change may begin to be expressed, though perhaps at first in a hesitant, tentative way. The feedback of those statements through the television allows a chance for those being taped to look at themselves, for reflection and self-examination. Where the feedback presents the participants in a realistic, non-stereotyped fashion, it can give a certain validity to the concerns and ideas being expressed, and give confidence to those expressing them. Playback of the tapes to other groups comparably situated can have similar impact, sparking discussion and an examination of their own grievances. Like Freire's use of written symbols in political education in Latin America, this use of electronic images in articulating, reflecting and connecting with others can become part of a 'conscientization' process amongst the powerless.[21]

Similar effects of the media upon the process by which issues emerge were seen when Granada Television's 'World in Action' expressed interest in making a documentary exposé of the role of the British company in the area. The film later became an effective tool for challenge by the community, but when it was begun in the autumn of 1972, a fearful silence about the Company persisted in the Valley.

Elements of the film-making process helped to overcome this fear.[22] First, a series of meetings were held quietly involving members of the community, the film director, and community organizers. At the meetings, the community demanded and received certain conditions. The director would come to be known by the group over a period of

[21] See, for instance, Ted Carpenter and Mike Clark, 'The Living Newsletter: Portable Videotape and Regional Spirit', in *Challenge for Change,* 11 (a publication of the National Film Board of Canada); 'Videotaping: A Medium for Social Change', *Instructional Technology Reports* (July–August 1974); and John Gaventa, 'Miners and Video: Appalachia and Wales', *Mountain Review* (1974), 10–12.

[22] For a useful discussion of the attitudes in Appalachia towards the media see Calvin Trillin, 'A Stranger With A Camera', *The New Yorker* (29 Apr. 1969), reprinted in Walls and Stephenson, *Appalachia in the Sixties, op. cit.,* pp. 193–201. The article tells the story of the slaying of a Canadian film maker in Eastern Kentucky by a mountaineer, essentially for no other reason than a distrust of outsiders with cameras who were thought to be 'making fun' of the culture and poverty of the local situation.

several weeks, and would get to know the community; only then would the community group decide whether to participate in making the film. A copy of the film must be returned to the group, who would control its use locally. Excitement was expressed about the fact that here was an opportunity to bypass the local élite and to communicate directly with the seats of power over the Valley, the Company and its peers in the previously inaccessible, vaguely perceived place called London.

The dual opportunity of a) using a medium that could be controlled b) to reach the ears of the controllers, gave the community a potentially significant reason, lacking before, to come together and discuss their concerns. In the process one learned from another about similar grievances. Surprise was expressed that 'so and so' from the next hollow was affected by the same problem, and owing to the same Company's policy! As common ground was established, new concerns began to be articulated. Remarks were made like, 'Why, I've lived here all these years and I didn't know that', or 'Well, I've never thought of it like that before.' The opportunity for potentially meaningful statements gave rise to expression of the grievances themselves—now better defined and collectively perceived. The group decided to make the film.

In it the citizens expressed their concerns forcefully and in their own fashion. A sixty-eight-year-old mountaineer who had worked for fifty years in deep mines on company property only later to be twice evicted from the company-owned dwelling in which he lived, spoke about the strip mines that had dislocated him from his homeplace:

It's damaged your timber, it's damaged your wildlife, your water, it's damaged little farms, and it's damaged peoples' health . . . and it's just puttin' people out of homes . . . They've destroyed it, really destroyed it. It weren't no intention for this earth to be torn up, I wouldn't want to damage God's work, I wouldn't want to touch God's work. God created this world, created this coal, created this timber and created our wildlife and it's torn it all. It's a'doin away with it all, wildlife and all. So I, no I wouldn't work in the strip mines, I wouldn't destroy this earth.

A retired Marine, and manager of the community-owned pallet factory said of the land monopoly:

Well its just like you're going hungry, and right across the fence there's a whole field full of corn and you can't get it because a guy is standing there with a hatchet, and he's going to chop your arm off when you reach through there. Well, either side you took on here, you're looking at the property of the American Association and they will not turn it loose by any means.

A local woman who had been postmistress in the community for thirty-nine years spoke of some of the hopes of the group:

I hope that we can all together make the American land Association in England realize what they have taken away from us, and how they've robbed us, and that they would be willing and eager to give something back to the people that live here, and I hope that I live to see that day.

While these grievances were forcefully expressed, there was also a certain naive expectancy about how they might be viewed in London. 'Do you think the Company in London know what's happening here?', Granada asked. 'I wouldn't think so', or 'The main headquarters don't know all about this and how its damaged the earth', said the Clear Fork citizens. 'Why not?', asked Granada. ' 'Cause they've never been notified about it', came the reply.

While the impact of the film's nationwide broadcast in Britain on 6 November 1972 is uncertain, there was an observable impact in the Valley when a copy of the film was returned. Even before then there had been some feedback from the Company. Whether real or rumour, word spread that 'the Company wants to know who's been in on that'. There was a wavering in the emerging protest, with some residents saying, 'I don't mind to say that I'm in on it', and others suggesting that they would just 'play dumb' if asked about it. With this ambivalence, there was also the question of whether watching the film, which openly portrayed the conflict of angry residents against the powerful Company, would encourage further challenge or a retreat into acquiescence.

The community's response contained both elements. On the one hand, there was excitement that here was a real expression of grievances, seen perhaps for the first time on any media. The vision by the group of themselves as direct challengers to the Company and its manager seemed to strengthen a sense of challenge. A plan emerged for the group to organize the film as a resource for protest, 'to let the whole country know what's goin' on here in the Valley'. At the same time, though, there was a continued fear and recognition of the powerlessness of a single community against a multinational giant, whose managers in London had refused Granada an interview, saying they trusted their local man Funk and were fully aware of everything happening in America.

Over the next few weeks, the articulation and feedback process continued. The film was quietly taken to potential supporters such as lawyers and newsmen outside the area, as well as to other mountain groups within the region. Video-tapes of the reactions, inevitably ones of sympathy, anger and support, were brought back to the group. Further confidence and desire for challenge developed.

Along with Save Our Cumberland Mountains, a larger citizens' group in the region, the Clear Fork group began to use the film widely as a resource for developing support for its goals. The mobilization process met barriers: despite the film's quality and the fact that it had been shown nationally in Britain, the local media refused to air it, either saying that it was too controversial, or that it would have no interest for their urban audience. The group resorted to distributing the film themselves, taking it on tours around the region, to the legislatures in Nashville and Washington, and to numerous other potentially supportive interest groups.

With the film went a platform: 'Our past is being destroyed and our future is being denied by the actions and policies of the American Association—the British landholding company which owns most of the land of our valley'. The citizens called upon public pressure to help to get the Company to:

Stop the destruction of our land, streams, homes, timber and wildlife that its strip-mining brings to our valley. *Allow community development* of alternative housing and industry simply by freeing to us some of their 65,000 acres of land . . . *Repair its houses in the valley* to make them liveable for the citizens who have to live there.
Pay its fair share of property taxes to the county. While owning 17% of the county land, 90% of the coal wealth, the company has in the past paid only 4% of the local taxes, thus denying us much needed revenue for our schools, etc.[23]

[23] Leaflet of Clear Fork Citizens United (undated).

The 'culture of silence' surrounding the Company's ownership and use of the land had been broken. In the process of
self-definition of and action upon perceived limit situations
provided by the community development organization and
the community media, the issues of challenge had been
formulated. But the next stage in the emergence of protest,
placing the issues upon appropriate decision-making agendas,
had just begun.

9
COMMUNITY PROTEST AND NON-DECISION-MAKING POWER: THE REGULATORY AGENCY AND THE MULTINATIONAL

The process of raising challenges is a dynamic one. Overcoming one facet of powerlessness may serve simply to reveal another. For a relatively powerless group, the combination of articulating grievances and organizing action upon them does not necessarily mean that the grievances will merit response—or even entry to the decision-making arenas. For the powerholders, the prevailing inequalities will be maintained to the extent that conflict can be contained through the 'hidden faces' of power. There persists in American political culture an abiding faith that 'something can be done' about situations of gross inequity. But the capacity of power to repel, neutralize and even remain aloof from protest may be seen as the Clear Fork citizens appeal to a government regulatory agency for help, and then, as they attempt to challenge the multinational more directly.

9.1 TRYING TO MAKE THE SYSTEM WORK: THE CASE OF BUFFALO HOLLOW

One potential path of protest for a relatively powerless group in American politics, especially where grievances are provoked by apparent violations of law or Constitutional rights, is appeal to the courts or regulatory agencies. The view is often put forward that these judicial and administrative processes are essentially pluralistic, and that the practice of judicial review and the ability of citizens to voice their views to government agencies makes them open and responsive to disaffected groups in society.[1] Yet political science knows

[1] For instance, Carl Auerbach, 'Pluralism and the Administrative Process', *The Annals of the American Academy of Political and Social Sciences,* 400 (March 1972), 1-13. For a text book statement of the 'openness' of the process to public groups, see Ira Sharansky, *Public Administration* (Markham Publishing Co., Chicago, 1972, 2nd edn.), pp. 211-12. The classic earlier statement, of course, is found in David Truman, *The Governmental Process* (Alfred A. Knopf, New York, 1953), chaps. 7 and 8.

very little about what really happens when relatively powerless groups attempt to call upon the courts or government
agencies to remedy their claims. A single case study may help
to expose the subtle community dynamics which may come
in to play as the relatively powerful and the relatively powerless seek to make the public system work for opposing
interests. Such a study may be found in the case of Buffalo
Hollow.[2]

Buffalo in Claiborne County, Tennessee is a small community. It lies off the single main road in the Valley, along
Buffalo Creek, a tributary of the Clear Fork. Most of the
forty or so families who live scattered along the banks or
higher in the hills own their own plots of land—some of the
few people in the area to do so. Upon the land, they care-
fully till small gardens to supplement their meagre incomes.
Economically, Buffalo is a poor community. Its residents are
mainly unemployed, work intermittently in the mines, or are
retired. Yet in another sense it is a rich community. Its
relative isolation, and closeness to its land have helped to
maintain the strength of a traditional rural mountain culture.

In recent years, the gardens, the people, and the culture
have come under a threat: the strip mining above the community, on the land of the Company, is causing the mountain to slide down into the little valley. A four-hundred-yard
avalanche of mud, boulders and trees has moved on to most
of the land of one retired miner, and hovers directly above a
cluster of homes. Giant cracks may be seen splitting the
hillsides from the mountain, where cuts were begun months
before by bulldozers. Rain washes mud and rocks on to the
single dirt road. During a heavy torrent, entrance into and
out of the area by car is almost impossible. The creek—once,
people say, clear and deep—is now full of silt and mineral
particles. It rises high above its banks during rains, covering
the gardens with its acidic substances and lapping dangerously
at the steps of the clapboard homes.

'No, the community isn't what it used to be,' the people

---

[2] The data that follow are based on extensive participant-observation especially from July 1972 to May 1973, when I lived in the Buffalo community. Unless
referring to specific statements or documents, sources are field notes taken during
this time.

say, and they talk about moving. But there is little money to go, or desire to leave their land, kin, or neighbours. And so they stay.

Although they stay, they fear and resent the damage from the unreclaimed mining of the Company and the operators who worked upon its land. Yet, at the beginning of this case study, there had been little overt protest. Occasional appeals to a country lawyer, to the Company, or to the courthouse across the mountain had met with little response. To the observer, an unnecessary fatalism appeared predominant, expressed in such views as, 'One night it'll rain and we'll just all be washed away and destroyed.'

The apparent quiescence seemed to alter with the opportunity for a significant challenge, one that bypassed the local élite, and went on film directly to the absentee Company. In it, spokesmen for the community strongly articulated their fears of the slide. The film apparently had effect: soon after it was made, the local manager, Mr. Funk, appeared for the first time in Buffalo to inspect the damage. There he was met by representatives of the community including a sympathetic lawyer, who presented a petition signed by twenty of the residents. It asked the Company to repair the 'awful and unreclaimed strip mining' it had allowed and continued:

We, the residents of Buffalo, had no say about your strip mining and made no money from it. But now, after it's over, it is we who must live with it. We own a little land and it is valuable to us. But now, we must suffer the damage and live with fear that the actions on your company lands have caused.

With the slide's threat to the community portrayed on television in London, and the citizens threatening legal action in Tennessee, the Company for the first time took some remedial action by building massive dams, an attempt to contain the moving mountain. But at about the same time, the strip mine operator who had carried out the mining as a lessee on company land applied for a permit from the State to begin to strip again. The operator's previous record had been atrocious. Not only had he caused this damage in Buffalo, but he had then claimed to have gone out of business (apparently to avoid legal action against him) and he had, like the Company, failed to respond to the citizens' previous

complaints. Now he proposed to continue, this time further
down the hollow on land adjacent to that of the Company—
land owned by the Godfather. Activated by participation in
the events that surrounded the film, afraid that yet more
damage would be caused to their community, the Buffalo
residents talked of opposing the Company's application to
the State Department of Conservation for a mining permit.
The ensuing conflict, which lasted with some intensity over
the next five months, thus featured a) a relatively powerless,
previously quiescent community b) attempting to act upon
grievances against representatives of the local élite and the
absentee Company c) by appealing to their state regulatory
agency.

The Letter of the Law and the Spirit of the Community. The
Tennessee State Surface Mining Law of 1972 may be seen as
an example of the recent attempts in the United States to
open the regulatory process to participation and appeals from
affected members of the public. Before permission is granted
from the Commissioner of the Department of Conservation
for a company to mine, 'any interested persons or group of
persons' may submit statements to be taken into account by
the Commissioner in the decision. While the Commissioner
is given broad discretion in his action, his decision in turn
may be taken to a review panel, the Board of Reclamation
Review. Consisting of the Commissioner of Public Health
and four members of the public (two from the mining
industry and two independent citizens appointed by the
Governor), the panel may overrule the Commissioner's
decision.

The rights of access and appeal are thus embodied into the
regulatory process as a potential means through which a
relatively powerless group can make its voice heard. But the
striking features of the Buffalo case were the barriers through
which the grievances and information relevant to them could
be excluded from the process—through forms of power not
always observable from within the process itself.

The first set of barriers involved access to the legal process.
The relatively powerless community lacked even the minimal
resources of protest—knowledge of the right of appeal, legal

or para-legal assistance in the formulation of claims, and the means of travel to a hearing. But perhaps the most powerful barriers within the community were the subjective ones: the potential appeals procedure, like that of almost any regulatory or judicial body, was viewed as part of the unitary power structure, imposed from the outside and inevitably subject to the pervasive influence of the Company and the Family. The law and its instruments were considered in Buffalo to be the instruments of the powerful, beyond the everyday sphere of the powerless. Outcomes were thought to be predictable, offering little incentive to challenge. The alternative for the community was tolerant resignation to what was imposed from the outside, and maximization of what was more easily understood and controlled on the inside—the harmony of the community and the values of the subculture. As one woman said, 'Don't get me wrong, but I'm a Christian church goin' woman, and I don't want to cause trouble that will make enemies of those around me.'

In this instance, the factors that would normally prevent the emergence of challenge were overcome. Assistance was available from a publicly-funded lawyer in the area. The film had already activated the community. There could be no harm, the residents decided, in voicing a complaint. As one resident argued, 'I reckon if we were throwin' this stuff in their backyard, they'd slap us with everything in the book.'

But the first step of challenge faced another major barrier —administrative blockage from the bureaucracy. On 22 November 1972, the Charles King Coal Company gave notice in a local paper of the intent to strip mine on the 'northwest slope of Miller Mountain drained by Buffalo Creek'. On the same day, a letter went from the Valley to the Department of Conservation, in the state capital 200 miles away, requesting copies of the company's permit application so that the community could register a specific protest. On 7 December the regulatory agency mailed the necessary documents to the community. A lengthy and detailed complaint was formulated, signed by eighteen residents, giving fifteen reasons for their concern. The petition concluded:

Charles King's past performance, under the name of C. and A. Coal Co., has been among the worst of any strip-miner's in Tennessee. He has

broken laws, damaged property and endangered citizens in almost every
conceivable way—and has then slipped across the State line, thus
avoiding legal consequences. Now, under a different name but with no
indication of a different style, he proposes to return.

On 18 December 1972 the petition was submitted to the
Commissioner for consideration. Shortly afterwards the
response came: the permit had already been granted—on 6
December, *the day before the Commissioner had mailed the
citizens the information needed to register their protest.*
The Commissioner had known of the intent to challenge.
The permit had been granted in under the minimum time
required by law for the period of consideration. An administrative fiat had rendered the voicing mechanism 'voiceless'.

Perhaps as amends for his actions, the Commissioner did
request the area head of the Surface Mining Department to
investigate the allegations made in the petition. Two months
later, however, there was still no evidence of the investigation
occurring. The Buffalo group decided to exercise the second
formal step available to them, an appeal to the Board of
Reclamation Review. This was the first time in Tennessee
that this appeal process had been invoked by a concerned
group. Their complaint, in addition to the complaints against
the coal operator, added a new grievance: that the Commissioner 'has abused his discretion' by granting the permit
and has 'demonstrated a clear disdain . . . for the protest of
citizens who must bear the ill effects of surface mining and
who under the law have a clear right to register their protest
before a permit is granted'.

The Hearing. 'First Test of Reclamation Law is Fiery',
announced the *Knoxville News Sentinel* headlines about the
nine-hour hearing held on 25 April 1972,[3] and indeed it was.
The local citizens, the Department of Conservation, and the
coal operators were each represented by lawyers who presented thirty-eight exhibits and eleven witnesses. As the
single poverty lawyer tried to argue on behalf of the citizens,
the lawyers of the State and the operator, each with their
staff of technical assistants, made the argument that the
problems in Buffalo were not really serious, that there was

[3] *Knoxville News Sentinel,* 26 April 1973, p. 1.

consensus in the community for the mining, and that the protest had arisen only because outside agitation had, in the coal operator's words, 'poisoned the minds of the Buffalo people'. Six weeks later the two mine owners, the college professor, and the city lawyer who heard the case issued their verdict: 'The Commissioner did not abuse his discretionary authority; no material evidence now exists to support a decision to overrule the Commissioner's issuance of a permit.'[4]

It is neither within the purpose nor scope of this case study to evaluate the integrity of the decision made by the Board. Neither is it necessary, for what is more revealing to the study of power in the case is to compare *what happened* within the hearing room with *what* of potential significance to the outcome *did not*. While the Review Board may have made the appropriate decision on the basis of the information organized into the formal proceedings, more significant power over the final decision may well have been exercised through the process which kept alternative information out.

The view of the regulatory agency as a neutral body in the process of resolving conflicts is widely held in American politics. Yet, as the conflict arose in Buffalo, the urban, middle-class government officials turned for interpretation of it not to the citizens of Buffalo hollow, but to the local élite. The field investigator into the complaint for the agency, whose report was presented as major evidence, testified:

Q. Did you talk to the citizens in the area, the strip mined area, about some of the problems that strip mining causes?
A. About problems it had caused—no I haven't found anybody complaining . . .
Q. Did you talk to any of the petitioners?
A. No, I don't believe so . . .[5]

When asked where he had obtained his local information, the inspector mentioned talks with the coal operator and conversations at the 'local store', a place historically and currently associated by the poor in the Valley with the control of the Company and the Godfather.

---

[4] 'Memorandum of Decision', Tennessee State Board of Reclamation Review, 1973-1, 11 July 1973, p. 1.
[5] Deposition of inspector, pp. 10, 11, 32.

On the basis of such information-gathering procedures, the investigation that was presented in the hearing was not into the grievances but about the petitioners. Each one was discounted as a witness for one reason or another, such as having a well-known 'negative attitude', being of 'blood kin', or being an 'agitator'. The report concluded that 'these people have been . . . agitated and stirred-up by an outside organization, who at this time are notorious for attempts to undermine any type of surface operations', and who had 'attempted to, in a manner of speaking, make a mountain of a molehill'.[6] The viewpoint re-enforced, and was in turn re-enforced by, the communication patterns:

Q. Do you think the residents . . . have a right to express their opinions to the Tennessee Department of Conservation about a Tennessee stripminer who they believe is causing damage to their community?
A. Well, I guess anybody in the United States could . . .
Q. Did you talk to any of the petitioners?
A. No, I don't believe so . . . The way I investigate a petition like that, you can't go to them, they've got but one viewpoint, I talk with other people in the community . . . I didn't believe I could make a proper investigation talking to just one side.
Q. Do you think that the people have a right to speak out against strip mining, if it damages people and if they are opposed to it?
A. I feel that any organization could.
Q. So 'undermining' could be that, merely speaking out against it.
A. No, not so much that . . . Undermine means stir up or cause trouble. Anything that would go against strip mining.[7]

In a later interrogation, the inspector could recall little of the spot 'investigated', could not specify any role of an 'outside' organization, and could remember only the names of informants who lived in a town some thirty miles away.

While the communication patterns and related attitudes of the state inspector thus shaped his testimony, other information was shaped into the hearings by the testimony of the professional or 'expert' witness. Like the agent of the State, the 'expert' enjoys a neutral status. Yet his supposedly independent opinion may be bound by the same processes of interaction and ideology that affected the views of the

[6] Report from inspector to director, Division of Surface Mining, 13 March 1973. The group to which he is apparently referring is Save Our Cumberland Mountains, Inc., a citizens' group in the Tennessee coalfields which had taken a stand against strip mining.

[7] Deposition of inspector, pp. 29–32.

bureaucrat. At the same time, the relatively powerless group may not have access to or resources for an expert of their own. And their own observations and experiences may be denied entrance into legal hearings because they are 'lay' opinion. Thus, in the Buffalo case, the certified geologist employed by the State made an extensive report based on a single inspection of the area, carried out in dry weather, and in the company of the coal operator. On the basis of that study he presented a 'scientific' opinion that there was little or no danger or damage, that the operator had not been negligent, and, if there was a problem, that it had probably been caused by mining some twelve years before, by another party.[8] Alternative information—based on measurements by observers in the community of the slide and its movement over a period of weeks—was excluded from evidence by the court as being 'non-professional'.

These components of a mobilization of bias thus served to shape the nature and content of the conflict which emerged in the regulatory process. However, they alone did not account for the disparity between the grievances originally expressed by the community and those which emerged in the hearing. As the level of protest increased—from spokesmanship, to petition, to legal complaint, to hearing—the extent of participation of the community residents in the emerging protest group decreased. By the time the case was actually heard by the Board, only a handful of the group appeared to testify. The Company's owners were able to present a counter-petition in support of the proposed mining, which contained numerous signatures from residents of the Clear Fork Valley, including those of some of the original Buffalo protestors. Within the hearing room, the argument could seem legitimate that there was 'consensus' in the community for the mining and that the protest had been only because of outside agitation. What had happened in the community? Why had the citizens appeared to back down? Interaction and interviews there during the time of the emerging challenge showed more coercive factors of power at work, which served to keep substantive conflict from appearing in the formal decision-making arena.

[8] Report of staff geologist, filed as evidence in the case, and his testimony.

Coercion for the containment of community conflict could be exercised through effective manipulation by the local élite of various values significant to the local subculture. Thus, hostilities towards the operator diminished when he visited the church in the hollow (for the first time in years, according to the informants) and contributed handsomely to the offering plate. A member of one of the key families was hired by the operator, and all the other members of the extended family withdrew from challenge rather than risk having one of their kin lose the chance of work. The operator, too, began to insist that he, like the other residents, was a poor man who had been a victim of bad luck and outside forces. The value of harmonious personal relations—especially with a fellow mountaineer—began to predominate over political grievances.

While the manipulation of the subcultural values could help to shape a choice other than protest, the selective use of more direct coercion helped further to ensure it. As if responding to threat, people began to talk of their fear of losing food stamps or credit at the Godfather's store. For the first time, residents began voluntarily to tell stories about violence that had occurred previously in the community; and this was followed a day or two later by overt threats and acts of violence (directed primarily against the author, the outsider perceived as 'the troublemaker' in the situation). As the risks of protest grew greater in a remote arena perceived to be rigged, the pattern of acquiescence within the community began to re-appear.

'The right of citizens to be heard in issues involving the regulatory power of the state is central to our forms of government', read the decision of the Board of Reclamation Review. It continued, 'We believe that the Commissioner though he did satisfy the letter of the law violated the spirit of the surface mining law by unnecessarily restricting public expressions of concern.'[9] In view of what had happened in the conflict, the decision was somewhat ironic. The 'unnecessarily restricting' factor to which the decision referred was that of the administrative blockage. The other perhaps more subtle examples of power that shaped the outcome of

[9] 'Memorandum of Decision', op. cit., pp. 12-13.

the case by limiting what was said, and by whom, were not mentioned. As the appeal was made by the local citizens, the experts and bureaucrats of the regulatory agency—separated by class, culture and distance from the protest group—turned to the local élite, with whom they felt more affinity, for interpretation of the conflict. The élite in turn could maximize their power: while serving as the brokers of information to the regulatory agency, they operated as wielders of more coercive power within the local arena. While presenting the view of a non-problem to the outside world, they could use their power locally to ensure that their view was not challenged. The stripping of Buffalo Hollow continued—amidst a quiescence that could be interpreted again by the outside observer as the fatalism of the culture rather than powerlessness within a larger power field.

9.2 BEYOND THE CLEAR FORK VALLEY: COMMUNITY PROTEST AND THE MULTINATIONAL

Several thousand miles away from the Clear Fork Valley, in a bustling square mile of London, stands the City, the financial centre of Britain. In the midst of the City, one block from the Bank of England, on the seventh floor of a grey stone building at 56 Gresham Street, is the head office of the American Association, Ltd., the Company which owns and controls much of the Clear Fork Valley. At the time of this case study, and until shortly before his death in 1975, the Chairman of the Board of Directors of the American Association, Ltd. was Sir Denys Colquhoun Flowerdew Lowson, an important figure in the City. A graduate of Christchurch College, Oxford and a barrister of the Inner Temple, Lowson had successively been Sheriff, Alderman and between 1950 and 1951, Lord Mayor of the City. He had married into the nobility (the Hon. Ann Patricia Macpherson, daughter of the Hon. First Baron Stratharron) and his name was well connected with good causes: officer and director of several hospitals and charities; Vice-President of the League of Mercy; Vice-President of the Royal Overseas League; Life Governor of the Royal Shakespeare Theatre; and President of the British Philatelic Society.[10]

[10] Much of this information is also used in John Gaventa, 'The Unknown Lowson Empire', *Social Audit* (Spring 1974), 18–31.

Sir Denys Lowson was also one of the City's wealthiest men, with an estimated fortune of over £200 million. From his Gresham Street office, he presided over a vast financial maze, termed by *The Guardian* as 'the most complicated of the City's international empires'.[11] (see Figure 9.1). He sat on the boards of some ninety companies, usually as chairman and often in the company of his son, Ian Patrick Lowson, and his nephew, D. A. Revell Smith. Through his empire, he controlled millions of pounds of investments, many in unit trusts or investment funds, which in turn controlled interests across the world—steamships on the Great Lakes, railroads in Chile, Costa Rica and Canada, bauxite in Ghana, agriculture in Australia, trading companies in the Far East, helicopters in Thailand, resort developments in Florida and hotel catering services in Britain—to name but a few. Among the smaller and least valuable of his concerns was the American Association, Ltd., with its 65,000 acres of coal and mineral land, the Holiday Inn, and the coal camp housing in and around the Clear Fork Valley.

How were citizens like those in Clear Fork to place their concerns upon the decision-making agendas of a place like the City and multinational empire like Lowson's? Who within the Company made the decisions relevant to their lives? The managers? The directors? The owners? Can one suspect that, like political power, corporate power is reflected in what is not decided as well as what is? What are the components of the mobilization of bias of a multinational corporate organization, and how do they affect the protest attempts of a small community?

Even within nations, the role of large corporations has only recently begun to re-emerge as a focus of attention in studies of community power and community conflict.[12] And

---

[11] *The Guardian* (London), 2 May 1975.

[12] Earlier studies of the corporation in local politics included Morton S. Baratz, 'Corporate Giants and the Power Structure', *Western Political Quarterly* (June 1956), 406–15; Donald A. Clelland and William H. Form, 'Economic Dominants and Community Power. A Comparative Analysis', *American Journal of Sociology*, 69, (1964), 511–21; Roland Pellegrin and Charles H. Coates, 'Absentee-Owned Corporations and Community Power Structure', *American Journal of Sociology*, 61 (Mar. 1956), 413–19. For more recent attention, see Crenson, *The Un-Politics of Air Pollution*, op. cit.; Edwin M. Epstein, *The Corporation in American Politics* (Prentice-Hall, Englewood Cliffs, New Jersey, 1969); and

despite a growing literature on the power of the multinational corporations, particularly as they affect national decision-making, there has been very little study of their impact upon subnational political entities—e.g. communities or pressure groups. The exception is the work being done on the multinational corporation and the trade unions, which suggests for instance, that 'where decision-making responsibility is located in a regional office or corporate headquarters outside of the country where the subsidiary is located, union efforts to influence management are likely to be rather ineffective'.[13] The attempts of the Clear Fork citizens both to locate and to influence the decision-makers in and about the corporate agenda of the Lowson empire offers a unique opportunity for a concrete case study of community challenge to multinational corporate control.

'But who do we shoot?'. According to the Company's local manager in Middlesboro, Kentucky, the American Association, Ltd. is 'actually managed in London'.[14] It made sense, then, for the Clear Fork citizens to begin there in their attempts to get action on their grievances. The citizens, of course, had no representative in London with access to the Company, so their approach had to be made through others, who by virtue of geography, credibility or influence might be able to reach Gresham Street. The singular response they received provided the Clear Fork citizens with their first clue that the campaign would be a difficult one: the Company refused to enter the conflict.

In October 1972 a request from Granada Television's

various Ralph Nader inspired studies, such as *The Water Lords*, a study of paper company influence in Savannah, Georgia.

[13] David H. Blake, 'Trade Unions and the Challenge of the Multinational', *The Annals of the American Academy of Political and Social Sciences*, 403 (September 1972) 36. For other major works on the multinational, see Richard J. Barnet and Ronald E. Müller, *Global Reach: The Power of the Multinationals* (Simon and Schuster, New York, 1974); Christopher Tugendhat, *The Multinationals* (Pelican, London, 1971); Anthony Sampson, *The Sovereign State: The Secret History of ITT* (Hodder and Stoughton, London, 1973); Dennis Kavanaugh, 'Beyond Autonomy: the Politics of the Corporations', *Government and Opposition* (Winter 1974), 42-5.

[14] Interview with Granada TV, *The Stripping of Appalachia*, op. cit.

'World in Action' for an interview with Sir Denys or the managers was turned down with the statement, 'No interview will serve any useful purpose in this country.'[15] Then Ralph Nader, the American consumer advocate, took an interest in the situation in Clear Fork. He wrote to Lowson in May 1973, beginning his appeal by acknowledging Sir Denys's position as Life Governor of the Royal Shakespeare Theatre and quoting from *Measure for Measure*: 'O, it is excellent to have a giant's strength, but it is tyrannous to use it like a giant.' The letter received no reply. An English visitor to Clear Fork wrote to Lowson on 11 June 1973: 'I think you should know . . . that I have never felt the shame of being English as I felt it in that ravaged landscape amongst those ravaged families whose plight only Dickens might have expressed.' His letter did receive a reply: 'I am passing your letter to our Managing Director, Mr. Brian Morgans, and also to our President in America, Mr. Al Funk. Thank you for writing.'

As more appeals on behalf of the Clear Fork citizens were made, the attitude of the Company hardened. A Thames Television reporter was told in June 1974, 'We have nothing to answer for at all', and this was followed later by a letter from the Company's managing director in London, Mr. Brian Morgans:

Nothing has occurred to induce us to change our attitude that further interviews will do anything to improve the situation in which we found ourselves the subject of unprovoked attack. As a competent reporter I am sure that you have discovered this yourself.

Meanwhile, in Middlesboro, Funk was telling a reporter from the *New York Times*, 'You can just say I refused to be interviewed and I'm just damn tired of this stuff.'[16] In the first instance, then, the citizens' attempts to reach these decision-makers were thwarted by the power of the corporate élite to remain aloof from the protestors' grievances.

The Shareholders. In such a situation a relatively powerless group may attempt to maximize its power by appealing to another element of the corporation, the shareholders. In

[15] ibid.
[16] *New York Times*, 22 June 1974, p. 32.

theory, the joint-stock company represents a 'shareholders' democracy', and in recent years, the 'proxy fight' has increasingly become a means whereby pressure groups concerned with corporate responsibility attempt to place their concerns on the corporate agenda. At first this seemed another potential strategy for the Clear Fork group: although the American Association is a small corporation with only ninety-odd shareholders, it is listed as a public corporation on the London Stock Exchange, and has an issued two million shares, whose price in 1972 of around thirty-five pence a share was not prohibitive. It appeared possible to buy a few shares, raise money for spokesmen to go to London, and air the grievances before the shareholders, asking them to take up the case before the management. The publicity which might surround the event, it was thought, would also help to attract support for the cause.

This possibility, too, faced a blockage. An offer to buy shares through an English bank got no response. Similar offers made through one of the world's largest stockbroking firms, and through the offices of a London solicitor, also brought a negative response: 'none were available or offered for sale', and 'we made a determined effort to try . . . but they were unavailable to us'. This failure to gain even entrance to the public corporation seemed especially peculiar as the Stock Exchange Daily Lists showed that trades of the share were being made at the time. But further investigations suggested the likelihood that these trades were primarily amongst the corporate actors already within the financial empire, so that as one Lowson company lost, another gained.[17]

Meanwhile, the annual reports from Lowson to the shareholders continued to assure them of the Company's continued concern for the environment and development of the Clear Fork area. They made no mention of the citizens' complaints or legal actions—such as those on taxation—to which the Company had been a party, and routinely concluded with the traditional vote of thanks to the manager, Mr. A.E. Funk,

[17] Study of share registers of the American Association, Ltd., 1963-73. For instance, in 1968 New Zealand River and Plate lost 1,321 shares while New World and General Investments gained 1,321. Both companies were part of the Lowson network. For further details see Gaventa, 'The Unknown Lowson Empire', op. cit.; and quotations from letters to author, 5 September 1973 and 12 June 1973.

who 'continues to lead the team with great success'.

The Owners. Failing to reach the directors or shareholders, the Clear Fork citizens had one final option for attempting to bring pressure directly upon the corporation: they could locate the principal owners to attempt to influence them to use their financial power to alter the Company's behaviour. Yet this, too, was to prove a difficult task, and one already unsuccessfully attempted by others. After his investigation, a knowledgeable reporter of the *Investor's Chronicle* had written, 'what is quite unknown is how the empire is controlled, how the various companies relate to each other . . . The diligent investor or assets stripper sending minions to search records in Companies House can get nowhere.'[18] *The Guardian* would later say, 'If seven men with computers studied the Lowson empire for half a year they would probably not disentangle the network . . . It is like a gigantic molecule whose characteristics depend not just upon its general shape but on the precise relationship of one part with another.'[19]

The experience of this author on behalf of the Clear Fork group indicates much the same. Though a director of the American Association, Ltd. was later to reveal that Lowson and his family owned about 70 per cent of the corporation's stock, extensive use of available public information in the United States, Britain and Canada could not have discovered this. In the United States, state laws in neither Tennessee nor Kentucky require full disclosure of corporate ownership. Stronger federal regulations administered under the Securities Exchange Commission do not apply to companies with under 500 shareholders.

In Britain, although corporations are required under the Companies Act of 1948 to disclose listings of shareholders, the use of cross-share holdings, nominees and holding companies can make identification of the real owners difficult.

A study of the 1973 shareholders lists showed Lowson's London-based companies appearing to own only 15 per cent

[18] John Roberts, 'Lowson's £200 million Empire', *Investor's Chronicle* (28 Jan. 1972).
[19] *The Guardian,* 24 July 1974.

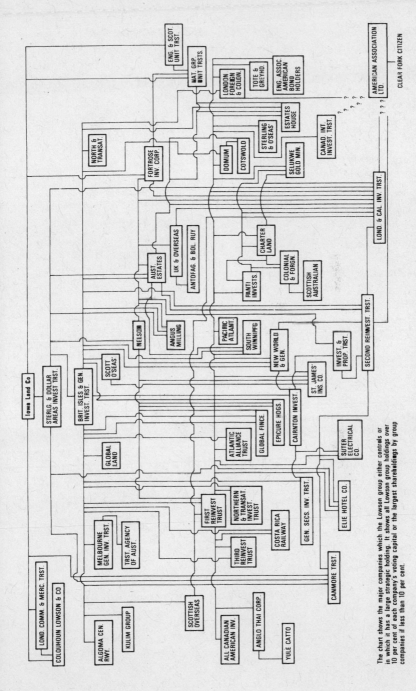

9.1 The Structure of the Lowson Empire (Adapted from *Investor's Chronicle*, 28 Jan. 1972, as reprinted in *Social Audit*, Spring 1974, p.28)

The chart shows the major companies which the Lowson group either controls or in which it has a large strategic holding. It shows all Lowson group holdings over 10 per cent of each company's voting capital or the largest shareholdings by group companies if less than 10 per cent.

of American Association's shares, while the major owners, holding 54 per cent of the equity, were Canadian companies. The major portion of these shares, representing 36 per cent of the total, was held in the name of a large investment and real estate group, the Royal Trust Company of Canada, which could have been holding them either for itself or for a beneficiary. The other Canadian shares were owned by three companies—Halsco and Co., Ottsco and Co., and Bensco and Co.—each of the same address in Toronto. While Lowson thus appeared not to be involved, inquiries to the Royal Trust Company in Montreal about its stock were referred back to Lowson in London. Meanwhile, inquiries to Public Search Offices in Ontario and Ottawa revealed no knowledge of Halsco and Co., Ottsco and Co., and Bensco and Co. as being registered Canadian companies. The Toronto Stock Exchange also could not help to identify the 'real' owners of Clear Fork Valley: 'I checked our reference sources but there was no mention of the companies at all. The Ontario Securities Commission had no record of the companies either.'[20] Neither could the Clear Fork citizens gain more information by starting with what inside sources revealed to the *Investor's Chronicle* as the keystone to the empire— the Iowa Land Company. The company controls other companies (not land as the name implies), and attempts to trace its ownership again led back to faceless offices in the City, Scotland or Canada.

The point for power is this: not only could the Clear Fork citizens not gain access to the decision-making agenda of the multinational, but they could not even discover for certain who financially controlled it or how the control was maintained. While the managers and directors of the American Association had little reason to allow even bargaining to occur, the secrecy, complexity and tightly-held nature of the empire's ownership also helped to ensure that the power was not challenged. The consequent powerlessness of the would-be protestors is like that of the farmer in Steinbeck's *Grapes of Wrath*, who, as the absentee-owned bulldozer mows down his crops, pleads but *'who can* we shoot?'[21]

[20] Letter to author from Toronto Stock Exchange, 16 November 1973. Inquiries *re* Royal Trust by John Roberts, op. cit.

[21] John Steinbeck, *The Grapes of Wrath* (Penguin Books, Harmondsworth,

Public Opinion and the Multinational. In 'normal times' and faced with a different empire, the citizens of Clear Fork may still not have been able to break through these barriers to carry their protest further to the source of absentee power. But the years 1973-5 were not 'normal times' for the Lowson empire. In July 1973 the London press revealed that by in-house trading disguised through corporate complexity, the Lowson interests had been able to defraud other interests for £5 million, or more.[22] The revelations were a scandal in the City. An investigation by the Department of Trade and Industry quickly followed, creating more widespread interest in the affairs of the Lowson group. In a sense, the mobilization of bias surrounding the company's financial affairs had weakened, giving the story of social irresponsibility in the Appalachias some appeal. The relatively powerless group could now attempt to mobilize public support and govern-mental intervention to a degree not possible before.

Of course, 'World in Action' 's documentary of the Clear Fork connection, aired in Britain in November 1972, had already provoked some public outcry. A woman in Middlesex wrote to the *Campbell County Times*, near the Clear Fork Valley:

I write to tell you how ashamed I am that an English owned company can so indiscriminately cause so much havoc to a small community. My feeling after watching a recent television documentary on the subject was one of total horror. I have today written to the Chairman and Managing Director of the Company in London expressing my views.[23]

But, before the Lowson scandal at home, the 1972 documen-tary brought little or no follow-up from other media, who said that the story would have little interest, or that it had already been told.

On the other hand, after the Lowson scandal in the City, the *Social Audit* inquiry (plus other initiatives taken by the Clear Fork group) stimulated three major stories released together in *The Guardian,* followed shortly by coverage in other British newspapers and features on BBC Radio, BBC

Middx., pp. 35-7).
[22] See for instance, *The Guardian*, 12, 18, 28 July 1973.
[23] 'Letters to the Editor', *Campbell County Times*, 22 November 1972.

Television and Thames Television—all of which focused on the social consequences of Lowson's Clear Fork holdings.[24] What was an interesting story under one set of circumstances became a public issue under another set of circumstances in the home country of the corporate power. Likewise, as interest in the Lowson affair died down, so did the affairs of the American Association in the Appalachias sink out of sight.

The Clear Fork citizens' brief flirtation with the media in London suggests some limitations to this path of action, especially in a multinational context. Exposés rarely translate into political power without the intervening variable of a pressure group or potential pressure group to link diffuse public knowledge to impact upon responsible corporate or governmental decision-makers. Yet, in the case of challenge to a multinational, the linking process may not take place as readily as it does within a single political milieu. Potential allies of the relatively powerless group, e.g. other pressure groups, unions, political parties, etc., may perceive insufficient information either relevant to their actions, or significant enough within their own goals, resources and constituencies to warrant their support. That is to say, the likelihood of alliance formation by the relatively powerless group, through the media or otherwise, may decrease as potential alliances are dispersed across political boundaries (nation, state, organization, etc.). It is otherwise for the powerholders, for whom a multitude of boundaries maximizes the possibility of avoiding significant, organized challenges from below.

Governmental Jurisdiction and the Multinational. If the local protest group in the multinational arena has difficulty in gaining support through public opinion, it can attempt finally to appeal to government agencies for its case, either in the host country or in the home country of the multinational. However, if governmental actions normally happen only in response to organizational pressures, as in traditional

[24] See *The Guardian,* 6 May 1974. After this story, five British newspapers immediately contacted spokesmen in the Clear Fork Valley about a story; in addition features were carried in 'The World Tonight', BBC Radio (transmitted 8 May 1974); 'News Extra', BBC TV (transmitted 14 May 1972); and 'This Week', Thames TV (transmitted 25 July 1974).

interest group theory, and if the difficulties of alliance formation have prevented the development of such pressures, then this path for protest may also fail. Moreover, the difficulties normally faced by the relatively powerless group in getting its case heard in the governmental process (as seen in the case of Buffalo Hollow) may be compounded by the limits of governmental jurisdiction in the multinational arena.

In the case of the Clear Fork citizens, appeals in the United States to the staff of the Senate Subcommittee on Multinationals brought the response that the primary interest of the committee was investigation into the behaviour of United States firms abroad, not of foreign firms at home. In Britain, on the other hand, the inquiry of the Department of Trade and Industry (DTI) into aspects of Lowson's financial affairs seemed to offer the possibility of getting the investigation expanded to include aspects of the American Association's performance. Appeals to the Government directly, as well as indirectly through Members of Parliament, brought the response from the DTI:

. . . in as far as the activities of American Association, Limited, which is said to be operating in Kentucky and Tennessee, are concerned, the Department is not in a position to exercise its investigatory powers under the Companies Acts, because the Company is not trading in this country. Any Inspector appointed under the Companies Acts would have no legal right to demand officers to answer questions or give information about the activities of that company in the USA.[25]

Further suggestion on behalf of the citizens that the 'particular nature of the American Association matter . . . and the amount of public attention attracted on both sides of the Atlantic' might warrant a special inquiry, patterned after the inquiry into the behaviour of British companies in mining regions of South Africa, also brought a negative response. The Parliamentary Under Secretary of State for Companies, Aviation and Shipping replied: 'I do not propose to recommend a Parliamentary enquiry into the company's affairs. The recent investigation into the working conditions of employees of British companies trading in South Africa was

[25] Letter to *Social Audit* from Mr. H. C. Gill, Companies Division, Department of Trade and Industry, 1 May 1974.

a unique exercise which the government has no intention of repeating.'[26]

It is not new, of course, to say that multinational corporate power faces limited accountability to nations or to groups. But the inaction upon the grievances of the citizens of Clear Fork is all the more noteworthy when contrasted with the action that did occur in response to the exposure of Lowson's unsavoury financial dealings in the City. In July 1974 the Department of Trade and Industry released a strongly-worded report finding Lowson 'in breach of his fiduciary duty' and guilty of 'grave mismanagement' in the deals for which he had been investigated.[27] Lowson and his family had benefited, it said, at the expense of the other shareholders involved. In response to the report, the headlines of the editorial page of *The Times* read, 'A Bad Case of City Misconduct', and the editorial suggested this to be an example of what former Prime Minister Heath had called 'the unacceptable face of capitalism'.[28] Even more damning was *The Guardian,* whose headlines read, 'The City's Scarred Integrity', and whose editorial continued its biological analogy, 'there are molecules which are fatal to the bodies in which they lodge, and the City is host body to this one. The City will survive, of course, but it will be damaged. . .'[29]

In this instance, after public and governmental attention, the City moved quickly to recover its image and its credibility. A plan on behalf of the shareholders was developed through the Hill Samuel Merchant Bank to re-organize the empire. A new investment group quickly took the reins, ending Lowson's domination of the financial empire. A disgraced Lowson left on a £25,000 round-the-world cruise to recover. Shortly afterwards he died, on 10 September 1975, hours after a summons concerning his share deals had been issued by the Director of Public Prosecutions.

Though the scarred integrity of the City was being rectified,

[26] Letter to author from Stanley Clinton Davis, Department of Trade, 26 July 1974.
[27] Department of Trade, 'Investigations into First Re-Investment Trust, Ltd., Nelson Financial Trust Ltd., English and Scottish Unit Trust Holdings Limited', Interim report by D. C.-H. Hirst and R.M.D. Langdon (H.M.S.O., London, 1974).
[28] *The Times,* 24 July 1974.
[29] *The Guardian,* 24 July 1974.

the re-organization meant little change for the citizens in the Clear Fork Valley. Although Lowson was gone, his son and other untraceable Canadian interests took his place in the Company. Indeed, the process of the demise and recovery of the multinational empire was much like that of the American Association in the 'Magic City of Middlesborough' eight decades before.[30] The ambitious Lowson, like the visionary Arthur, was replaced; a slightly different organization was substituted for the old; in response to certain actors and issues, the system proved its 'responsiveness'; the mobilization of bias, once weakened, was re-shaped. But in the Clear Fork Valley, the non-issues experienced daily by the relatively powerless citizens continue much the same.

9.3 REPERCUSSIONS

Although the power of decisions and non-decisions may allow the powerholder to remain beyond protest, the power-lessness of the protestors does not protect them from repercussions from their actions. While a target such as the Company may appear, publicly, aloof from challenges, local mediators may quietly attempt to re-instil acquiescence.

Within the Clear Fork Valley, the initial emergence of challenge by the protestors at first appeared to bring response. With the airing of the Granada film abroad and the threats of suits at home, the Company agreed to discuss freeing some land to the community development group, after five years of saying 'no'. For over a year, the community negotiated with various bodies, governmental and private, to obtain the financial, legal and professional resources needed to ratify the lease and begin developing housing and industry on the land.

Gradually, however, the Company began to delay, and placed highly restrictive conditions on the lease. The community leaders began to suspect that the bargaining was not in good faith. A decision was made to try to bring further pressure in London, leading to a wave of publicity in the spring of 1974. By this time, naïvete about the Company's distant owners—that they only needed to know the state of affairs in order to remedy them—had faded. A leader of

[30] See Chapter 3, pp. 00–000.

the community development group appeared on BBC's 'News Extra' saying that the Company had been carrying on 'double talk mostly. Just plain double talk. They say they will and don't.'[31] When asked if they thought they would get anywhere with the Company, another community leader told Thames Television: 'I doubt it . . . people that's been hounding and talking to them—it just don't faze them. Poor people can't talk to rich people; they just don't get any place with them.'[32]

While these statements were being aired in London, repercussions were being felt in the Valley. On 10 June 1974 the local manager called the community leaders to the Company's office. He was, he said, tired of being bothered by the media. The biggest mistake the Company had made, he added, had been to allow the people to remain in the Valley after the mines had closed. If it had torn the houses down and cleared the Valley, it would not have been subject to such harassment. The negotiations for the land were off. No lease would be forthcoming.

In the ensuing months, the challenges of the valley residents subsided. Yet in the surrounding area other groups, particularly the five-county Save Our Cumberland Mountains (SOCM), continued to protest about the inequalities of the region. In March 1975 a victory was won as the State Equalization Board ordered more equal taxation of corporate coal reserves. In Washington and in Nashville, the state capital, lobbying efforts in support of legislation regulating strip mining looked for the first time as if they might have some success. But then came more reprisals.[33] Perhaps because of the widespread attention brought to it through the use of the media, the relatively quiescent and highly powerless Clear Fork Valley became the focus of retaliation by the strip-mining companies. In April 1975, groups of roving vigilantes threatened the lives of community activists. Organizers were threatened with lynching or rape. Not only were the members of SOCM threatened, the primary protestors

---

[31] Transcript of 'News Extra' Report, BBC 2, transmitted 14 May 1974.

[32] Transcript of 'This Week', Thames TV, transmitted 25 July 1974.

[33] No evidence exists as to the precise source of these particular reprisals; this description is not meant to implicate the Company or its officers.

against the strip mining, but also those involved in any of the community controlled institutions—the clinics, the factory, the crafts shop. As throughout the history of the Valley, any autonomous collective action amongst the non-élite appeared threatening to the élite. The responses of power were effective. A general mode of fear was re-invoked. By the end of 1975, the challenges of the community against the Company had virtually ceased.

10

CONCLUSIONS

If the response of local and absentee powerholders to challenge in the contemporary situation helps to confirm the extent of their power, so, too, does it help to confirm a pattern found throughout the history of the Appalachian Valley. The pattern is one in which challenges by the people of the Valley to the massive inequalities they face have been precluded or repelled, time and again, by the power which surrounds and protects the beneficiaries of the inequalities. The unitary nature of the power and the transferability of its components among various aspects of community life liken the powerlessness in the contemporary Valley to that of the coal camps of earlier years. The pattern serves now, as it did then, to maintain and strengthen the absentee-dominated social and political order which was established in the 'colonization' of the region in the late nineteenth century. Time, of course, has brought changes in the Valley—of technology, of culture, of social life—but, in the flux, the basic patterns of inequality and the supporting patterns of power and powerlessness have persisted, if not grown stronger.

The roots of quiescence amidst the inequalities and obstacles to rebellion have been a major concern of this study. If there are general conclusions, they must be that the quietness of this segment of America's lower and working class perceived at a distance cannot be taken to reflect consensus to their condition or seen to be innate within their socio-economic or cultural circumstances. As one draws closer, in fact, the silence is not as pervasive as it appears from other studies, or even from initial inquiry within this one. Generalized discontent is present, but lies hidden and contained. Where the discontent does emerge into rebellion, as it has at various moments in the Valley's history, the extent of the normally more latent conflict is revealed. The fact that the discontent is so often overlooked says less about the Valley than it does about the methodological biases found in the dominant approach in America to the study of power.

In this study I have attempted to develop an expanded notion of power and to ask whether its workings could be witnessed in the everyday life of the community. I conclude that power can *and should* be viewed in its multiple dimensions, and that mechanisms or processes within each are specifiable. Methodologically, a historical approach has been found to be helpful in revealing the shaping of patterns and routines which underlie the power relationships of the present. In the contemporary situation, a 'view from below' has allowed a unique perspective of power's hidden faces, as they work in the maintenance of quiescence and in the containment of rebellion. Historically and presently, a comparison of varying modes or potential modes of participation in 'normal' and 'abnormal' times has helped to document what the powerless might otherwise think or do were it not for the strength of the powerholders. This approach has not only illuminated various aspects of the community situation, but its empirical application has also illustrated the interrelationships of power and powerlessness, quiescence and rebellion set out tentatively in Chapter 1. (See Figure 1.1.)

The Dimensions and Mechanisms of Power. In the first dimension of power, conflicts over fundamental issues of inequality were seen primarily in the past. For example, the first elections in the Magic City in the 1890s or the cases in the courts in the 1930s well revealed the conflict between the local non-élites and the corporate interests in the area, as well as the power of the latter to prevail. Similarly, the Jellico assembly and other meetings early in the process of organizing the union showed the conflict between the rank and file and the élite within the organization over the establishment of certain governing procedures. Once patterns of prevalence had been established within the decision-making arenas, power could be wielded more readily over the decision-making agenda itself. Since the formative historical moments, conflict over matters of inequality has been contained primarily within the second- and third-dimensional arenas of power. For this reason, those studies which apply only the pluralists' assumptions to a study of the Valley will neither discover the hidden faces of power, nor understand how they serve to maintain the area's inequalities.

In the second dimension of power, the grievances of the Appalachian poor continue today more covertly. Though they remain outside the decision-making arenas, they are not hard to discover. But the holding of grievances does not in itself mean that action over them will occur, or that they will be translated into issues for study in dominant political forums. In the Appalachian Valley, the anticipation of defeat by the relatively powerless, often thought to reflect the fatalism of the traditional culture, is not an irrational phenomenon. It has been instilled historically through repeated experiences of defeat. When actions or attempted actions do take place, the powerholders also benefit from the numerous resources of a historically shaped mobilization of bias which serves or can be wielded to re-instil non-challenge.

Institutional practices have often worked against the powerless to the benefit of the powerful: in the complexity and secrecy of the corporation, the administrative fiat of the regulatory agency, or the 'stacking of the deck' of union committees. Certain values of the traditional culture, such as those of personal harmony, family, or religion, may be wielded by an élite (less bound to those values) to shape 'choices' that the powerless 'cannot refuse', as seen in the case of Buffalo Hollow. The mobilization of bias may be strengthened, where necessary, by the use of force, as seen in the response to the challenges of the 1930s and the 1970s. Sanctions may be used or threatened, whether over pension benefits, health cards, food stamps, or the home or job tenure of an individual or an individual's kin or neighbour. Symbolic resources—'Catholic', 'communist', 'outsider', or 'troublemaker'—offer more subtle means for discrediting discontent. Where a prevailing mobilization of bias begins to crumble, it can be reshaped in ways that accommodate certain demands while excluding others. For instance, following their temporary demise both the 'magic' of the city in the 1890s and the 'integrity' of the Lowson empire in the 1970s were restored, though the social inequalities contained within them continued much the same. Similarly, in the rebellion of the 1930s the civil rights of the miners received a flurry of national focus, while the fundamental economic demands initially voiced were 'organized out' of the conflict. At other times, power can be exercised with no apparent action on the part of the powerholders, such as seen in the means by which institutional inaction contributed to Yablonski's murder or in the unwillingness of the Valley's London owners to acknowledge the challenge of the people in the Valley.

In all of its mechanisms, the second dimension of power serves to enhance and re-enforce the third-dimensional power relationship. The establishment of the fundamental inequalities in the Appalachian Valley in the 1890s brought its own legitimations, as seen in the glorification of the dominant ways and values of the new order coupled with the degradation of the culture of the old one. Other legitimations can be found in the relationships that developed in the union, seen, for instance, in an ideology of loyalty predominating at the expense of the interests of the rank and file. In the contemporary Valley, the prevailing values and ideas continue to be strengthened through specificable processes. An illustrative focus on information flows—in the local newspaper in the 1930s, in the communication of leaders with members of their union, or in the modern mass media—has suggested one means through which conceptions of conflict can be directly shaped.

But the strength of the direct processes of power's third dimension is increased, too, through what has been termed in the study as its indirect mechanisms. Continual defeat gives rise not only to the conscious deferral of action but also to a sense of defeat, or a sense of powerlessness, that may affect the consciousness of potential challengers about grievances, strategies, or possibilities for change. Participation denied over time may lead to acceptance of the role of non-participation, as well as to a failure to develop the political resources—skills, organization, consciousness—of political action. Power relationships may develop routines of non-challenge which require no particular action on the part of powerholders to be maintained, as seen between leaders and led in the union situation, or in the voting patterns of local elections. If the routines are broken, manipulation of the power field through the invocation of myths, rumours or symbols may serve to channel the conflict of a situation away from the agents responsible for it, such as seen in the shaping of union discontent into support for the corrupt union regime.

While each dimension of power has its mechanisms and uses, it is only through the interrelationship of the dimensions and the re-enforcing effect of each dimension on the other that the total impact of power upon the actions and conceptions of the powerless may be fully understood. What is voiced by the powerholders in the decision-making arenas may not always reflect the real conflict, but may articulate norms or myths which disguise or deflect the more latent conflict. The ceremony of 'thanksgiving' to city and Company in 1893 gave a dramatic example of this phenomenon. What does not happen or what goes unsaid in the first-dimensional arenas (as in the 'non-issueness' of tax inequalities in the courthouse or in the 'non-coverage' of certain events and themes by the media) may also shape conceptions about which matters are appropriate for consideration upon the dominant agendas. Similarly, second-dimensional exercises of power affect vulnerability to the shaping of wants and beliefs, as in the third dimension of power, which in turn strengthens the symbolic resources available in the second.

From this perspective, the total impact of a power relationship is more than the sum of its parts. Power serves to create power. Powerlessness serves to re-enforce powerlessness. Power relationships, once established, are self-sustaining. Quiescence in the face of inequalities may be understood only in terms of the inertia of the situation. For this reason, power in a given community can never be understood simply by observation at a given point in time. Historical investigation must occur to discover whether routines of non-conflict have been shaped, and, if so, how they are maintained.

Despite their strength, the power relationships of the Appalachian Valley have not been altogether successful in shaping universal acquiescence. Even in 'normal times' the

extent to which Appalachian culture has resisted penetration
of dominant social values can be seen. Indeed, the adherence
to traditional values in itself, in view of the power situation,
may be seen as a form of rebellion. And while developed
conceptions of an alternative order are not widely expressed,
grievances about the *status quo* do abound: about working
conditions, unfair taxation, environmental destruction,
corrupt governmental or union leadership, welfare and health
benefits, job security, and all the other manifestations of
inequality daily experienced in the lives of the people. On
the occasions when the power field has altered—the demise
of the Company in 1894, the wage nexus in 1931, the passage
of labour legislation in 1933, the 'maximum feasible participation' clause of 1964, the opportunities for action in the
1970s—challenges to dominance have emerged.

But the challenges have not been sustained; nor do they
reflect the complete conflict contained within the situation.
The dimensions of power say something not only about how
quiescence is maintained, but also about the aspects of
powerlessness which must be overcome in the development
of successful protest.

In the first instance, a process of issue and action formulation must occur, to overcome the effects of the third-
dimension of power. The powerless must be able to explore
their grievances openly, with others similarly situated. They
must develop their own notions of interests and actions, and
themselves as actors. This process of 'conscientization' was
seen to have occurred in a small way in the Valley, as the
community organization and the community media rapidly
brought otherwise more latent grievances to the fore.

Even as issues and actions are developed, the powerless
must undergo a process of mobilization upon them. That is,
they must develop their own resources for challenge—organization, information, sustaining values—to counter the
prevailing mobilization of bias, as seen in the study of the
Yablonski candidacy. They must also locate and overcome
the barriers which normally prevent them from entry to
decision-making arenas, as witnessed in the case of Buffalo
Hollow. Only as these multiple aspects of powerlessness are
overcome may the conflict that emerges in power's first

dimension be said to be amongst relatively competing groups, upon clearly conceived interests, in an open arena.

In situations of great inequality, conflict rarely reaches such a pluralist stage. At any point along the process of emerging challenge, the powerful may intervene to re-instil quiescence, as seen, for instance, in the response of John L. Lewis to demands for rank and file voice in the 1930s, or in the response to the protests against the corporation in the 1970s. What for the powerless are obstacles to be overcome in the raising of issues, for the powerful are mechanisms for maintaining the *status quo*. Rebellion, to be successful, must both confront power and overcome the accumulated effects of powerlessness.

The rebellion that has occurred over inequalities in the Appalachian Valley so far has not done so. In order to overcome the biases of the power they face, the Valley's people must gain strength by alliance with similarly deprived groups, or win intervention on their behalf by powerholders elsewhere. Until this happens, the inequalities of the Valley will remain hidden from the political agenda, and the conflict contained in the situation will remain latent there.

The Levels of Power. If this study has said something about the dimensions of power, it has also said something about its levels. The power of the Appalachian Valley is of a hierarchical, clearly stratified nature. Yet the sources of that power are not contained within the Valley, or indeed within the Appalachian region. The study of power and powerlessness in the Valley must go beyond the Valley to consider the absentee bases of the local patterns.

The dominant institutions and social values that affect the Valley from beyond it have often been found to be mediated by a local or regional élite. Though appearing from within as spokesmen for the local situation, the élite are intertwined in interests and outlook with the absentee forces upon which their own relative dominance in the local situation depends. The formation of the local élite has been seen historically, for instance, in the incorporation of the rural patriarchs and the importation of a professional and business middle class into the Magic City, and in the installing by John L. Lewis of his henchman into positions of control over local union affairs in the 1930s. In the contemporary situation, the local élite continue to play multiple roles, e.g. as brokers of political resources such as jobs or votes, as mediators of values and policies, and as 'gatekeepers' of information between the 'outside' and 'inside' worlds.

With the local élite as the dominant actors within the situation, the absentee powerholders may maintain their power through appearing inactive or remaining aloof from conflict, as did the Chinese rulers described by Pocock. The very absence of their visible intervention may give rise to or re-enforce mystifications about them, as seen in the abiding faith of the miners in John L. Lewis, or in the initial naïvete of the community towards the goodwill of the owners of the Company in London. The grievances which are articulated may be confined to those inequalities visible daily within the loacl community; and action upon these grievances may be directed only against the local agents perceived as being responsible for inflicting them. Yet the power and practices of the local élite must be understood in reference to the absentee interests from which they gain their strength and form. And the restriction of conflict to the local situation must be seen in reference to the difficulties faced by the relatively powerless group in taking their challenge to the more distant seats of control. In general, just as the dimensions of power and powerlessness re-enforce one another, so, too, do the levels of power maximize the capacity of the holders of power to lie beyond challenge, and minimize the ability of the relatively powerless subjects of power to formulate or act upon the full extent of their interests within the conflict situation.

In the absence of challenge, the levels of authority and the variety of potential paths for protest may lend a pluralistic appearance to power in the contemporary Valley. Yet, as challenges have emerged, so, too, have the levels and paths appeared to converge in their response. As has been occurring since the 1890s, when one aspect of the mobilization of bias weakens, other aspects are able to 'hold the line' until power relationships are re-established.

In understanding this is found a further lesson significant

for understanding power within the society as a whole. The argument is often made, particularly in reference to the United States, that the multiplicity of national élites and the decentralization of political authority ensures a pluralism necessary for democracy. Yet to ascribe national characteristics to the local community is to commit a serious ecological fallacy. The institutions which affect the Valley—corporate, governmental, communications, labour—may appear 'at the top' diverse, relatively unconnected, even competing. But when the same institutions are viewed 'from the bottom', i.e. from the perspective of the non-élite of the community, they appear unitary in nature. The local élite—interrelated in their civic, economic and political roles—help to strengthen the unitary portrayal of the wider diversity. Yet, it is 'at the bottom' in a participatory, federalist system where democracy should be working if it is working at all. When it is not, then the pluralism 'at the top' only gives a false appearance to what occurs locally.

While the notion of universal democracy in America may consequently be a myth, it is not an impotent one. As long as the belief in 'openness' can be sustained, the phenomenon of power may continue to be separated from the understanding of non-participation. And as long as the roots of quiescence can continue to be blamed upon the victims of power, then democracy of the few will continue to be legitimated by a prevailing belief in the apathy or ignorance of the many.

The pluralists' portrayal, however, has been challenged by the case of the Appalachian Valley, and that challenge has implications for pursuit beyond this study. If the power relationships of the Appalachian Valley cannot be understood except in terms of the decisions, non-decisions, and prevailing values of national and international centres of power, as they are mediated through a local élite, then neither the reasons for the inequalities nor the responsibilities for their alteration rest simply with the people of the region. If the processes of power that affect quiescence and rebellion in Central Appalachia are more general in source, then they may be similar in nature and consequence for rural or urban, subcultural or mainstream, black or white relatively powerless people elsewhere. And if, within or beyond Appalachia, power relationships do impede challenge to social and economic inequalities, then theorists and practitioners of democracy should turn their energies to considering how the power relationships of contemporary society are to be altered if the social and economic deprivations of the people within it are to be overcome.

INDEX

UNIVERSITY OF ILLINOIS PRESS
1325 SOUTH OAK STREET
CHAMPAIGN, ILLINOIS 61820-6903
WWW.PRESS.UILLINOIS.EDU